PROJECTS FOR MICROSOFT® ACCESS 97

MICROSOFT® CERTIFIED BLUE RIBBON EDITION

Philip A. Koneman
Colorado Christian University

Pamela R. Toliver

Yvonne Johnson

ADDISON-WESLEY

An imprint of Addison Wesley Longman, Inc.

Reading, Massachusetts • Menlo Park, California • New York • Harlow, England
Don Mills, Ontario • Sydney • Mexico City • Madrid • Amsterdam

Acquisitions Editor: Anita Devine
Editorial Assistant: Holly Rioux
Senior Marketing Manager: Tom Ziolkowski
Senior Marketing Coordinator: Deanna Storey
Production Supervision: Patty Mahtani and Diane Freed
Copyediting: Krista Hansing, Barb Terry, and Robin Drake
Technical Editing: Pauline Johnson and Emily Kim
Proofreader: Holly McLean-Aldis
Indexer: Irv Hershman
Composition and Art: Gillian Hall, The Aardvark Group
Cover Illustration: © Frederic Joos/SIS
Cover Designer: Anthony Saizon
Design Supervisor: Regina Hagen
Manufacturing: Sheila Spinney

0-201-43864-x

Ordering from the SELECT System
For more information on ordering and pricing policies for the SELECT Lab Series and supplements, please contact your Addison Wesley Longman sales representative or fax 1-800-284-8292 or email: exam@awl.com. Questions? Email: is@awl.com

Addison-Wesley Publishing Company
One Jacob Way
Reading, MA 01867
http://hepg@awl.com/select

1 2 3 4 5 6 7 8 9 10-DOW-01009998

Preface

Microsoft Certified

Welcome to the *Microsoft® Certified Blue Ribbon Edition of Select: Projects for Access 97*. This project-based visual text is approved courseware for the Microsoft® Office User Specialist program. After completing the projects in this book, students will be prepared to take the Expert level exam for Access 97. Successful completion of this exam gives students marketable skills that they can use for summer jobs or after they graduate. The *Microsoft® Certified Blue Ribbon Edition of Select: Projects for Access 97* allows students to explore the essentials of the software application and learn the basic skills that are the foundation for business and academic success. Step-by-step exercises and full-color illustrations show students what to do, how to do it, and the exact result of their action.

QWIZ Assessment Software is a task-based test that simulates the Office 97 environment and tests students on measurable skills using the features of Office 97.

The Select Lab Series

Greater access to ideas and information is changing the way people work and learn. With Microsoft Office 97 software applications, you have greater integration capabilities and access to Internet resources than ever before. The *Select Lab Series* manuals help you take advantage of these valuable resources, with special assignments devoted to the Internet.

Dozens of proven and class-tested lab manuals are available within the *Select Lab Series*, from the latest operating systems and browsers to the most popular applications software for word processing, spreadsheets, databases, presentation graphics, and integrated packages to HTML and programming. The *Select Lab Series* also offers individually bound texts for each *Office 97* application. Knowing that you have specific needs for your lab course, we offer the quick and affordable TechSuite program. For your lab course, you can choose the combination of software lab manuals in *Brief, Standard,* or *Plus* Editions that best suits your classroom needs. Your choice of lab manuals will be sent to the bookstore, in a TechSuite box, allowing students to purchase all books in one convenient package at a significant discount.

In addition, your school may qualify for full Office 97 upgrades or licenses. Your Addison Wesley Longman representative will be happy to work with you and your bookstore manager to provide the most current menu of application software in addition to *Select Lab Series* offerings. Your representative will also outline the ordering process, and provide pricing, ISBNs, and delivery information. Call 1-800-447-2226 or visit our Web site at http://hepg.awl.com and click on ordering information.

Organization

Before launching into the application, the *Microsoft® Certified Select: Projects for Access 97 Blue Ribbon Edition* familiarizes students with the operating system and Internet functionality with an Overview of Windows 95, Windows 95 Active Desktop, and Windows 98. Students learn the basics of starting Windows 95, using a mouse, using the basic features of Windows 95, and organizing files. Your computer may also be set up with Windows 95 Active Desktop or Windows 98—we have included a new section that shows what the different desktops may look like, what makes them similar, and what differentiates them.

Working with databases using Access 97 is covered in depth in six projects that teach beginning to intermediate skills. It begins with an Overview that introduces the basic concepts of the application and provides hands-on instructions to put students to work using the applications immediately. As they work through the projects, students learn problem-solving techniques that provide practical, relevant, real-life business scenarios.

Approach

The *Microsoft® Certified Select: Projects for Access 97 Blue Ribbon Edition* uses a document-centered approach to learning that focuses on *The Willows*; a running case study that helps students understand how the applications are used in a business setting. Each project begins with a list of measurable **Objectives**, a realistic case scenario called **The Challenge**, a well-defined plan called **The Solution**, and an illustration of the final product. **The Setup** enables students to verify that the settings on the computer match those needed for the project.

The project is arranged in carefully divided, highly visual objective-based tasks that foster confidence and self-reliance. Each project closes with a wrap-up of the project called **The Conclusion**, followed by summary questions, exercises, and assignments geared to reinforcing the information taught throughout the project.

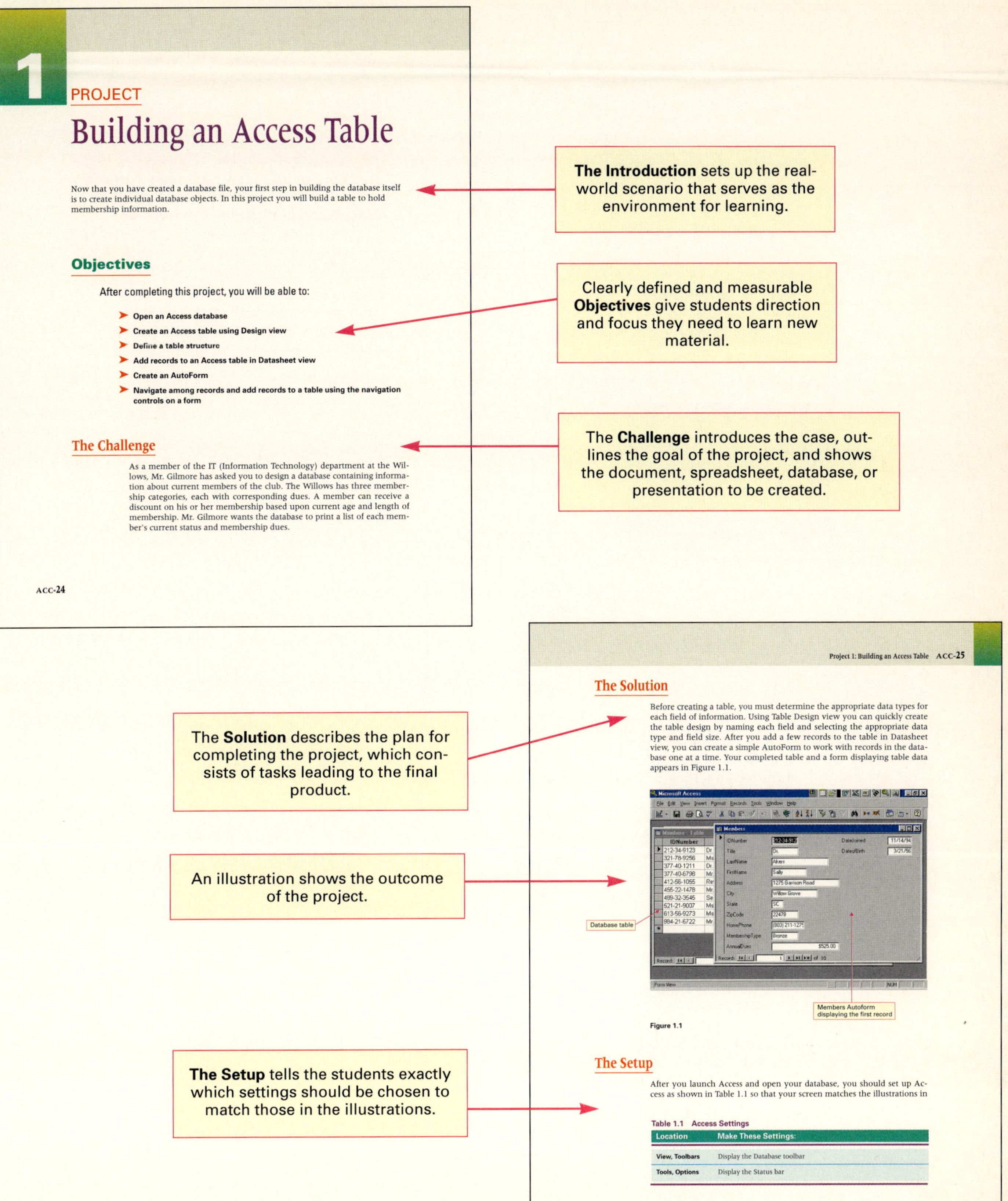

1 PROJECT

Building an Access Table

Now that you have created a database file, your first step in building the database itself is to create individual database objects. In this project you will build a table to hold membership information.

The Introduction sets up the real-world scenario that serves as the environment for learning.

Objectives

After completing this project, you will be able to:

- Open an Access database
- Create an Access table using Design view
- Define a table structure
- Add records to an Access table in Datasheet view
- Create an AutoForm
- Navigate among records and add records to a table using the navigation controls on a form

Clearly defined and measurable **Objectives** give students direction and focus they need to learn new material.

The Challenge

As a member of the IT (Information Technology) department at the Willows, Mr. Gilmore has asked you to design a database containing information about current members of the club. The Willows has three membership categories, each with corresponding dues. A member can receive a discount on his or her membership based upon current age and length of membership. Mr. Gilmore wants the database to print a list of each member's current status and membership dues.

The **Challenge** introduces the case, outlines the goal of the project, and shows the document, spreadsheet, database, or presentation to be created.

ACC-24

Project 1: Building an Access Table ACC-25

The Solution

Before creating a table, you must determine the appropriate data types for each field of information. Using Table Design view you can quickly create the table design by naming each field and selecting the appropriate data type and field size. After you add a few records to the table in Datasheet view, you can create a simple AutoForm to work with records in the database one at a time. Your completed table and a form displaying table data appears in Figure 1.1.

The **Solution** describes the plan for completing the project, which consists of tasks leading to the final product.

An illustration shows the outcome of the project.

Figure 1.1

The Setup

After you launch Access and open your database, you should set up Access as shown in Table 1.1 so that your screen matches the illustrations in

The Setup tells the students exactly which settings should be chosen to match those in the illustrations.

Table 1.1 Access Settings

Location	Make These Settings:
View, Toolbars	Display the Database toolbar
Tools, Options	Display the Status bar

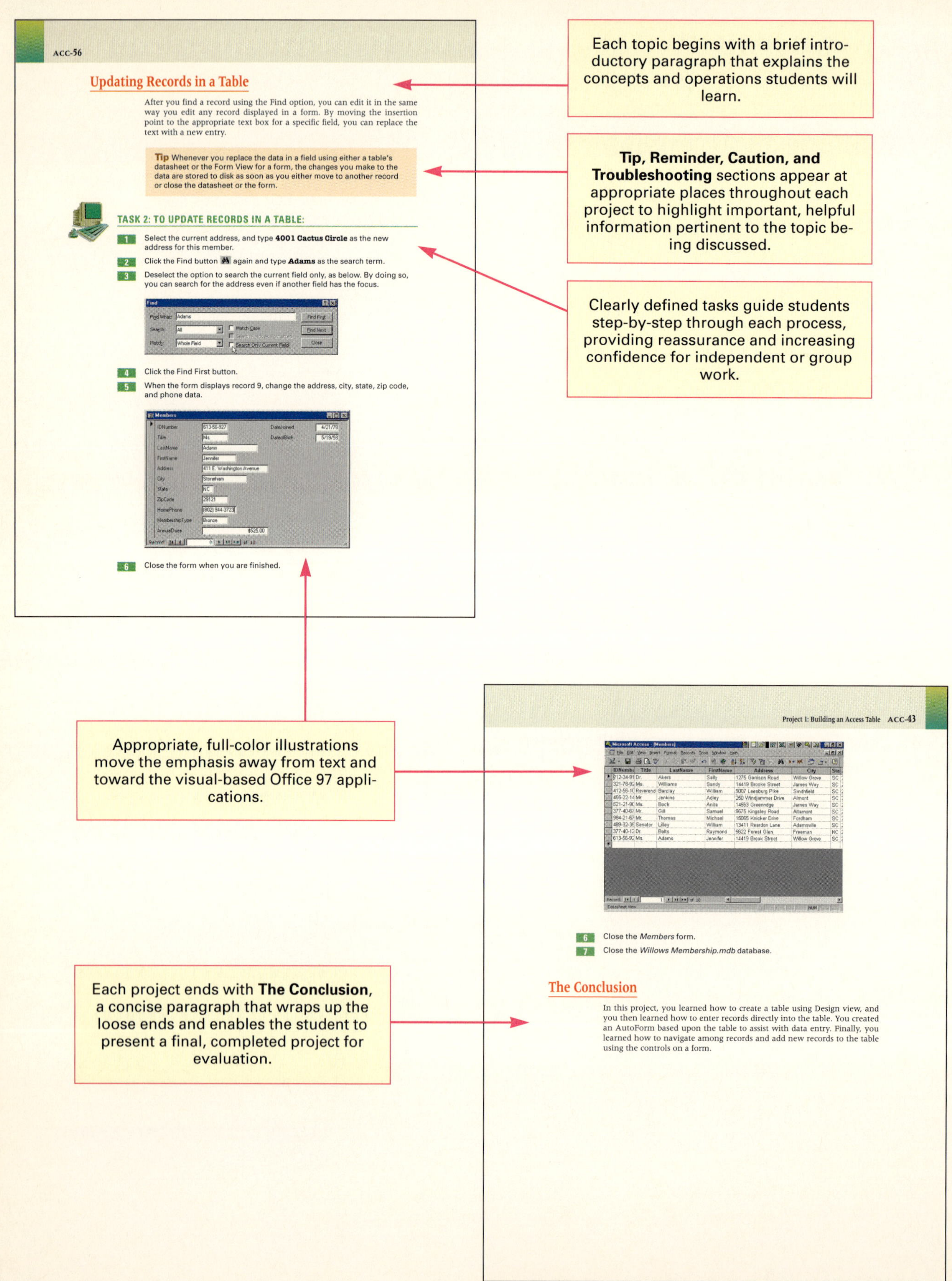

Each topic begins with a brief introductory paragraph that explains the concepts and operations students will learn.

Tip, Reminder, Caution, and Troubleshooting sections appear at appropriate places throughout each project to highlight important, helpful information pertinent to the topic being discussed.

Clearly defined tasks guide students step-by-step through each process, providing reassurance and increasing confidence for independent or group work.

Appropriate, full-color illustrations move the emphasis away from text and toward the visual-based Office 97 applications.

Each project ends with **The Conclusion**, a concise paragraph that wraps up the loose ends and enables the student to present a final, completed project for evaluation.

ACC-56

Updating Records in a Table

After you find a record using the Find option, you can edit it in the same way you edit any record displayed in a form. By moving the insertion point to the appropriate text box for a specific field, you can replace the text with a new entry.

Tip Whenever you replace the data in a field using either a table's datasheet or the Form View for a form, the changes you make to the data are stored to disk as soon as you either move to another record or close the datasheet or the form.

TASK 2: TO UPDATE RECORDS IN A TABLE:

1. Select the current address, and type **4001 Cactus Circle** as the new address for this member.
2. Click the Find button again and type **Adams** as the search term.
3. Deselect the option to search the current field only, as below. By doing so, you can search for the address even if another field has the focus.
4. Click the Find First button.
5. When the form displays record 9, change the address, city, state, zip code, and phone data.
6. Close the form when you are finished.

Project 1: Building an Access Table ACC-43

6. Close the *Members* form.
7. Close the *Willows Membership.mdb* database.

The Conclusion

In this project, you learned how to create a table using Design view, and you then learned how to enter records directly into the table. You created an AutoForm based upon the table to assist with data entry. Finally, you learned how to navigate among records and add new records to the table using the controls on a form.

Summary and Exercises

Summary

- Queries are database objects that you use to view, change, and analyze data in different ways.
- Queries are often used as the source of records for forms and reports.
- A select query retrieves data from one or more tables and displays the results in a datasheet.
- You use the Query Design window to create queries in Access.
- The Query Design window consists of two panes — the upper pane contains a list of tables and fields; the lower pane contains the query design grid.
- Fields that appear in the query design grid return information in a query datasheet when the query is run.
- Queries can contain calculated fields that return data according to an expression.
- You can easily create expressions using the Expression Builder.
- You can add sort order and criteria specifications to return specific records in a specified order.
- A query object can be the source for an Access AutoForm.

Key Terms and Operations

Key Terms

AND condition
calculated field
expression
Expression Builder
query
query datasheet
query design grid
Query Design View
run
select query

Operations

add calculated fields to a query using the Expression Builder
add fields to a query using the query design grid
add tables to a query
create a new query
create an Autoform based upon a query
define the sort order and criteria for a query
run a query
specify sort order and criteria

Study Questions

Multiple Choice

1. The query design grid appears in the
   a. Database window.
   b. Query datasheet.
   c. upper pane of the Query Design window.
   d. lower pane of the Query Design window.

A **Summary** in bulleted-list format further reinforces the Objectives and the material presented in the project.

Key terms are boldface and italicized throughout each project, and then listed for handy review in the summary section at the end of the project.

Study questions (Multiple Choice, Short Answer, and For Discussion) bring the content of the project into focus again and allow for independent or group review of the material learned.

4. What happens if you delete a field from a table that contains data?
5. Should you consider validating numeric field data?
6. If you want to improve the accuracy of data entered into a table, which field property or properties should you modify?
7. Which data type ensures that a primary key is always unique?
8. Many organizations have used what common identifier as a primary key in their databases?
9. Which property setting supplies a template that assists in data entry?
10. Which field property specifies a range of acceptable values for the field?

For Discussion

1. What is the difference between an input mask and a validation rule?
2. When you add a field to a table, what happens to the existing records?
3. In many Access database tables, an AutoNumber field is used as the primary key. Is this a good choice, and if so, why?
4. If you add a validation rule to a field, should you add validation text as well? Explain your answer.

Review Exercises

1. Creating an additional table and relating tables

You cannot appreciate the power of a relational database such as Access until you see why being able to relate table data is so significant. In this exercise, you will copy the Willows Membership database file, create an additional table, and relate the two tables. In Project 4, you will create a query that lists data from both tables. Complete the following:

1. Using the Windows Explorer or My Computer, copy the *Willows Membership.mdb* file. Rename the copy as **Membership Payments.mdb**.
2. Select the copy of *Members* table, and press the DEL key. Then click Yes on the confirmation alert box to delete the copy.
3. Create a new table using Design view. Use the field specifications in Table 3.2, set PaymentNumber as the primary key, and save the table as **Payments**.

   When you are finished defining the table structure and naming the table, the Table Design window should appear as below.

Table 3.2 Payments Table Field Specifications

Field Name	Data Type
PaymentNumber	AutoNumber
MemberID	Number
PaymentDate	Date/Time
Amount	Currency

Review Exercises present hands-on tasks for building on the skills acquired in the project.

4. Create an AutoReport named *Food Categories* for the table and print a copy of the AutoReport.
5. Save changes to the database and exit Access.

Assignments

1. Adding Validation Rules to the Willows Employees database

The Willows Employees database contains at least one field that requires a value within a specific range. Open the database, and then open the *Employees* table in Design view. Add a validation rule to the Salary field that specifies a salary greater than or equal to 25,000 and less than 100,000. Add validation text specifying that the value entered falls outside the salary range. Save your changes to the table, and close the table.

2. Changing Field properties in the Willows Employees database

When the Database Wizard created the Employees database, it set some of the field sizes to a value that is larger than necessary. Open the Willows Employees database if it is not currently open, and then open the *Employees* table in Design view. Change the field properties for the fields specified in Table 3.4.

For the StateOrProvince field, type **>LL** as the input mask. The mask requires an entry of two letters—A through Z—and if the user enters lowercase letters, they will be displayed in uppercase. Save your changes to the table, close it, and close the database.

Table 3.4 Field Size Property Values

Field Name	Field Size Property
SocialSecurityNumber	9
Title	10
LastName	20
FirstName	15
Address	50
City	15
StateOrProvince	2
PostalCode	9

Assignments invoke critical thinking and integration of project skills.

Other Features

In addition to the document-centered, visual approach of each project, this book contains the following features:

- An **Overview** of Windows 95 and the software application to help students feel comfortable and confident in the working environment.
- A **Function Reference Guide** for each application. Functions are arranged alphabetically rather than by menu.
- **Keycaps** and **toolbar button icons** within each step so students can quickly perform the required action.
- A comprehensive, well-organized end-of-the-project **Summary** and **Exercises** section for reviewing, integrating, and applying new skills.
- Illustrations or descriptions of the results of each step so students know they're on the right track throughout the project.

Student Supplements

QWIZ Assessment Software is a network-based skills assessment-testing program that measures student proficiency with Windows 95, Word 97, Excel 97, Access 97, and PowerPoint 97. Professors select the tasks to be tested and get student results immediately. The test is taken in a simulated software environment. On-screen instructions require students to perform tasks just as though they were using the actual application. The program automatically records responses, assesses student accuracy and reports the resulting score both in a printout or disk file as well as to the instructor's gradebook. The students receive immediate feedback from the program, including learning why a particular task was scored as incorrect and what part of the lab manual to review.

Instructor Supplements

On the Web: Instructors get extra support for this text from supplemental materials that can be downloaded from our password-protected Web site at http://hepg.awl.com/select/instructor. These materials include:

- Screen shots corresponding to key figures in the book that can be used for classroom presentation. Screen-by-screen steps in a project can be displayed in class or reviewed by students in the computer lab.
- The entire Instructor's Manual in Microsoft Word format
- Computerized Test Bank files. With these, you can create printed tests by viewing and editing test bank questions, make multiple versions of tests, easily search for and rearrange questions, and add or modify the questions. In addition, you can administer tests on a network, as well as convert your tests to HTML to post to the Web for students to use for practice. Self-assessment quizzes for the Internet are available also.

- Project Outlines
- Solution files
- Text updates

Student data files are available at http://hepg.awl.com/select

Contact your Addison Wesley Longman sales representative for your ID and password for the Instructor's site.

Printed Materials: The printed Instructor's Manual includes a Test Bank and Transparency Masters for each project in the student text. The Test Bank contains two separate tests with answers, and consists of multiple choice, true/false, and fill-in questions that refer to pages in the student text. Transparency Masters illustrate key concepts and screen captures from the text.

In addition, the printed Instructor's Manual includes expanded student objectives, answers to study questions, and additional assessment techniques.

Acknowledgments

When a *team* combines their knowledge and skills to produce a work designed to meet the needs of students and professors across the country, they take on an unenviable challenge.

To **Anita Devine** for the steady editorial focus needed to make the *Microsoft Certified Blue Ribbon Edition* happen.

To **Phil Koneman**, Series Consulting Editor, your suggestions and comments were invaluable.

Thanks to **Emily Kim** and **Pauline Johnson** who were more than just technical editors, but who also made sure things worked the way we said they would. To those in production, especially to **Gillian Hall**, **Diane Freed**, and **Pat Mahtani**, your efforts have paid off in a highly user-friendly book!

To **Tom Ziolkowski** and **Deanna Storey**, thanks for your strong marketing insights for this book.

Many people helped form the cornerstone of the original work, and we would like to thank **Barb Terry**, **Robin Drake**, **Chuck Hutchinson**, **Martha Johnson**, **Robin Edwards**, and **Deborah Minyard**.

And, finally, thanks to everyone at Addison Wesley Longman who has followed this project from start to finish.

P.T.

Acknowledgments

Addison-Wesley Publishing Company would like to thank the following reviewers for their valuable contributions to the *SELECT Lab Series.*

James Agnew
Northern Virginia Community College

Joseph Aieta
Babson College

Dr. Muzaffar Ali
Bellarmine College

Tom Ashby
Oklahoma CC

Bob Barber
Lane CC

Robert Caruso
Santa Rosa Junior College

Robert Chi
California State Long Beach

Jill Davis
State University of New York at Stony Brook

Fredia Dillard
Samford University

Peter Drexel
Plymouth State College

David Egle
University of Texas, Pan American

Linda Ericksen
Lane Community College

Jonathan Frank
Suffolk University

Patrick Gilbert
University of Hawaii

Maureen Greenbaum
Union County College

Sally Ann Hanson
Mercer County CC

Sunil Hazari
East Carolina University

Gloria Henderson
Victor Valley College

Bruce Herniter
University of Hartford

Rick Homkes
Purdue University

Lisa Jackson
Henderson CC

Martha Johnson
(technical reviewer)
Delta State University

Cynthia Kachik
Santa Fe CC

Bennett Kramer
Massasoit CC

Charles Lake
Faulkner State Junior College

Ron Leake
Johnson County CC

Randy Marak
Hill College

Charles Mattox, Jr.
St. Mary's University

Jim McCullough
Porter and Chester Institute

Gail Miles
Lenoir-Rhyne College

Steve Moore
University of South Florida

Anthony Nowakowski
Buffalo State College

Gloria Oman
Portland State University

John Passafiume
Clemson University

Leonard Presby
William Paterson College

Louis Pryor
Garland County CC

Michael Reilly
University of Denver

Dick Ricketts
Lane CC

Dennis Santomauro
Kean College of New Jersey

Pamela Schmidt
Oakton CC

Gary Schubert
Alderson-Broaddus College

T. Michael Smith
Austin CC

Cynthia Thompson
Carl Sandburg College

Marion Tucker
Northern Oklahoma College

JoAnn Weatherwax
Saddleback College

David Whitney
San Francisco State University

James Wood
Tri-County Technical College

Minnie Yen
University of Alaska, Anchorage

Allen Zilbert
Long Island University

Contents

Overview of Windows 95

Overview of Windows 95

Microsoft Windows 95 is an ***operating system,*** a special kind of computer program that performs three major functions. First, an operating system controls the actual ***hardware*** of the computer (the screen, the keyboard, the disk drives, and so on). Second, an operating system enables other software programs such as word processing or spreadsheet ***applications*** to run. Finally, an operating system determines how the user operates the computer and its programs or applications.

As an operating system, Windows 95 and all other programs written to run under it provide ***graphics*** (or pictures) called ***icons*** to carry out commands and run programs. For this reason, Windows 95 is referred to as a ***Graphical User Interface*** or GUI (pronounced *gooey*). You can use the keyboard or a device called a ***mouse*** to activate the icons.

This overview explains the basics of Windows 95 so that you can begin using your computer quickly and easily.

Objectives

After completing this project, you will be able to:

- **Launch Windows 95**
- **Identify the desktop elements**
- **Use a mouse**
- **Use the basic features of Windows 95**
- **Organize your computer**
- **Work with multiple programs**
- **Get help**
- **Exit Windows 95**

Launching Windows 95

Because Windows 95 is an operating system, it launches immediately when you turn on the computer. Depending on the way your computer is set up, you may have to type your user name and password to log on — to get permission to begin using the program. After Windows 95 launches, the working environment, called the ***desktop,*** displays on the screen.

Identifying the Desktop Elements

Figure W.1 shows the Windows 95 desktop with several icons that represent the hardware and the software installed on the computer. ***My Computer*** enables you to organize your work. The ***Recycle Bin*** is a temporary storage area for files deleted from the hard disk. At the bottom of the desktop is the ***Taskbar*** for starting programs, accessing various areas of Windows 95, and switching among programs.

Figure W.1

Note The desktop can be customized, so the desktop on the computer you're using will not look exactly like the one shown in the illustrations in this overview.

Using a Mouse

A pointing device is almost an indispensable tool for using Windows 95. Although you can use the keyboard to navigate and make selections, using a mouse is often more convenient and efficient.

When you move the mouse on your desk, a pointer moves on the screen. When the pointer is on the object you want to use, you can take one of the actions described in Table W.1 to give Windows 95 an instruction.

Table W.1 Mouse Actions

Action	Description
Point	Slide the mouse across a smooth surface (preferably a mouse pad) until the pointer on the screen is on the object.
Click	Press and release the left mouse button once.
Drag	Press and hold down the left mouse button while you move the mouse, and then release the mouse button to complete the action.
Right-click	Press and release the right mouse button once. Right-clicking usually displays a shortcut menu.
Double-click	Press and release the left mouse button twice in rapid succession.

TASK 1: TO PRACTICE USING THE MOUSE:

1. Point to the My Computer icon, press and hold down the left mouse button, and then drag the mouse across the desk.
   The icon moves.
2. Drag the My Computer icon back to its original location.
3. Right-click the icon.

Your shortcut menu may not match this menu

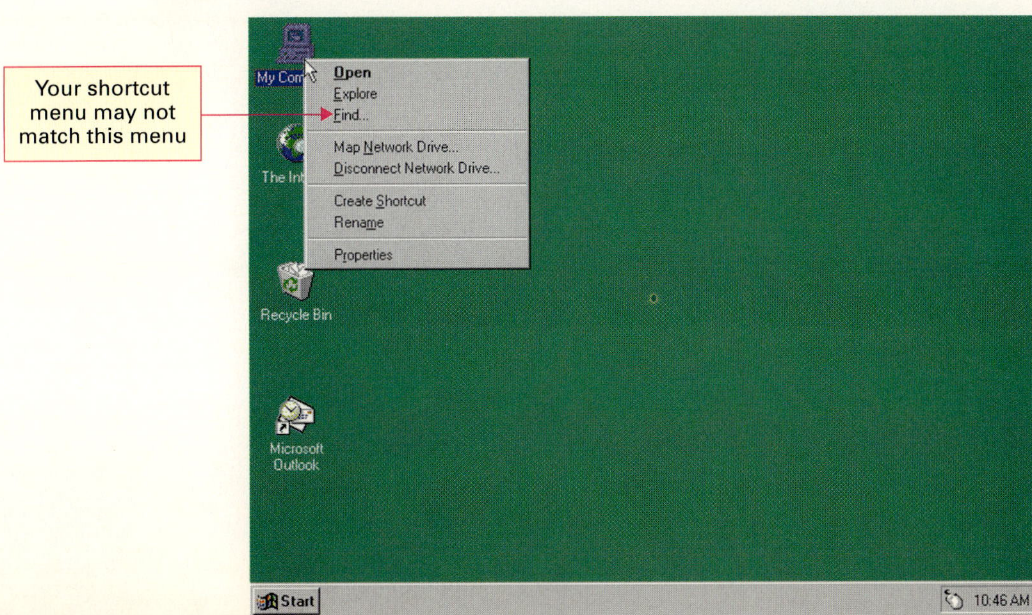

4. Click a blank space on the screen. The shortcut menu closes.

5. Double-click the My Computer icon.

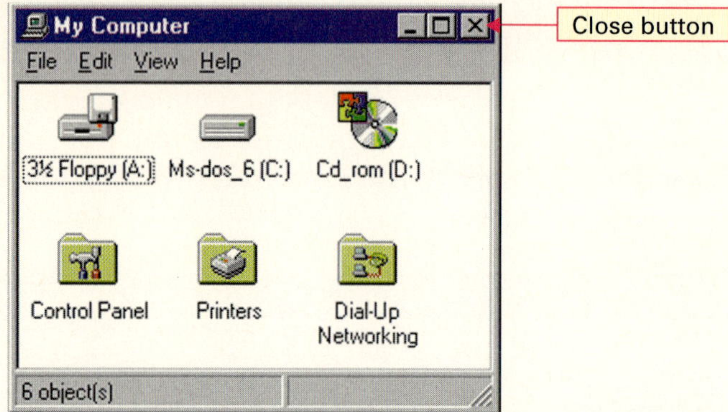

6. Click the Close button to close the My Computer window.

Using the Basic Features of Windows 95

The basic features of Windows 95 are menus, windows, menu bars, dialog boxes, and toolbars. These features are used in all programs that are written to run under Windows 95.

Using the Start Menu

Menus contain the commands you use to perform tasks. In Windows 95, you can use the Start menu shown in Figure W.2 to start programs and to access other Windows options.

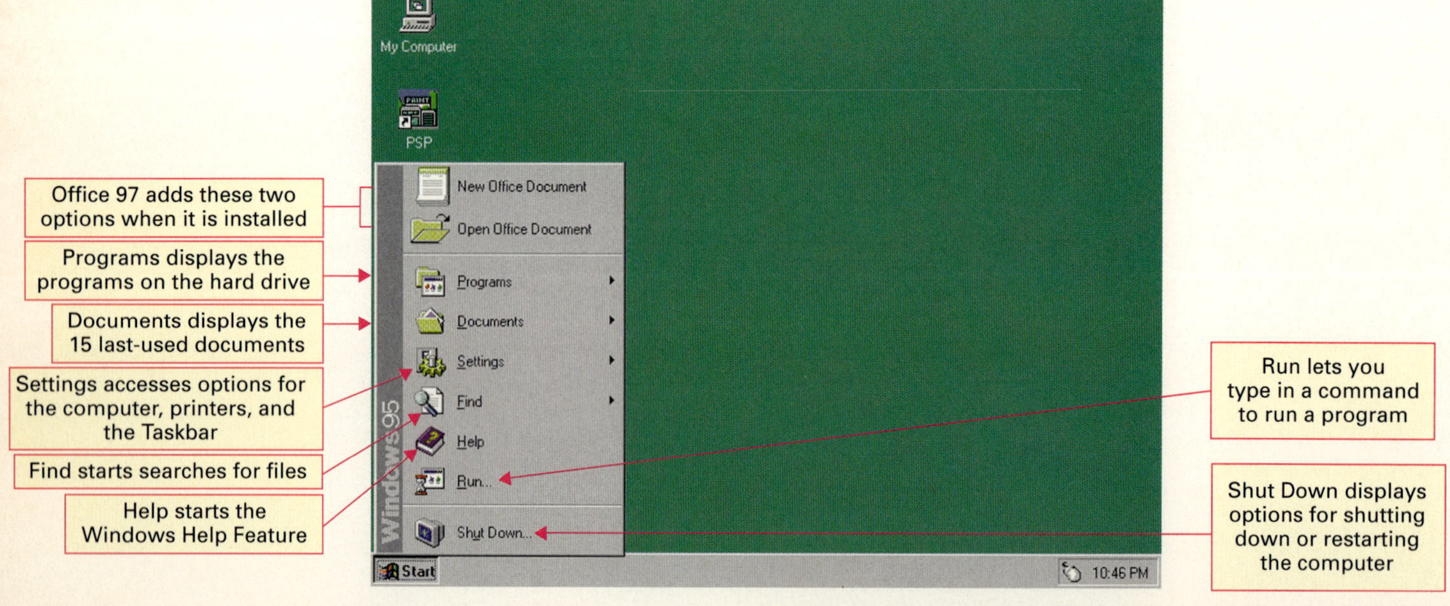

Figure W.2

TASK 2: TO USE THE START MENU TO LAUNCH A PROGRAM:

1 Click the Start button.
The triangles beside several of the menu options indicate that the options will display another menu.

2 Point to Programs and click the Windows Explorer icon on the cascading menu.
The Exploring window opens (see Figure W.3). You can use this feature of Windows 95 to manage files.

Using Windows

Clicking on the Windows Explorer icon opened a ***window,*** a Windows 95 feature that you saw earlier when you opened the My Computer window. Figure W.3 shows the common elements that most windows contain.

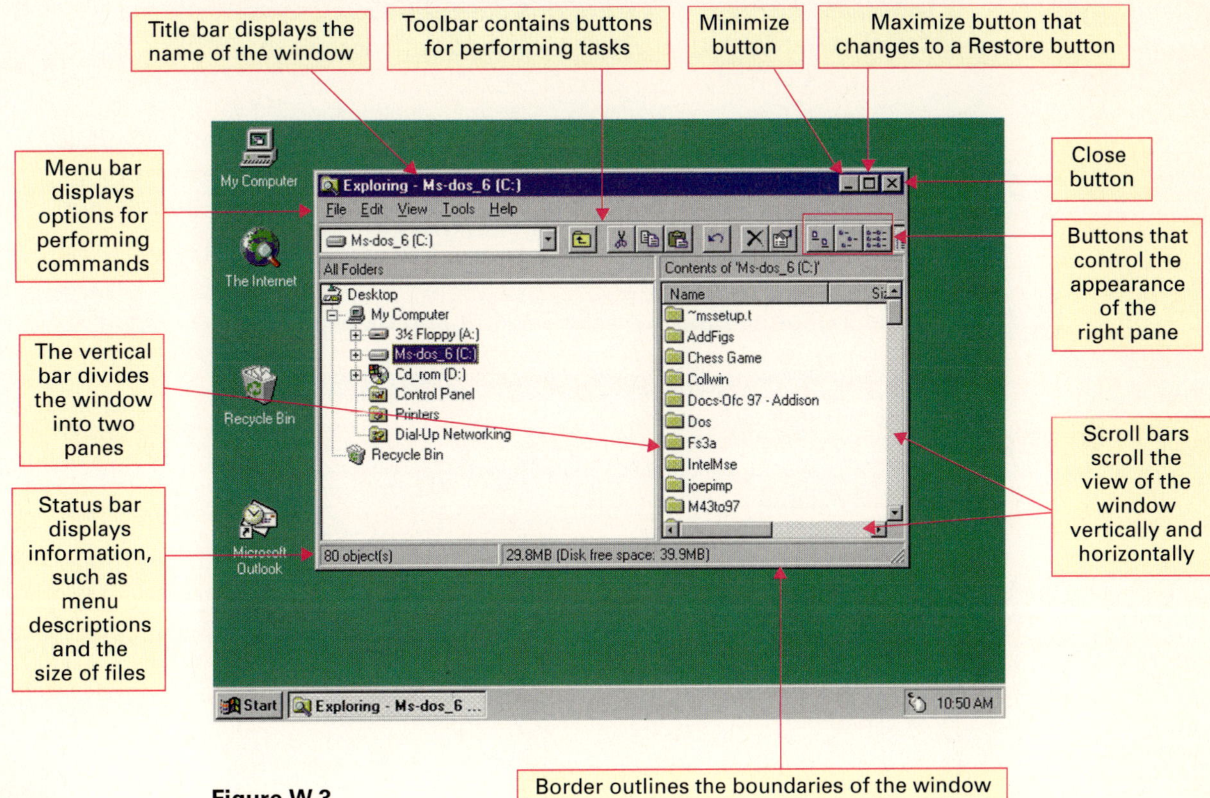

Figure W.3

TASK 3: TO WORK WITH A WINDOW:

1 Click the Maximize button if it is displayed. If it is not displayed, click the Restore button, and then click the Maximize button.
The Maximize button changes to a Restore button.

2 Click the Minimize button.

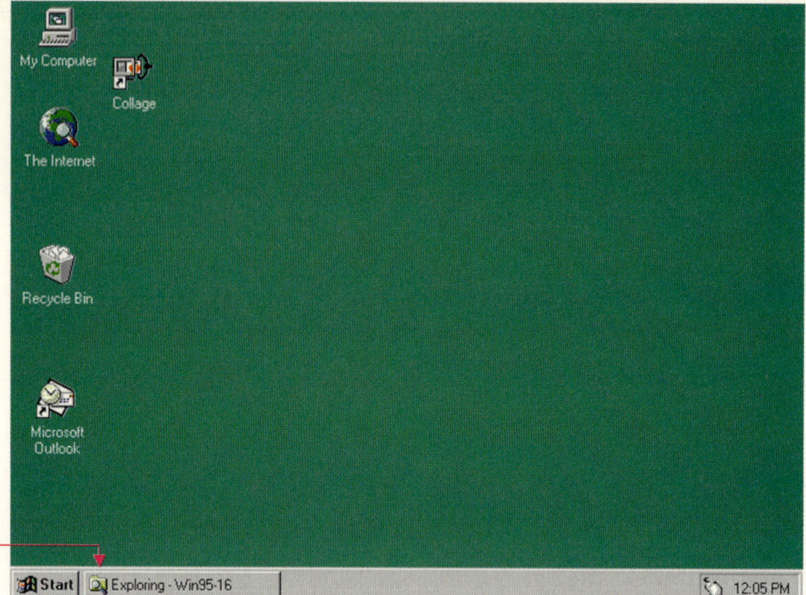

Warning When you minimize a window, the program in the window is still running and therefore using computer memory. To exit a program that is running in a window, you must click the Close button, not the Minimize button.

3 Click the Exploring button on the Taskbar and then click [icon].

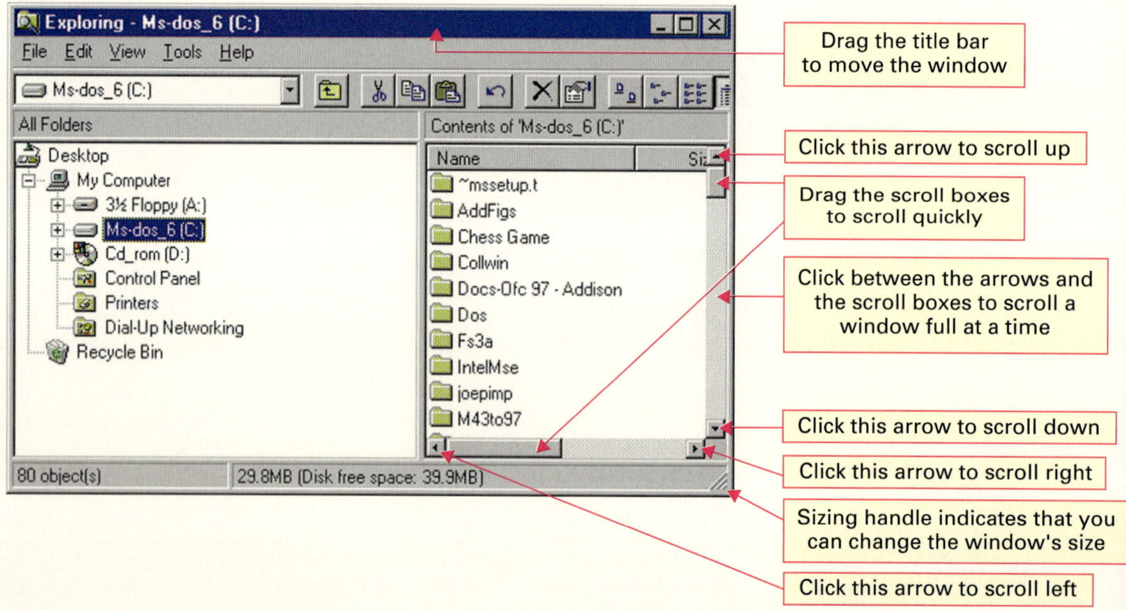

4 Point to the border of the Exploring window until the pointer changes to a double-headed black arrow, and then drag the border to make the window wider. (Be sure that all the buttons in the toolbar are visible.)

5 Practice scrolling.

6 When you are comfortable with your scrolling expertise, click [icon].

Using Menu Bars and Toolbars

Menu bars and toolbars are generally located at the top of a window. You can select a menu option in a menu bar by clicking the option or by pressing ALT and then typing the underlined letter for the option. When you select an option, a drop-down menu appears. Figure W.4 shows a menu with many of the elements common to menus.

Note Because you can select menu commands in two ways, the steps with instructions to select a menu command will use the word choose instead of dictating the method of selection.

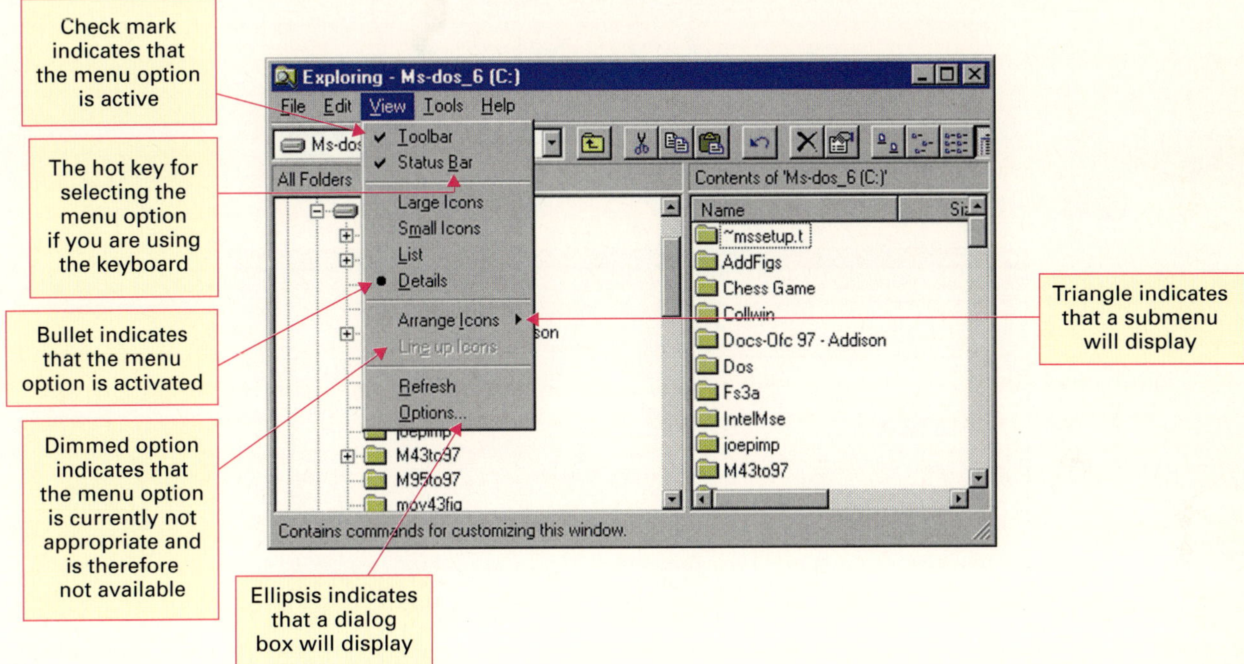

Figure W.4

Toolbars contain buttons that perform many of the same commands found on menus. To use a toolbar button, click the button; Windows 95 takes an immediate action, depending on the button's function.

Tip If you don't know what a button on the toolbar does, point to the button; a ToolTip, a brief description of the button, appears near the button.

TASK 4: TO USE MENUS AND TOOLBARS:

1. Choose View in the Exploring window.
   The View menu shown in Figure W.4 displays.
2. Choose Large Icons.

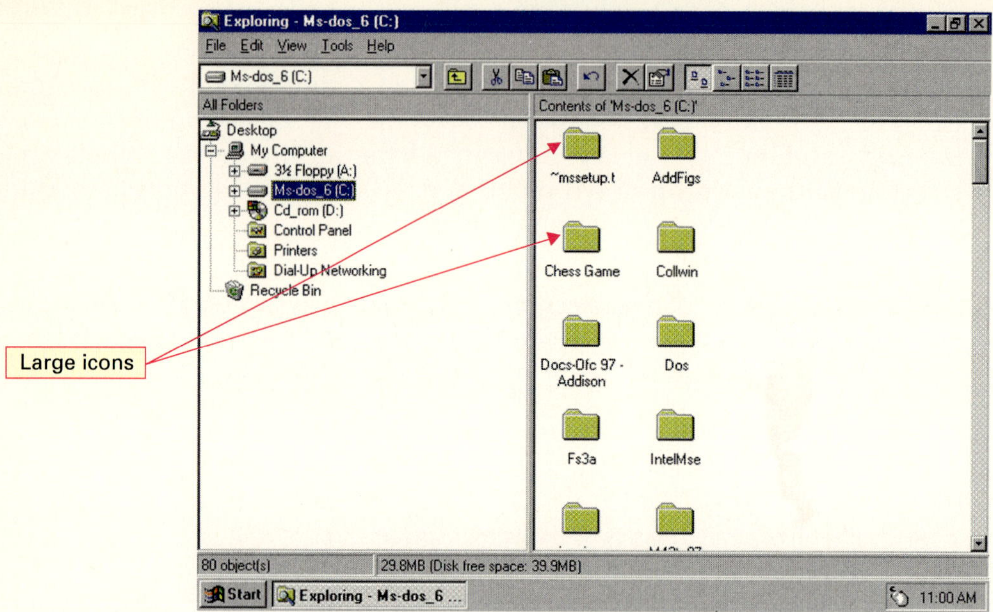

3 Click the Details button on the toolbar.

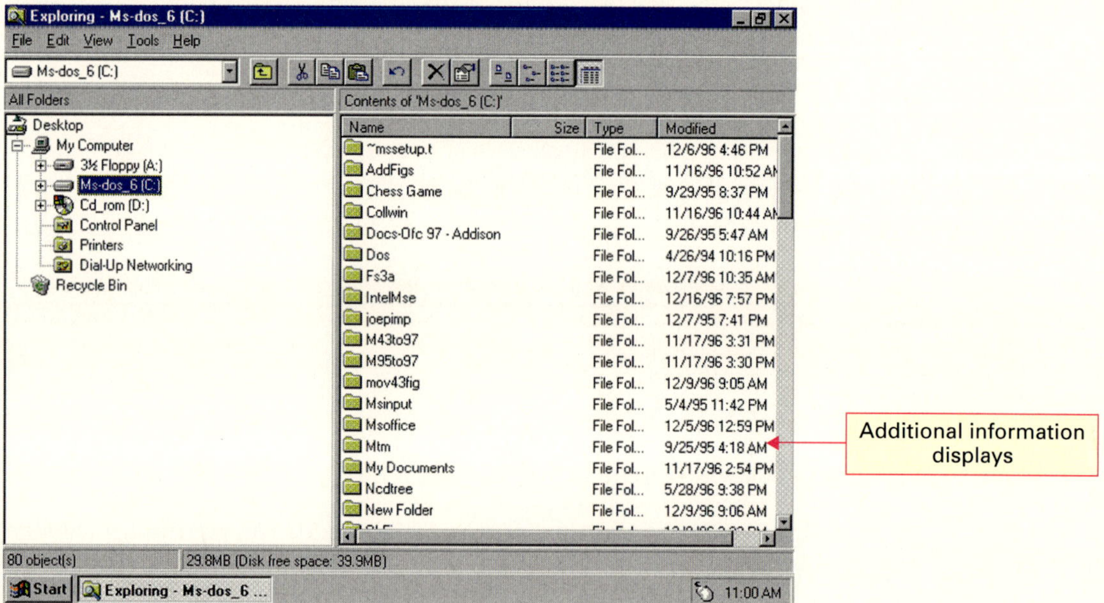

Using Dialog Boxes

When many options are available for a single task, Windows 95 conveniently groups the options in one place, called a ***dialog box.*** Some functions have so many options that Windows 95 divides them further into groups and places them on separate pages in the dialog box. Figures W.5 and W.6 show dialog boxes with different types of options. Throughout the remainder of this project, you practice using dialog boxes.

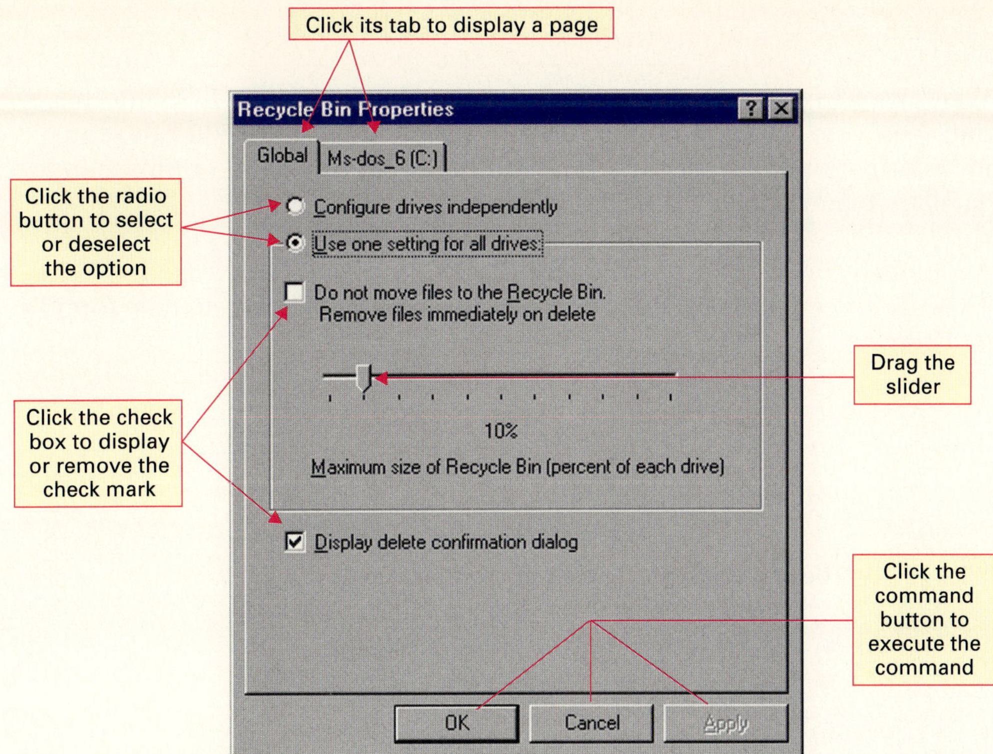

Figure W.5

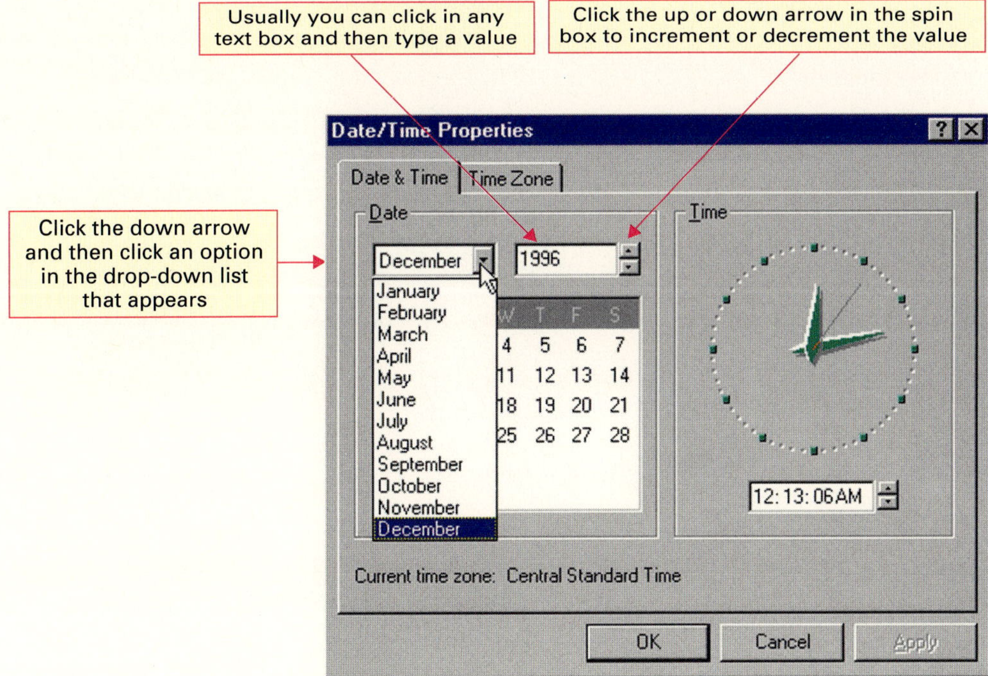

Figure W.6

Getting Help

Windows 95 provides you with three methods of accessing help information: You can look up information in a table of contents; you can search for information in an index; or you can find a specific word or phrase in a database maintained by the Find feature.

Additionally, Windows 95 provides ***context-sensitive help,*** called ***What's This?*** for the topic you are working on. This type of help is generally found in dialog boxes.

After you learn to use Help in Windows 95, you can use help in any Windows program because all programs use the same help format.

TASK 12: TO USE HELP CONTENTS, INDEX, AND FIND:

1. Click the Start button on the Taskbar and click Help.

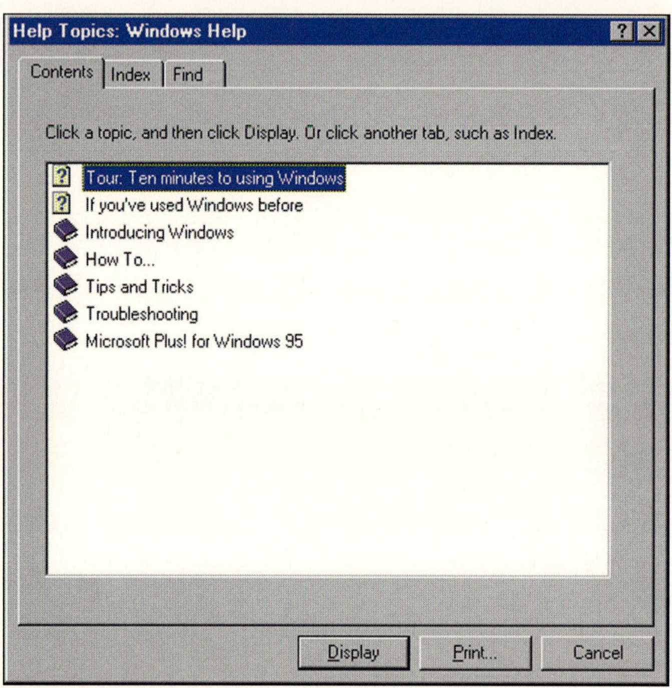

2. Click the Contents tab if a different page is displayed. The Contents page displays.

3 Double-click Tips and Tricks.

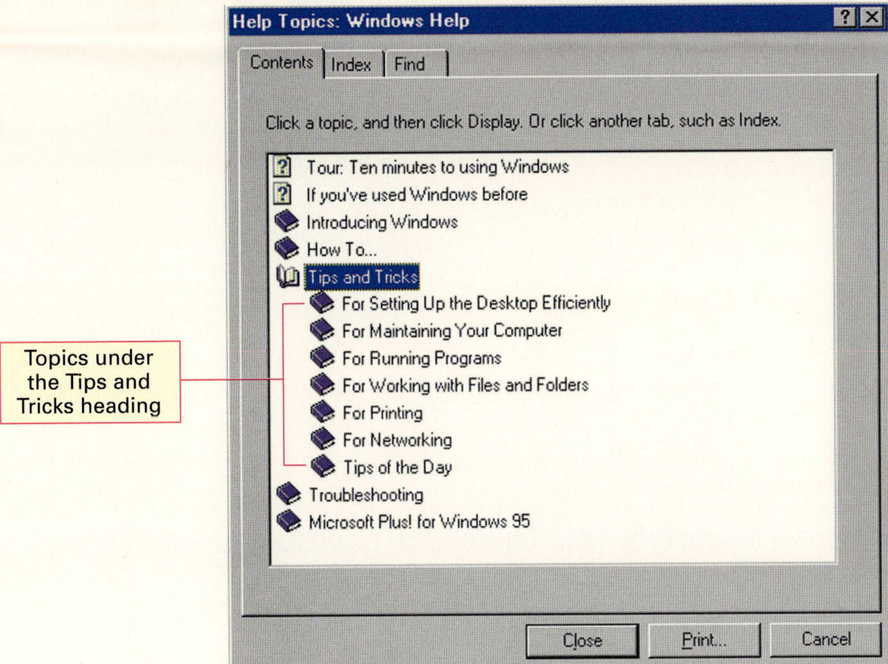

4 Double-click Tips of the Day.

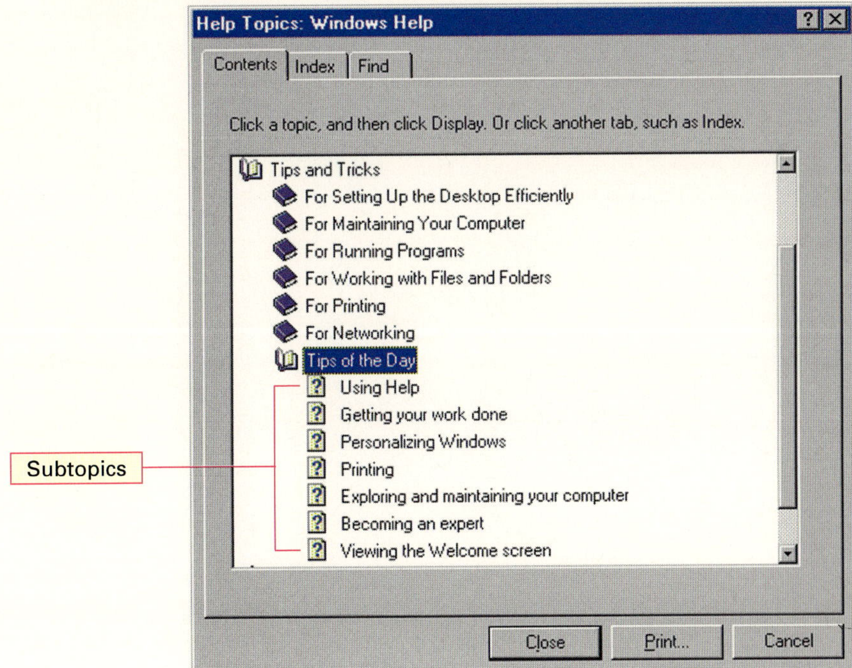

5 Double-click Using Help.

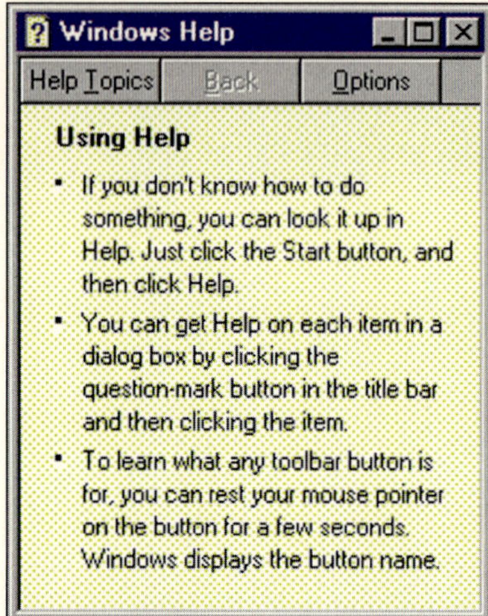

6 Read the information, click the Help Topics button, and then click the Index tab.

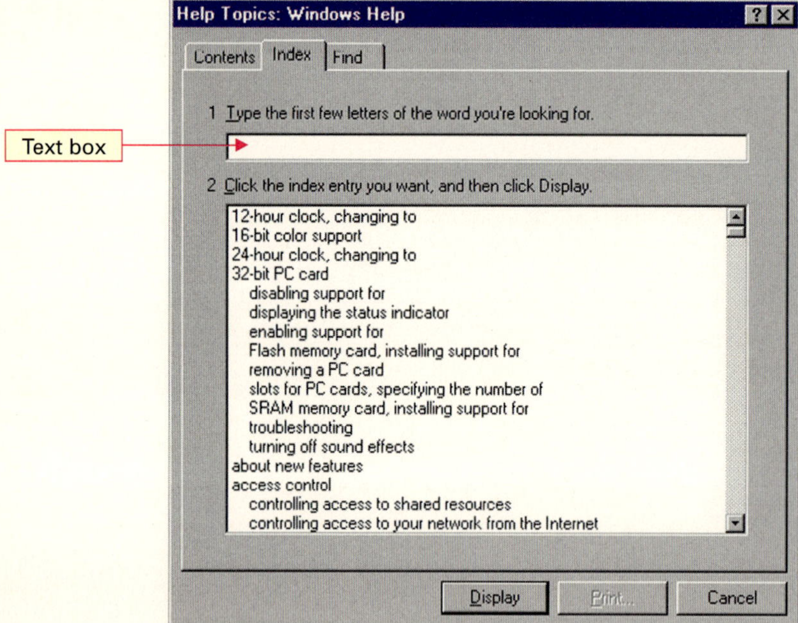

7 Type **shortcut** in the textbox.

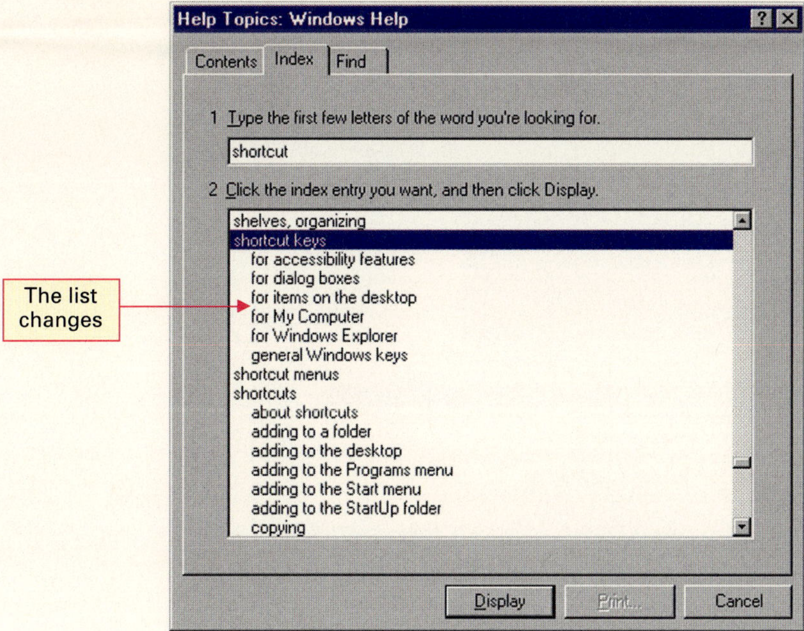

8 Double-click "shortcut menus" in the list.

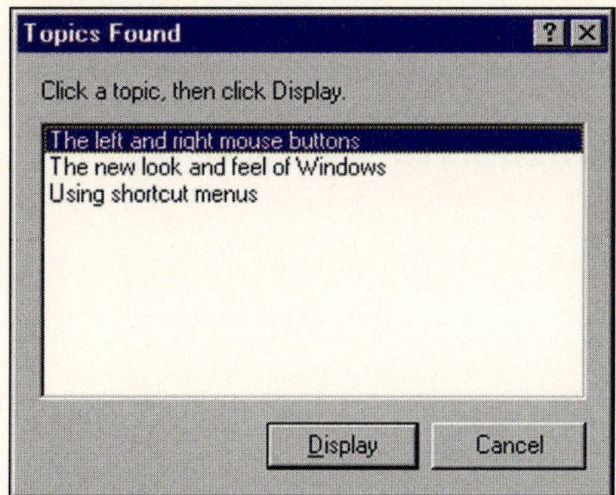

9 Double-click "Using shortcut menus."

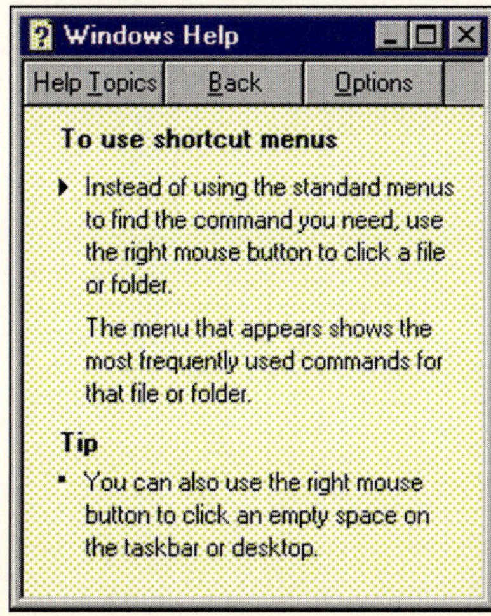

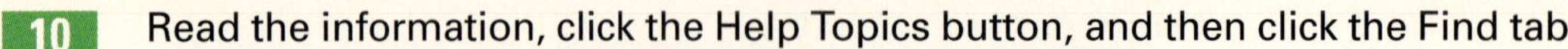

10 Read the information, click the Help Topics button, and then click the Find tab.

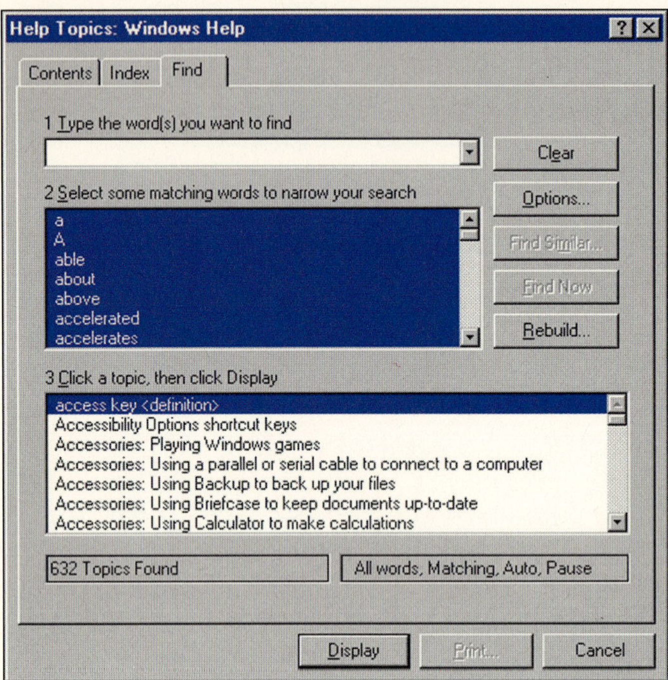

11 Click the What's This **?** button in the Help Topics title bar. A question mark is attached to the mouse pointer.

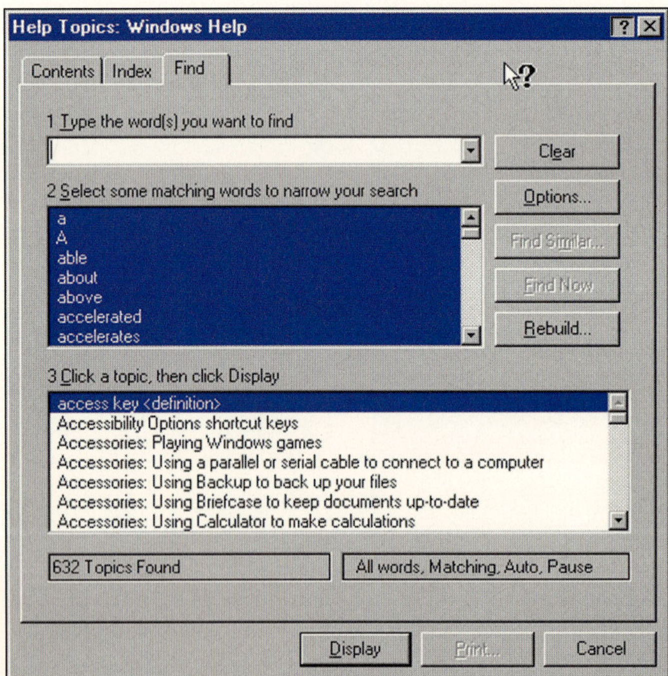

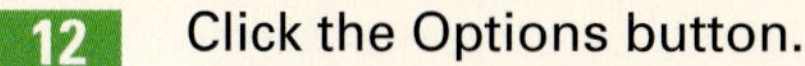

12 Click the Options button.

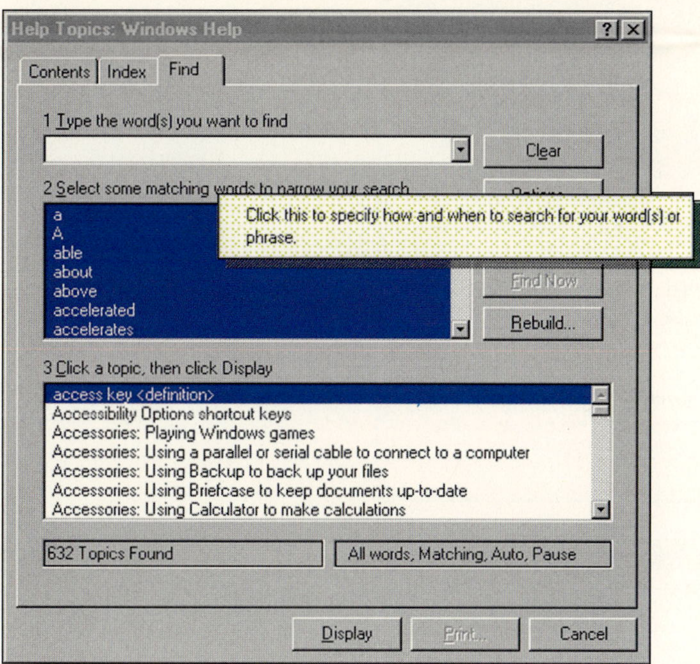

13 Read the pop-up message and then click it.
The message closes.

14 Type **printing help.** (If the list at the bottom of the screen doesn't change, click the Find Now button.)

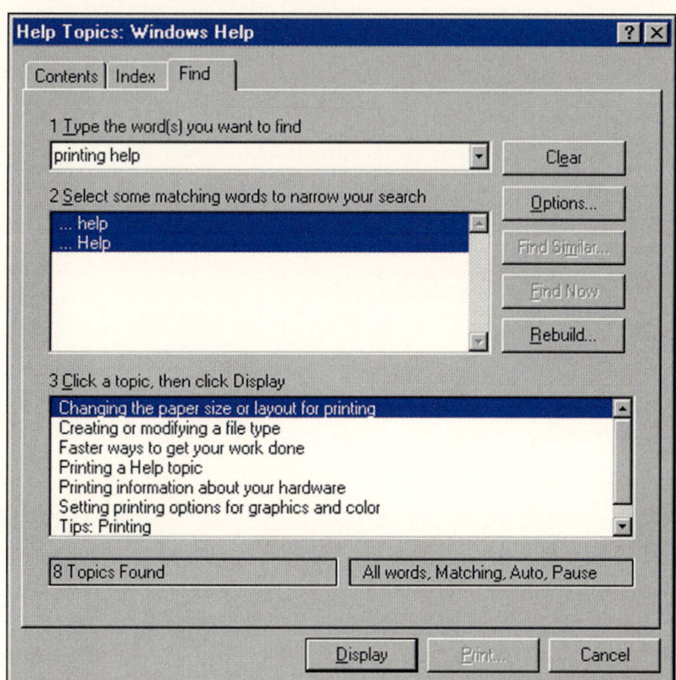

15 If necessary, scroll to "Printing a Help topic" in the list that displays and then double-click it.

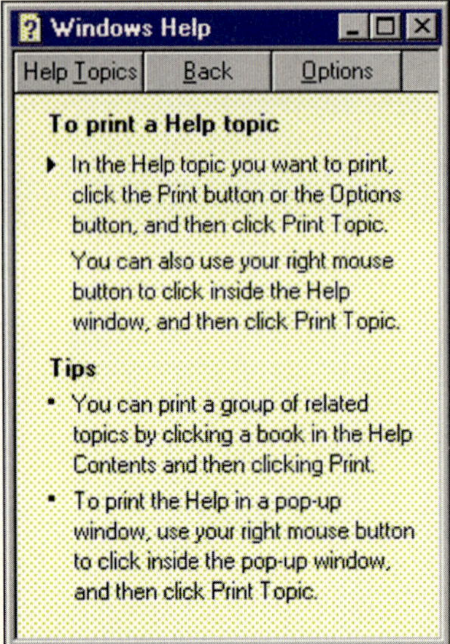

16 Click ✕.
The Help dialog box closes.

Tip You can print any help article by right-clicking anywhere in the article and choosing Print Topic.

Exiting Windows 95

When you are ready to turn off the computer, you must exit Windows 95 first. You should never turn off the computer without following the proper exit procedure because Windows 95 has to do some utility tasks before it shuts down. Unlike most of us, Windows 95 likes to put everything away when it's finished. When you shut down improperly, you can cause serious problems in Windows 95.

TASK 13: TO EXIT WINDOWS 95:

1 Click the Start button and then click Shut Down.

2 Click Shut down the computer? and then click Yes.

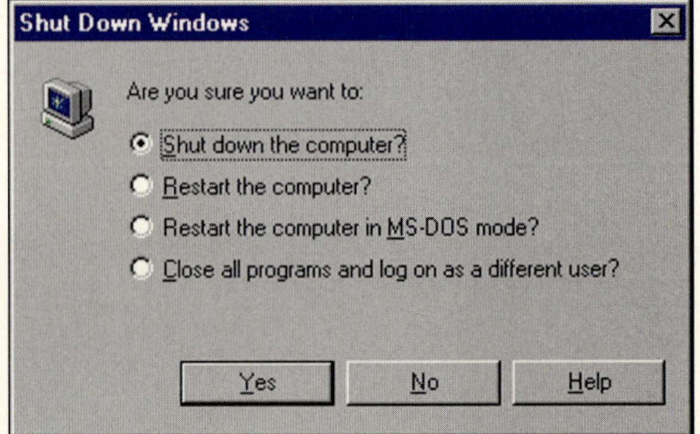

3 When the message "It's now safe to turn off your computer" appears, turn off the computer.

Active Desktop and Windows 98 Preview

Active Desktop and Windows 98 Preview

If you are running Windows 95 and your desktop looks significantly different from the desktop pictures found in the Overview of Windows 95, you may have Internet Explorer 4.0 installed with the Active Desktop. The Active Desktop contains features such as Taskbar toolbars, Internet Explorer Channel bar, and a Web-designed desktop background—features also available in Windows 98.

Other Windows 98 features—such as memory managers and file allocation tables—operate behind the scenes to improve the efficiency of your computer. Like Windows 95, Windows 98 is an operating system. Windows 98, however, operates with increased memory management capabilities. As a result, unless your computer is an older computer running less than 166 MHz, you should notice smoother transition when you move between programs, increased speed when performing basic tasks, and fewer program errors.

Many of the basic Windows 95 features, such as toolbars, are updated with a new look in Windows 98 because of the Active Desktop enhancement and the integration of Internet Explorer 4.0. Other features—such as the title bar and the minimize, maximize, and close buttons—remain unchanged. You will find that both Windows 98 and the Windows 95 Active Desktop are intimately integrated with the Internet and the World Wide Web. With the Active Desktop features, these "worlds" are literally just a click away.

This Active Desktop overview provides a preview of what to expect with Windows 98. You'll find that, in most cases, the procedures for using Windows 95 Active Desktop/Windows 98 features are identical to the procedures for using Windows 95 features.

Objectives

After completing this project, you will be able to:

- **Identify elements of the Windows 95 Active Desktop**
- **Use desktop ToolTips**
- **Launch programs**
- **Customize the Windows 95 Active Desktop**

- Edit the Start menu
- Restore the desktop to its original format

Identifying Elements of the Windows 95 Active Desktop

Both Windows 95 and Windows 98 start automatically each time you power up your computer. The appearance of the Active Desktop is controlled by options you choose when you install Internet Explorer 4.0. When you install Windows 98 the Active Desktop is installed, and the Web Channels bar displays automatically on your computer. You can choose to view your desktop as a Web page and to view the Internet Explorer Channel bar to provide easy access to pre-defined Web sites. These features are identified in the Active Desktop displayed in Figure A.1. If these features were not selected when you installed Internet Explorer 4.0 or Windows 98 on your computer, you can display the features from the Active Desktop.

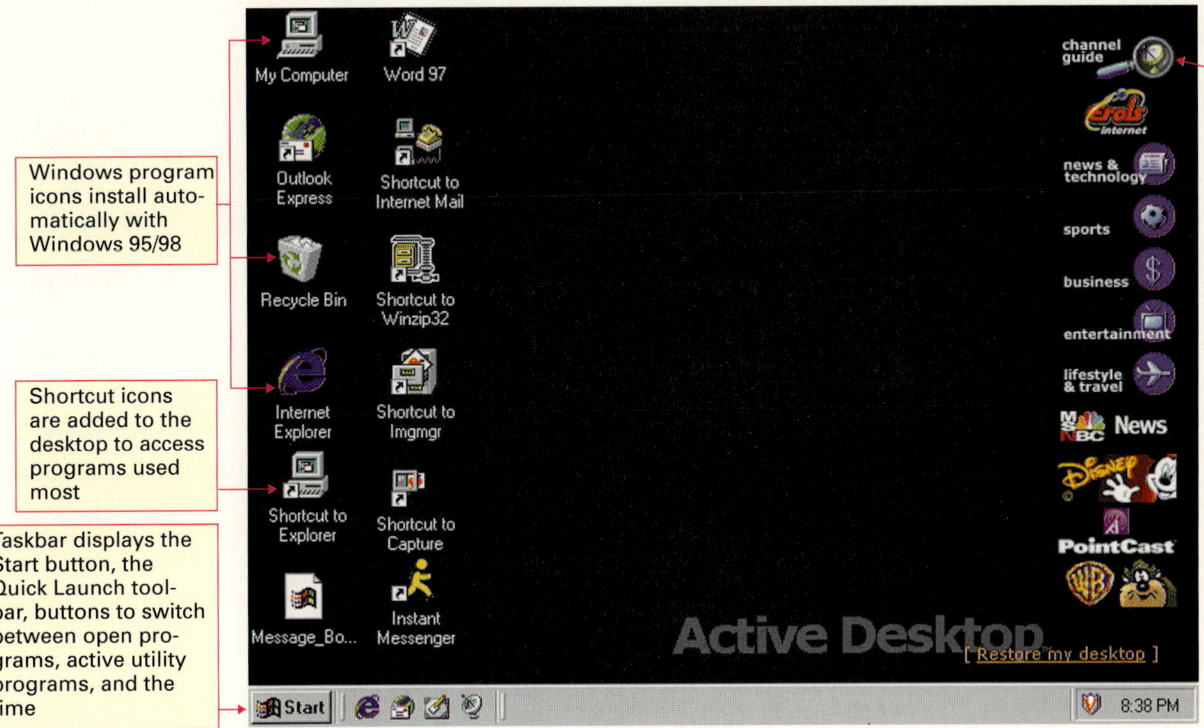

Figure A.1

Note Because the desktop can be customized, your desktop may not appear exactly as the one shown in the illustrations in this preview — even if you choose to display the Internet Explorer Channel bar and the desktop as a Web page.

Displaying the Internet Explorer Channel Bar

The Internet Explorer Channel bar appears in its own window when it is active. As a result, you can close the window by clicking the Close button that appears when you position the mouse pointer near the top edge of the Channel Guide button at the top of the Channel bar. Then use these procedures to restore the Internet Explorer Channel bar.

TASK 1: TO DISPLAY THE INTERNET EXPLORER CHANNEL BAR AFTER INSTALLATION:

1. Right-click a blank area of the Active Desktop and choose Active Desktop, as shown in the following figure.

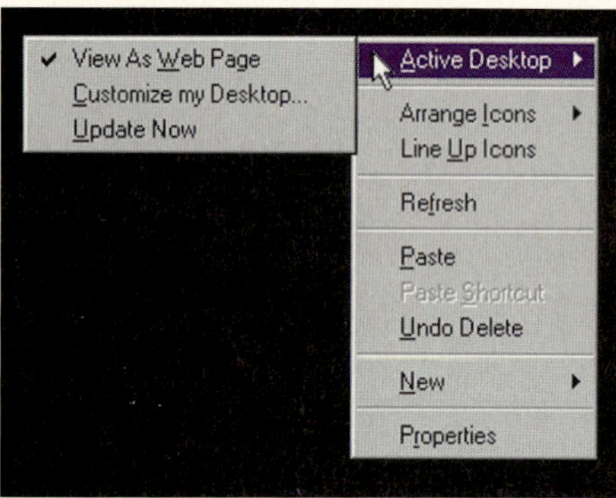

2. Choose Customize my Desktop.
   The Display Properties dialog box opens.
3. Click the Web page of the dialog box, if necessary, as illustrated in the following figure.

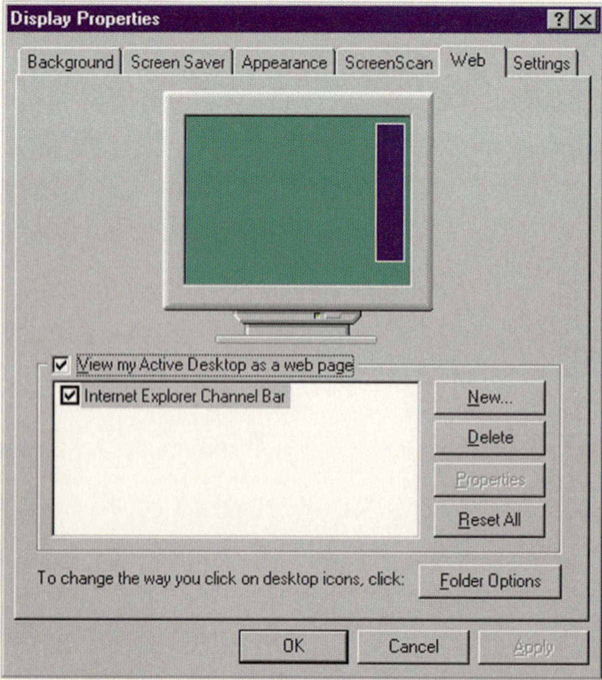

4. Check the View my Active Desktop as a web page check box, if necessary.

5 Check the Internet Explorer Channel Bar check box.
The Internet Explorer Channel bar shape appears in the preview monitor.

6 Choose Apply and then choose OK.

Displaying the Active Desktop Wallpaper

The default Active Desktop Web wallpaper displays a pre-formatted background. If your desktop is formatted with a different background, you can change the wallpaper to the Active Desktop Web wallpaper.

TASK 2: TO DISPLAY THE ACTIVE DESKTOP WALLPAPER AFTER INSTALLATION:

1 Right-click on a blank area on the Active Desktop and choose Properties.
The Display Properties dialog box opens.

2 Click the Background page tab, if necessary, to produce the screen shown in the following figure.

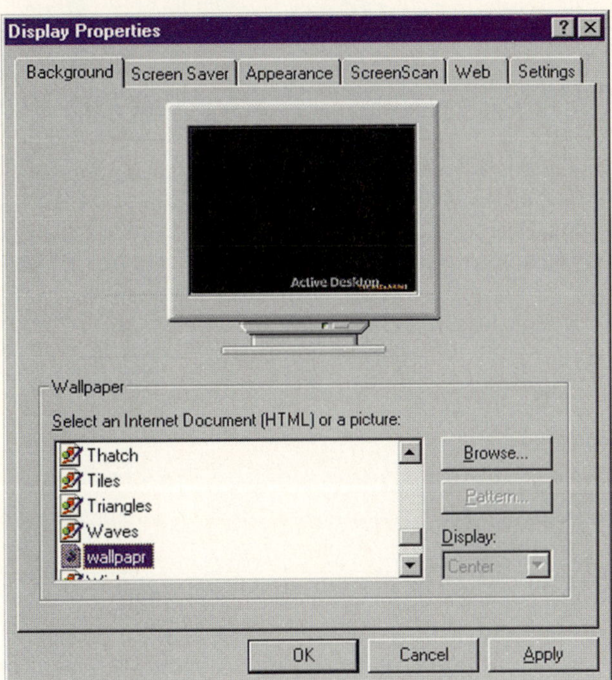

3 Select wallpapr from the Wallpaper list.
The preview monitor displays the Active Desktop Web wallpaper.

Note The list of background designs varies depending on programs previously installed on your computer. If wallpapr is unavailable, select the background identified by your instructor.

4 Choose Apply and then choose OK.
The desktop is reformatted.

Using Desktop ToolTips

Other features that have been enhanced by the Active Desktop and Windows 98 include desktop ToolTips and shortcut menus. With the Active Desktop, simply pointing to an icon or desktop feature identifies the feature and, in some instances, displays explanatory information about the feature.

TASK 3: TO DISPLAY DESKTOP TOOLTIPS:

1. Click on a blank area of the Desktop to make it active.
   The Desktop must be active before ToolTips appear.
2. Position the mouse pointer on the selected icon, as shown in the following figure.

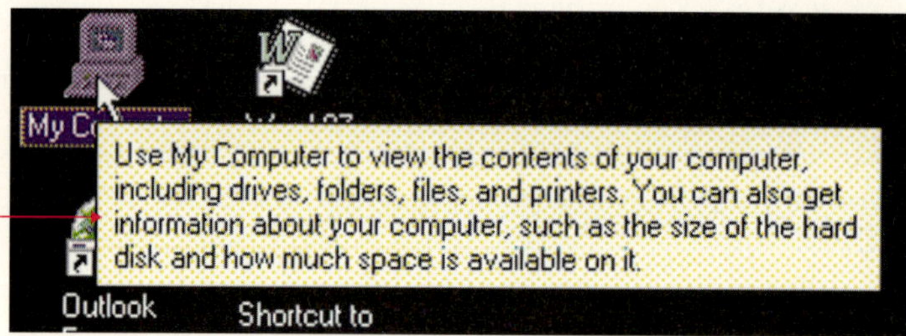

The ToolTip explains how to use the My Computer program.

Note The ToolTip appears different, depending on how the Active Desktop is installed on your computer. If it is installed using Internet Explorer 4.0 with Windows 95, it displays as shown in the figure. If the Active Desktop is installed with Windows 98, the information provided by the ToolTip will be different.

3. Point to the Start button.

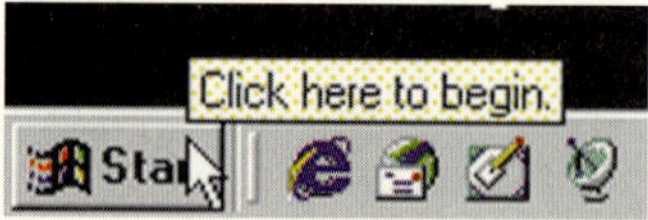

4. Point to a button on the Internet Explorer Channel bar, as shown here.

5. Point to the Time at the right end of the Taskbar, as shown in this figure.

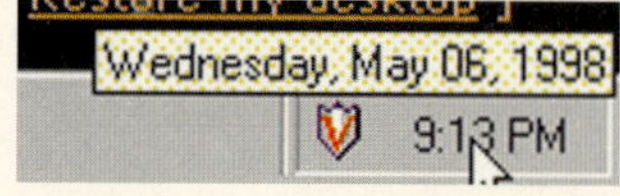

6 Point to an icon on the Quick Launch toolbar, as shown here.

Launching Programs

The same basic techniques used to launch programs in Windows 95 can be used to launch programs from the Active Desktop and Windows 98 Start menu and desktop shortcuts. The Active Desktop, however, enables you to use the Quick Launch toolbar located on the Taskbar to launch programs. In addition, you can change the setup of your desktop so that all program icons, shortcuts, and filenames act as hyperlinks. Clicking a filename, program icon, shortcut, or folder that is formatted as a hyperlink automatically opens the item. You'll also find that when Start menus contain more items than will fit on a cascading menu, the cascading menu displays an arrow at the top and/or bottom to indicate the presence of additional items.

TASK 4: TO LAUNCH PROGRAMS FROM THE ACTIVE DESKTOP:

1 Click the Outlook Express button on the Quick Launch toolbar, as shown here.

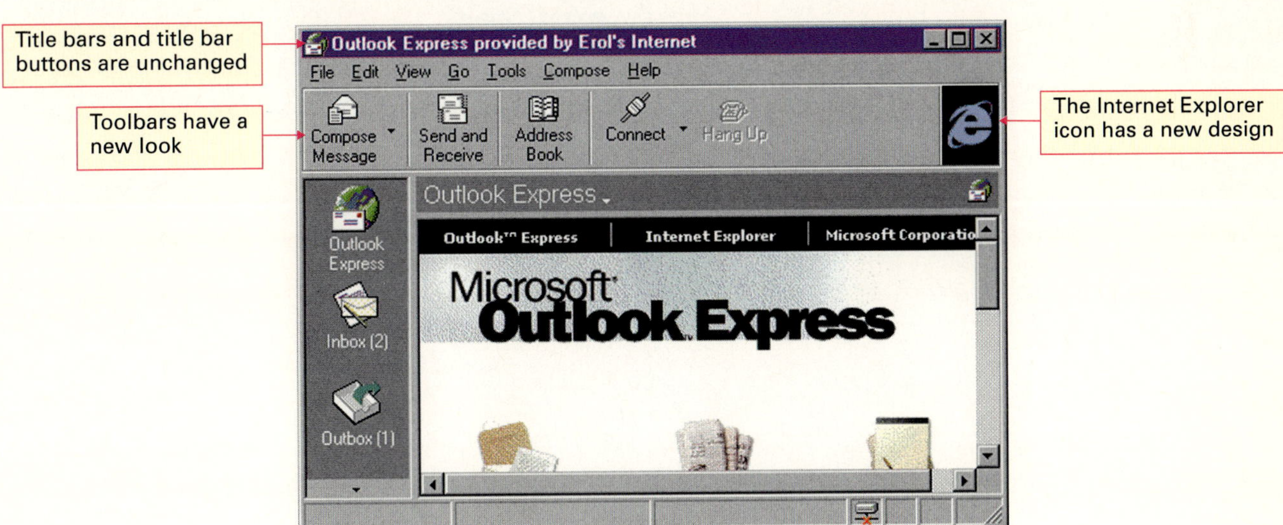

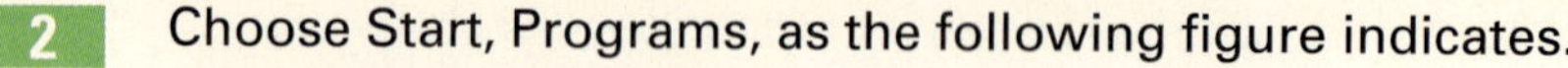

2 Choose Start, Programs, as the following figure indicates.

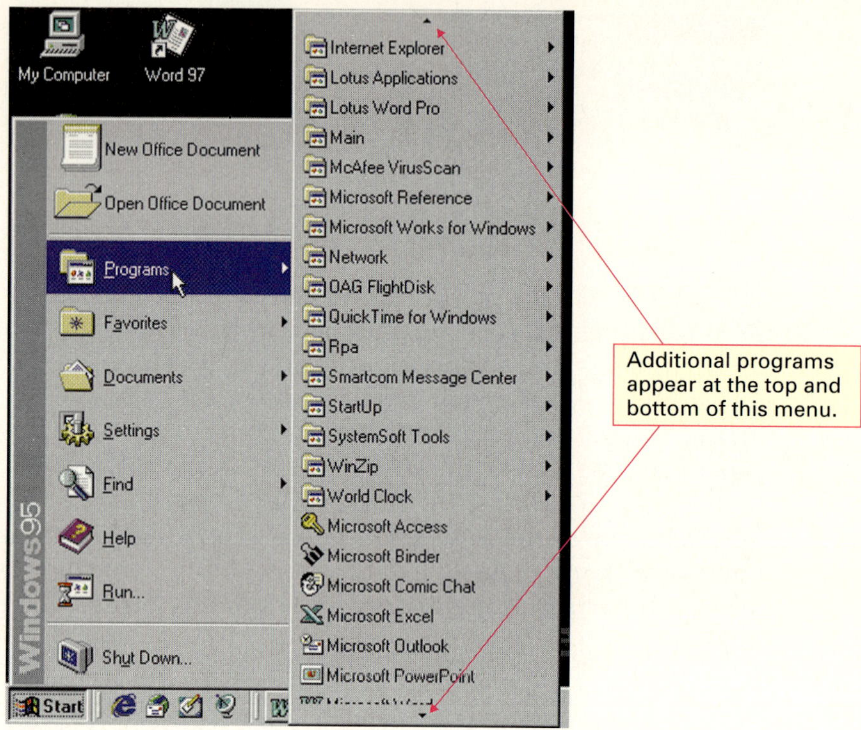

3 Click the arrow at the top or bottom of the cascading menu. Additional menu items scroll onscreen.

4 Double-click My Computer
The My Computer window opens.

5 Maximize the window and click once on the hard disk drive for your computer, as shown in the next figure.

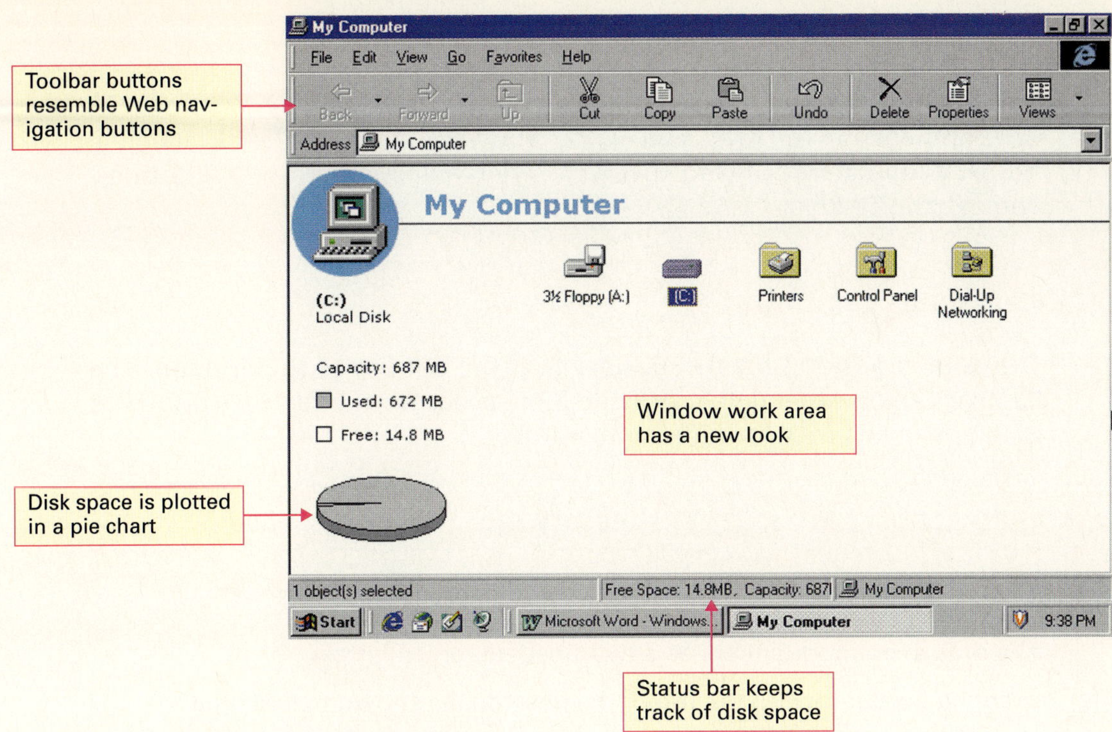

6 Choose View, Folder Options to display the screen shown here.

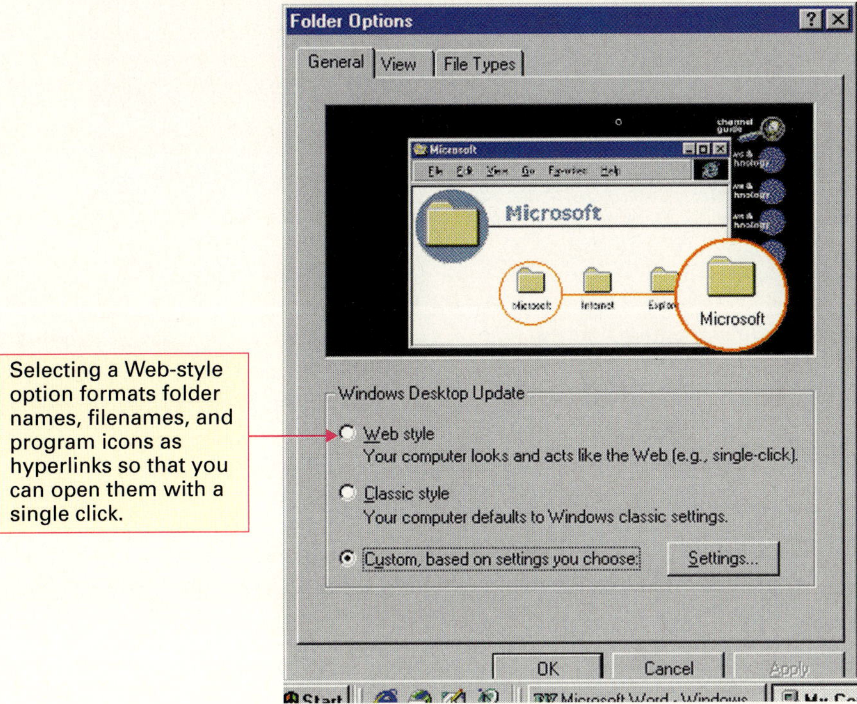

7 Choose Cancel and close the My Computer window.

Customizing the Windows 95 Active Desktop

Windows 95 Active Desktop enables you to customize the Windows 95 environment for the way you work. You've already explored changing the Desktop background to the Web-style wallpaper. Now you'll move and size the Taskbar.

Sizing and Repositioning the Taskbar

The default position for the Taskbar is at the bottom of the desktop. The Taskbar can be expanded to provide more space for the features displayed and moved to a new location on the desktop.

TASK 5: TO MOVE AND SIZE THE TASKBAR:

1. Position the mouse pointer on the border between the desktop and the Taskbar.
   The mouse pointer appears as a two-headed vertical arrow.
2. Drag the border toward the top of the desktop, as shown in this figure.

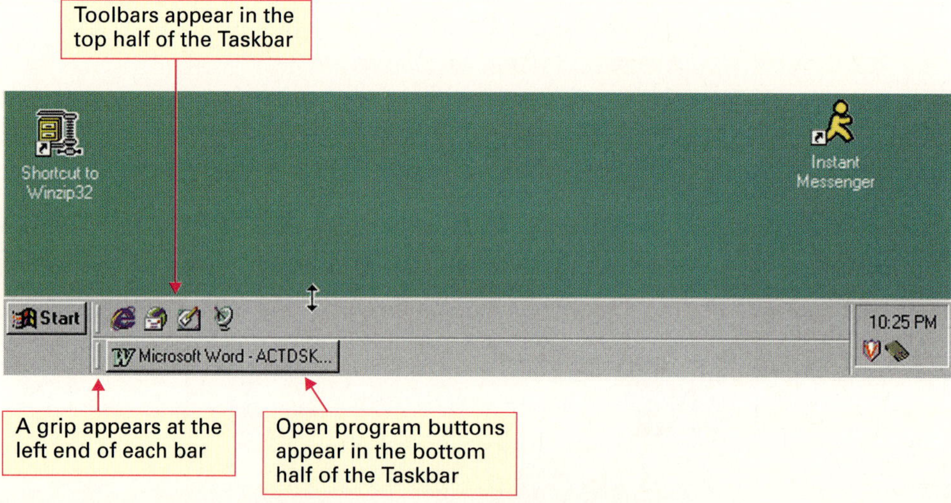

3. Drag the border of the Taskbar to its original size.
4. Position the mouse pointer on a blank area of the Taskbar.
   The mouse pointer should be a white arrow.
5. Click and drag the Taskbar to the top of the desktop, and drop it.
   The Taskbar appears at the top of the desktop.
6. Drag the Taskbar to the right or left side of the desktop, and drop it. The Taskbar appears as a vertical bar down the side of the desktop.
7. Return the Taskbar to its original position.

Displaying Additional Toolbars on the Taskbar

The Active Desktop provides four toolbars that you can display on the Taskbar. The Quick Launch toolbar is displayed by default. You can also display the Address, Links, and Web toolbars.

TASK 6: TO DISPLAY ADDITIONAL TOOLBARS:

1. Point to a blank area of the Taskbar, and right-click.
   The Taskbar shortcut menu opens.
2. Choose Toolbars, as shown in this figure.

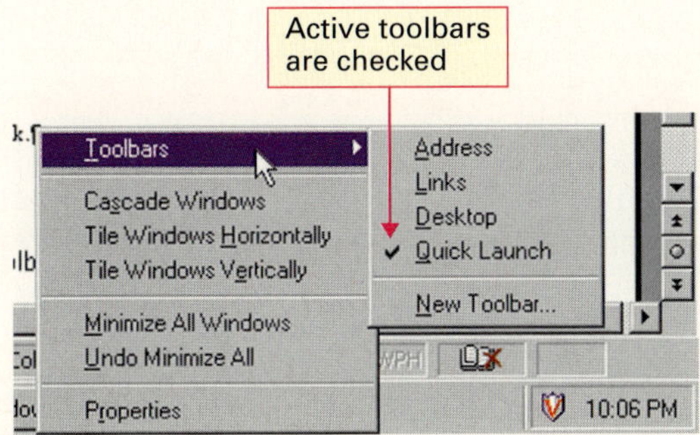

3. Choose Desktop, illustrated in this figure.

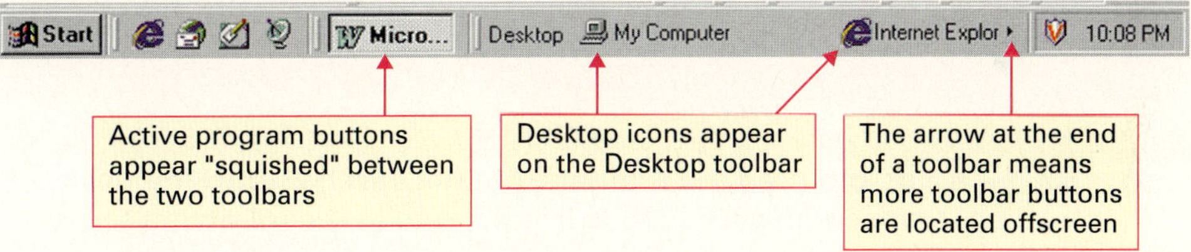

4. Right-click a blank area of the Taskbar, choose Toolbars, and choose Desktop to remove the toolbar.
   The Desktop toolbar is removed from the Taskbar, and the Taskbar program buttons are restored.

Customizing Taskbar Toolbars

Each of the toolbars displayed on the Taskbar can be customized to contain the tools you use most. To remove tools from the toolbars, drag the button from the toolbar. To add a tool, drag a program item or feature onto the toolbar.

TASK 7: TO CUSTOMIZE THE QUICK LAUNCH TOOLBAR:

1. Click the Show Desktop button on the Quick Launch Toolbar.
   All open programs minimize and the Active Desktop is visible.

2 Click and drag the Launch Internet Explorer Browser button from the Quick Launch Toolbar onto the desktop, and drop it.
The program button appears as a shortcut on the desktop, and the button no longer appears on the toolbar.

3 Select the Launch Internet Explorer Browser shortcut icon on the desktop, and drag and drop it in its original position on the Quick Launch toolbar.
The toolbar button appears on the toolbar, and the shortcut remains on the desktop.

4 Click the shortcut icon on the desktop, and press DEL.
The Confirm File Deletion dialog box opens.

5 Choose Yes to confirm the deletion.

Floating and Restoring Toolbars

Toolbars take up valuable space on the Taskbar. When you have more programs active than will comfortably fit on the Taskbar, you can drag a toolbar to the desktop so that program buttons have more space.

TASK 8: TO MOVE AND RESTORE A TASKBAR TOOLBAR:

1 Position the mouse pointer on the Quick Launch toolbar grip.

> **Note** The mouse pointer appears as a horizontal mouse shape when you point to the grip.

2 Click and drag the toolbar from the Taskbar onto the desktop.
Your screen should look like the one in the following figure.

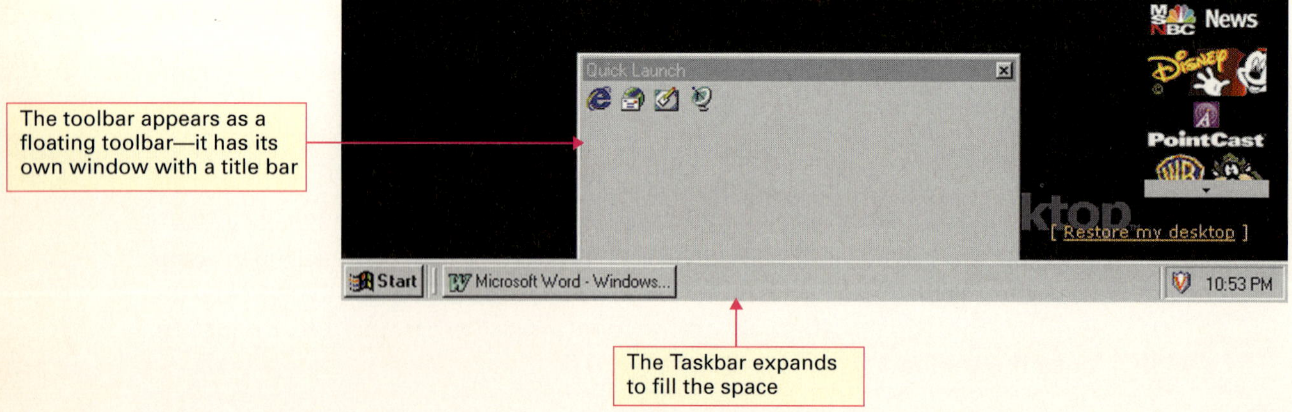

3 Click and drag the Quick Launch title bar until the mouse pointer crosses the border of the Taskbar, as shown in this figure.

The toolbar stretches across the desktop just above the Taskbar after the mouse pointer crosses the Taskbar border—the toolbar will hop onto the Taskbar when you release the mouse button.

4 Release the mouse button.
The Quick Launch toolbar appears at the right side of the Taskbar.

5 Drag the grip beside the Start button to the right end of the Taskbar.
When the Taskbar grip is dragged past the Quick Launch toolbar, the toolbar assumes its original position.

6 Drag the toolbar and Taskbar grips until the Taskbar returns to normal.

Editing the Start Menu

The Active Desktop makes customizing the Start menu quick and easy. You can remove items from the Start menu to the desktop, or you can drag items from dialog boxes, the desktop, and folders and then place them on the Start menu.

Creating Shortcuts from the Start Menu

Dragging an item from the Start menu removes the item from the menu. To leave items on the Start menu and create shortcuts for the item on the desktop, you generally want to copy the Start menu item as you drag it to the desktop. You can drag Start menu items to the desktop or to an open dialog box or folder.

TASK 9: TO CREATE SHORTCUTS FROM THE START MENU:

1 Choose Start, Programs.
The Programs cascading menu opens.

2 Press and hold CTRL, then click and drag the Windows Explorer icon and title to the desktop.

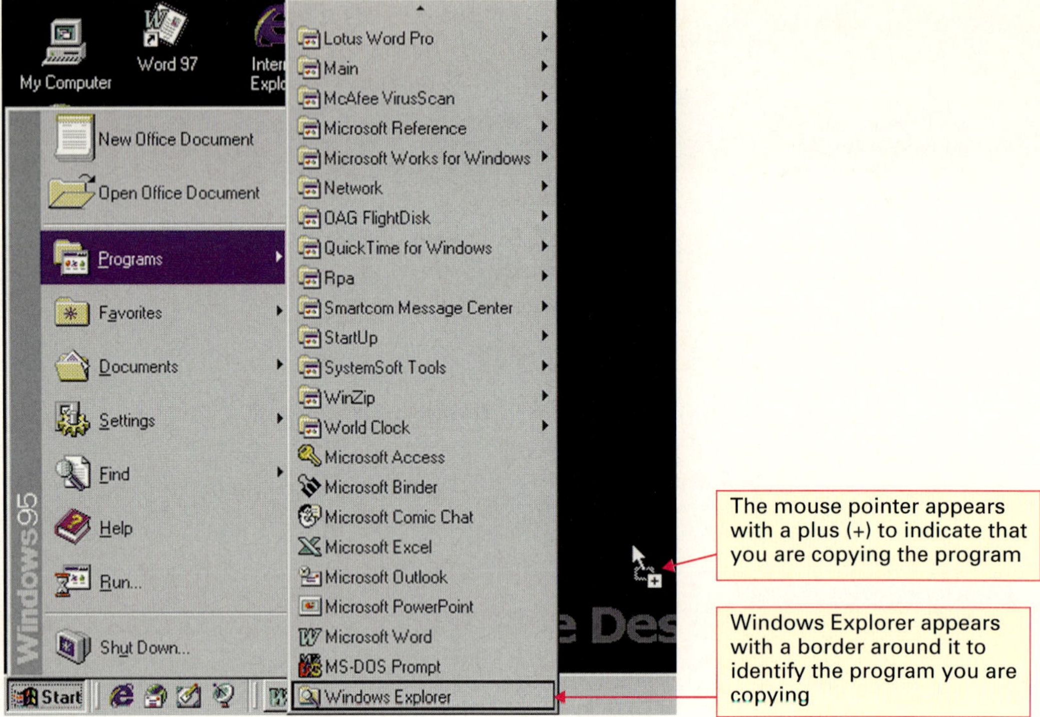

3 Drop the program on the desktop.
A Windows Explorer shortcut appears on the desktop.

4 Choose Start, Programs to ensure that the Windows Explorer icon remains on the menu.

Adding Items to the Start Menu

Adding items to the Start menu is as easy as copying shortcuts from the menu. Simply drag the item to the Start button and position the item on the menu in the desired position. It is important to keep the mouse button depressed from the time you start dragging the icon until it is properly positioned. You can also use the techniques presented here to reorganize items on the Start menu.

TASK 10: TO ADD ITEMS TO THE START MENU:

1 Drag the Windows Explorer Shortcut icon to the Start button.
The Start menu opens.

> **Troubleshooting** Do not release the mouse button until the item is properly positioned.

2 Drag the icon to the top of the Start menu, as shown in this figure.

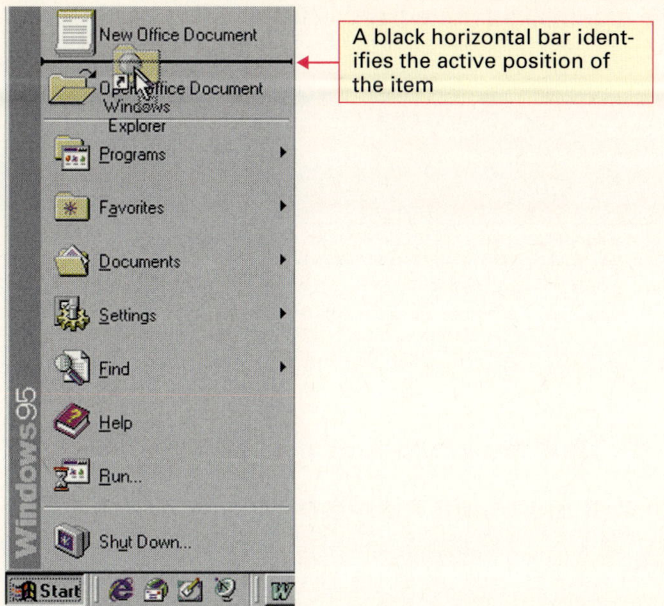

3. Release the mouse button when the item is appropriately positioned.
4. Choose Start and drag the Windows Explorer from the top of the menu to the desktop.
5. Select the Windows Explorer shortcut on the desktop, and press (DEL).

Restoring the Desktop

Tasks in this preview have most likely left your desktop in a bit of a mess. You can restore the desktop to its original format using the desktop itself.

TASK 11: RESTORING THE DESKTOP:

1. Point to the Restore my desktop hyperlink on the Active Desktop, as shown in this figure.

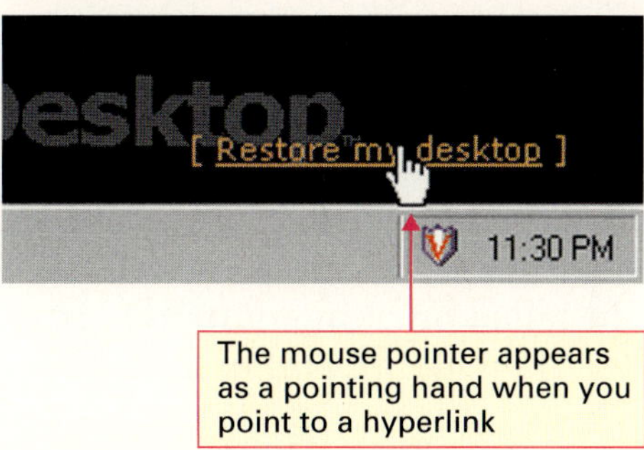

2 Click the hyperlink, illustrated in this figure.

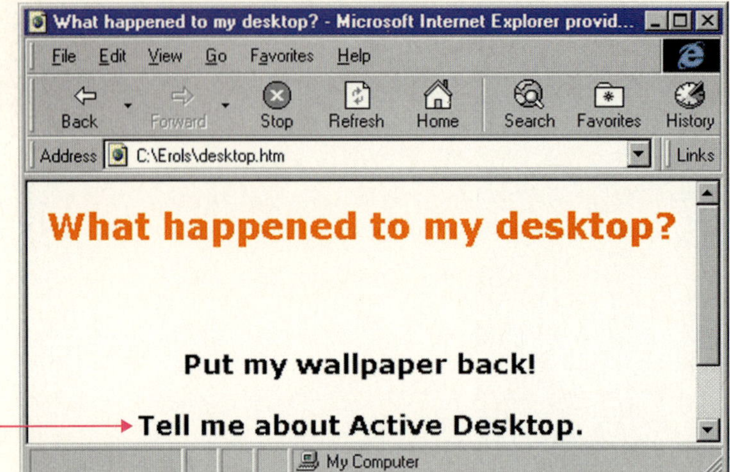

Review other features of the Active Desktop by choosing Tell me about Active Desktop

3 Choose Put my wallpaper back.
The dialog box shown in this figure appears.

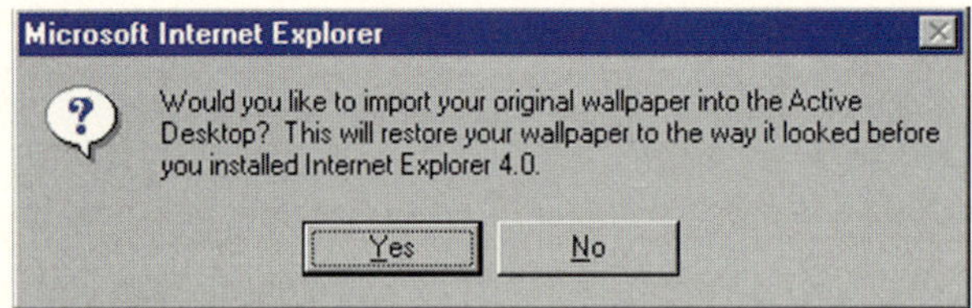

4 Choose Yes.
The original wallpaper forms the desktop background.

5 Close all open programs, if necessary, and shut down Windows 95.

Conclusion

While Windows 95 Active Desktop offers the capabilities you've worked with in this Project, Windows 98 Active Desktop enables users to add new and different objects to the Desktop. For example, with Windows 98 Active Desktop, you can add Java programs such as stock market tickers to the Desktop. In addition, you can subscribe to Web services and newsgroups and add shortcuts to these features to your Desktop. When Windows 98 is available and installed on your computer, explore Windows 98 and look for these features. Then identify other features and benefits Windows 98 has available.

Databases
Using Microsoft Access 97

Overview

Microsoft Access is the database management tool that ships with Microsoft Office 97 Professional. Because Access is based upon the relational database model, you can create powerful applications that can be implemented in a variety of ways. This overview introduces you to basic database concepts and the Microsoft Access user interface.

Objectives

After completing this project, you will be able to:

- **Define database terminology**
- **List the steps required to design a database**
- **Launch Microsoft Access and create a new database**
- **Identify Microsoft Access screen elements**
- **Work with Access menus and the Database toolbar**
- **Get Microsoft Access help**
- **Close a database and exit Access**

Defining Database Terminology

A ***database*** is a collection of information related to a particular subject or purpose. For example, most people keep a list of the names, addresses, and phone numbers of the people they contact frequently. The categories of information that you keep on each individual are most likely consistent. In database terms, each individual item of information in the list such as first name or last name is called a ***field***. The collection of field information for one person in the list is a ***record***. Therefore, a database contains fields and records. Figure O.1 refers to five fields and one record in a sample phone list.

When using Microsoft Access to store information, field and record information is contained in a grid called a ***table***. Figure O.2 displays employee name, address, and phone number data in a Microsoft Access table.

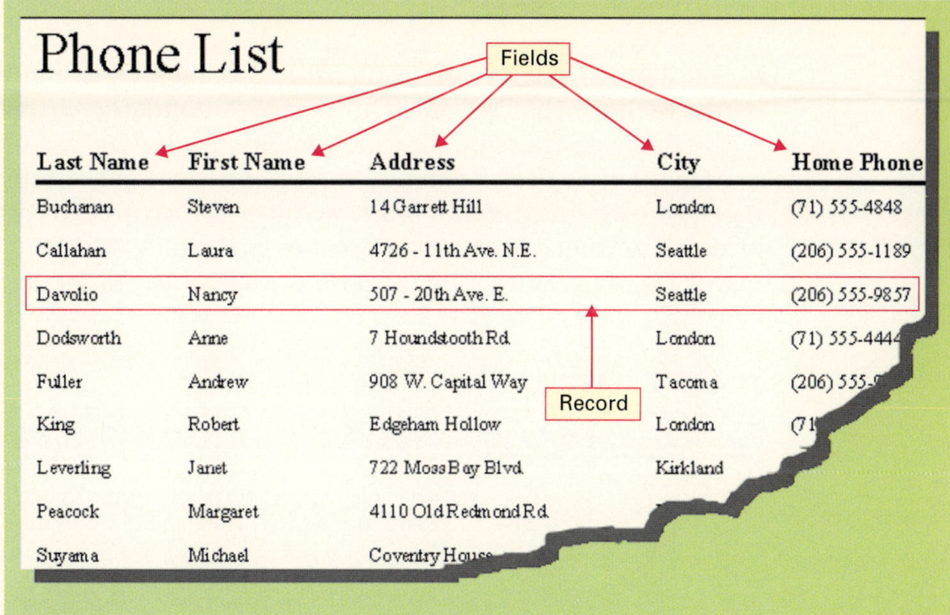

Figure O.1

Employees : Table

Last Name	First Name	Address	City	Postal Code	Home Phone
Davolio	Nancy	507 - 20th Ave. E.	Seattle	98122	(206) 555-9857
Fuller	Andrew	908 W. Capital Way	Tacoma	98401	(206) 555-9482
Leverling	Janet	722 Moss Bay Blvd.	Kirkland	98033	(206) 555-3412
Peacock	Margaret	4110 Old Redmond Rd.	Redmond	98052	(206) 555-8122
Buchanan	Steven	14 Garrett Hill	London	SW1 8JR	(71) 555-4848
Suyama	Michael	Coventry House	London	EC2 7JR	(71) 555-7773
King	Robert	Edgeham Hollow	London	RG1 9SP	(71) 555-5598
Callahan	Laura	4726 - 11th Ave. N.E.	Seattle	98105	(206) 555-1189
Dodsworth	Anne	7 Houndstooth Rd.	London	WG2 7LT	(71) 555-4444

Record: 1 of 9

Figure O.2

A computer application that you use to create and maintain databases is a ***database management system (DBMS)***. With Access, you can store information in separate tables and then use the data from one or more tables through relationships, which combine field data from one or more tables. A database management system that enables you to establish relationships among tables is a ***relational database management system (RDBMS)***. Relational database management systems are the most powerful kinds of database applications available for microcomputers.

Access Database Objects

In addition to tables, Microsoft Access databases contain other components, each of which is called an object. A ***database object*** is a component of the database that gives it functionality. Each database object belongs to a category of objects, known as a ***class***. For example, a table used for storing phone list information is a table object. Microsoft Access has six classes of database objects. These six classes are tables, queries, forms, reports, macros, and modules. The purpose of each object is listed in Table O.1.

Table O.1 Six Classes of Database Objects

Object Class	Purpose
Table	An organized collection of rows and columns used to store field data. Tables are the primary database object in that they hold the data.
Query	An object that allows the user to view, change, or organize data. Queries are often used as the data source for a screen form or a printed report.
Form	A graphical object that displays data from a table or a query on the screen. Forms make it easy for database users to add, edit, and delete table data.
Report	The database object used to present data in a printed format. Reports can be based upon either tables or queries.
Macro	A set of one or more actions used to automate common tasks, such as opening a form or printing a report.
Module	A collection of Visual Basic for Applications programming components that are stored together as a unit. Programmers create modules to customize an Access database.

Tip Macros and modules are complex database objects. In this book you will learn to design and use tables, queries, forms, and reports.

In Microsoft Access, the database objects you create are stored in a single database file with an ***mdb*** extension, which stands for "**M**icrosoft **d**ata**b**ase."

Before you design a database, you must understand how Access database objects relate to one another. Because tables are used to store field and record information, you must create at least one table before you create any other object. For instance, queries are always based upon one or more tables because they enable you to organize and view data in different ways. Queries can also display data from other queries.

Working with records in a row-and-column format is often tedious, because you often have to scroll horizontally or vertically to display information on the screen. For this reason, forms are used to make table or query data more accessible. In a well-designed database, users work with record and field data via forms, not at the table level. While forms are appropriate for viewing data on the screen, reports are used to format table or query data for printed output. Macros and modules are resources you can use to add more functionality to a database application. Working with these objects requires a solid working knowledge of Microsoft Access and Visual Basic, though, so this book does not cover them.

Designing a Database

Creating a database that is easy to use requires careful consideration, and the time you spend planning one will greatly benefit you in the long run. In general, you must complete five steps when designing a database.

1. **Defining the purpose**
   Define the overall purpose of the database, including a list of user specifications for input and output. Specifications include tasks such as entering data from a common source (such as employment applications) or printing a report of payroll data for the current pay period.

2. **Planning the database objects**
   The objects contained in your database must be carefully planned. You must determine the appropriate number of tables, the ways in which the records will be reorganized using queries and the kinds of forms and reports your database will contain. Make sure you talk with the people who will actually use the database, as they will often give you the most appropriate information about which fields will be needed for input and output.

3. **Creating and relating tables**
   As you know, tables are the primary database objects in Access. As you will see in Project 1, you must specify the kind of data each field will contain before you design a table. If your database contains more than one table, you will need to establish relationships among the tables.

4. **Creating queries to reorganize data**
   You rarely need to see all the field data in a database for all records at the same time. For this reason, queries are used to reorganize or manipulate data to fulfill a specific request. For instance, you may need a listing of all customers from California, or you may want to perform a calculation of a member's outstanding balance.

5. **Creating forms and reports**
   Users can access forms and reports to work with records both onscreen and in printed format, so they are essential to a database. Forms and reports obtain their data from tables and queries.

Tip Designing a full-fledged database is a complex and time-consuming process that requires careful planning and documentation. For the databases you design in this book, use either paper and pencil or a word processor such as Microsoft Word to document your intended design.

In the projects that follow you will create a simple database in which the data is stored in one table. After launching Microsoft Access, you will see that the user interface has been designed to facilitate the creation and maintenance of relational databases.

Launching Microsoft Access and Creating a New Database

As with each of the Office applications, you can launch Microsoft Access in a variety of ways from the Windows desktop. In Task 1, you use the Start button to launch Access and create a new database.

TASK 1: TO LAUNCH MICROSOFT ACCESS AND CREATE A NEW DATABASE:

1. Click the Start button.
2. Select Programs from the Cascading Start menu, and select Access.

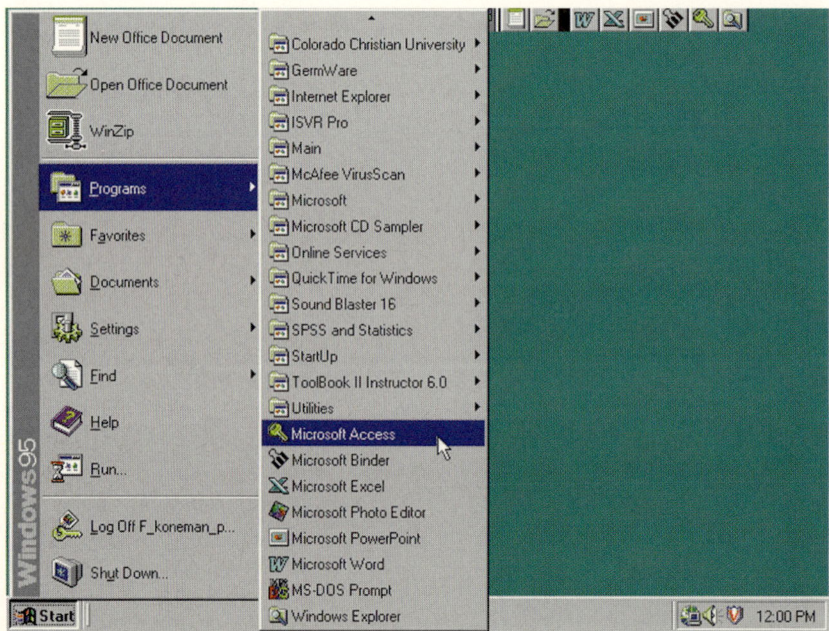

The dialog box shown below appears. You have three options: to open an existing database using the list of recently used databases, to create a new database using the Database Wizard, or to create a blank database.

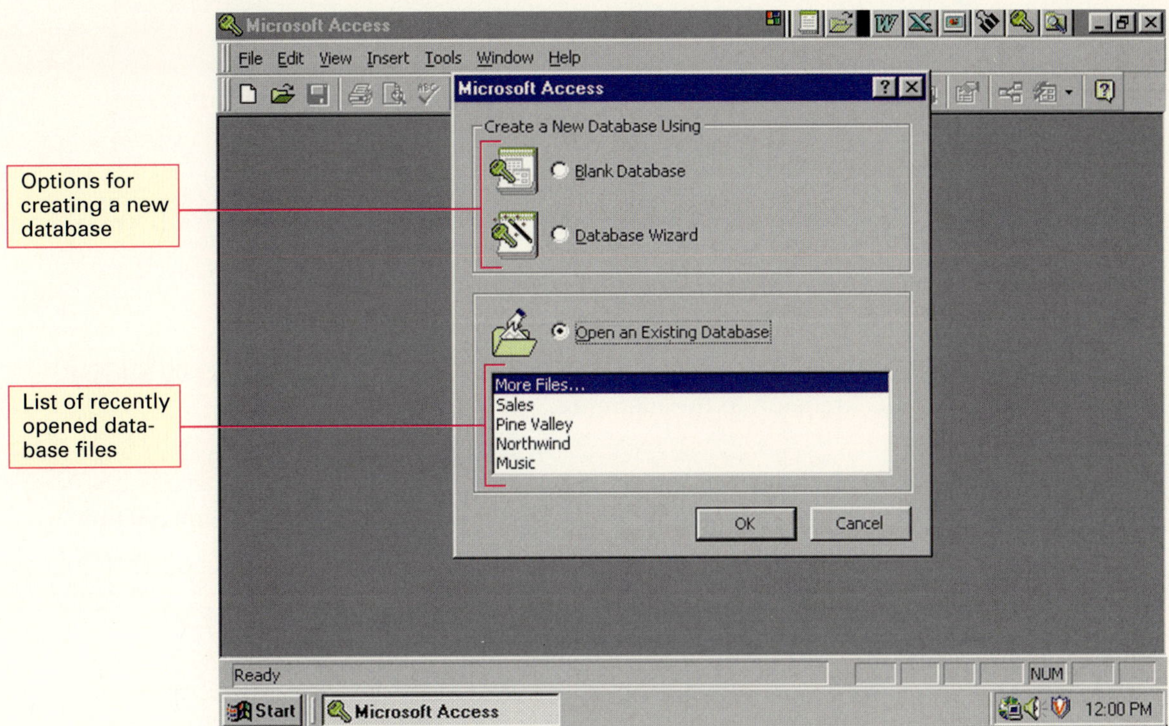

3 Select the Blank Database option and click OK.

The File New Database dialog box appears. Notice that the dialog box specifies a default location and default filename.

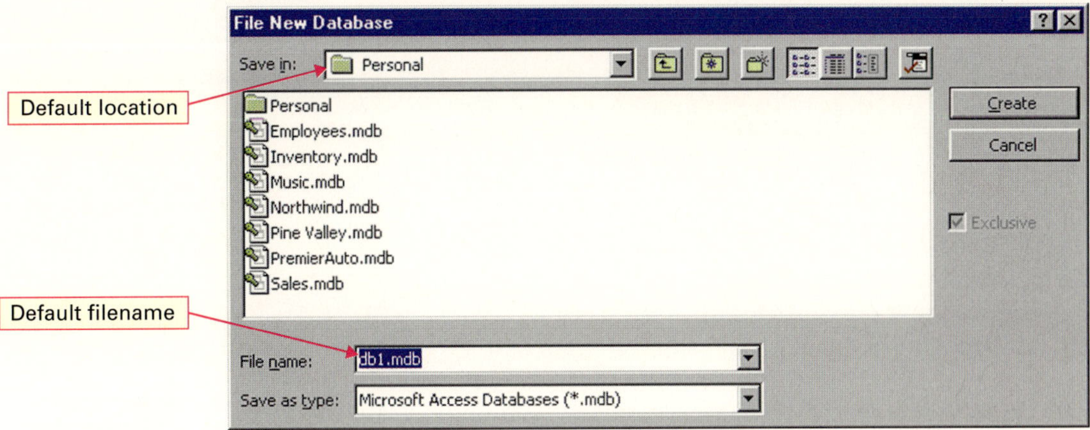

4 Select your floppy disk as the storage location, and type **Willows Membership** as the database name.

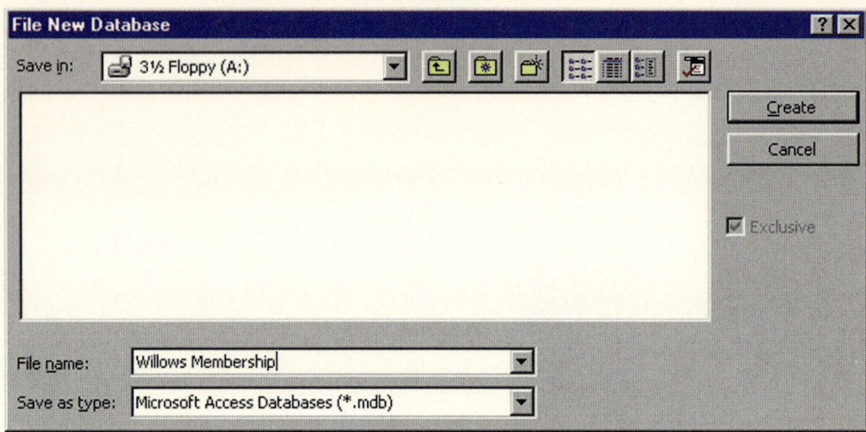

Tip When you name your database file, Access automatically adds a *.mdb* extension to the filename.

5 Click the Create button. Access creates a new database and displays the Database window shown below.

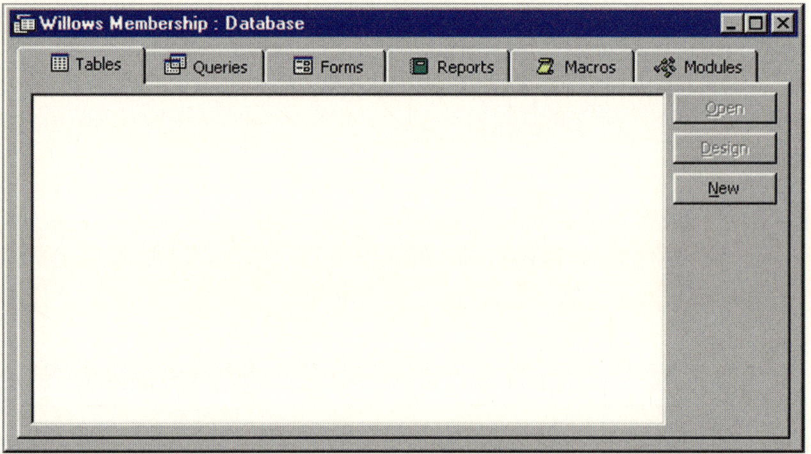

Tip Unlike other applications in the Office suite, only one database file can be open at a time.

Identifying Microsoft Access Screen Elements

You will notice three things about the database file you have just created:

- The Database window appears in a restored state within the Application window (although you can maximize or minimize the Database Window in Access, it will always appear as shown when you create a new database).

- The name of the database appears in the title bar of the Database window.
- The Database window contains tabs that display the database objects you will create; the leftmost Tables tab is active.

You will notice that the Microsoft Access application window shown below has unique elements not seen in other Office applications.

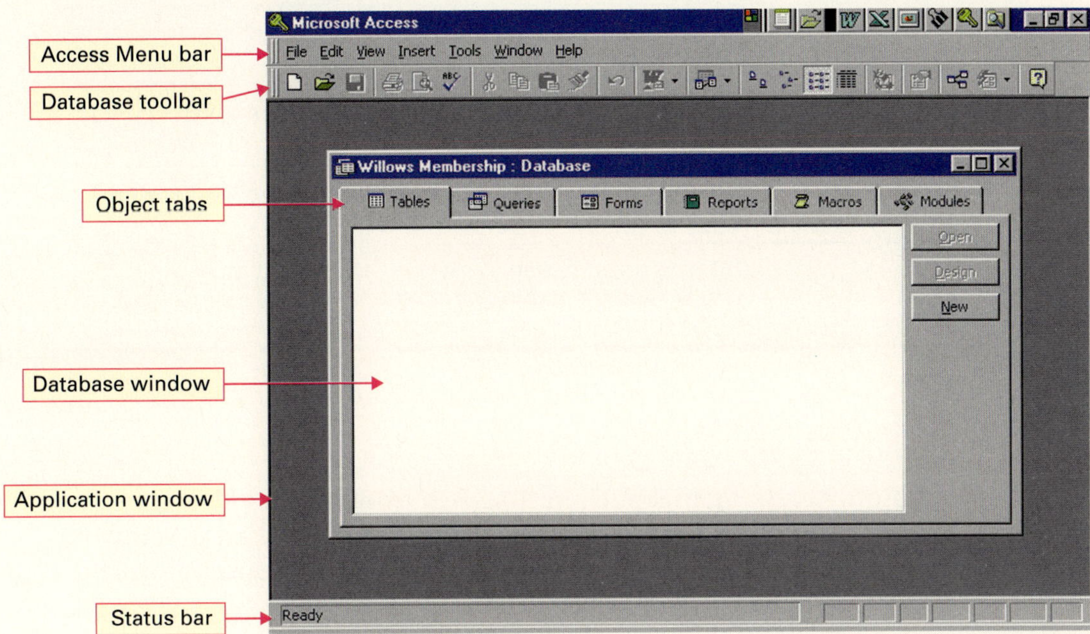

The most striking feature of the Access interface is the Database window. As you create database objects, they are displayed in the appropriate Object tab. You will also notice that the Application Window contains only one toolbar. You use this in the same way as other Toolbars in the Windows environment. Table O.2 identifies the purpose of each screen element you see.

> **Tip** Notice that the object tabs in the Database window appear in the same order as the kinds of database objects listed in steps for designing a database (see Table O.1). Because tables are the primary repositories for the data in a database, the Tables tab is listed first.

Table O.2 Access Screen Elements

Screen Element	Purpose
Access Menu Bar	Provides access to the commands used to perform tasks.
Application Title Bar	Identifies the current application and contains Control menu items for minimizing the Application Window, maximizing and restoring the Application Window, and exiting the application.
Database Toolbar	Provides shortcuts to the most common database commands and tasks.
Database Window	Displays Object tabs for the six kinds of database objects you can create.
Object Tabs	Display the specific objects you create. You can use the Object tabs to design or open each object.
Status Bar	Displays program status as well as instructions and information for performing specific tasks.

Working with Access Menus

The Microsoft Access menus and the Database toolbar provide access to the tasks you perform when creating and maintaining databases. Many of these procedures display dialog boxes in which you can specify exactly how to accomplish a task or procedure.

TASK 2: TO USE THE ACCESS MENU:

1. Select the File menu by clicking it. The menu opens.
2. Select Database Properties.

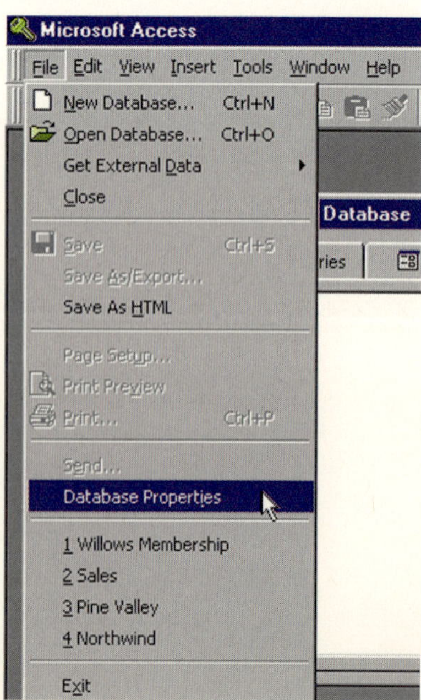

The Database Properties dialog box appears.

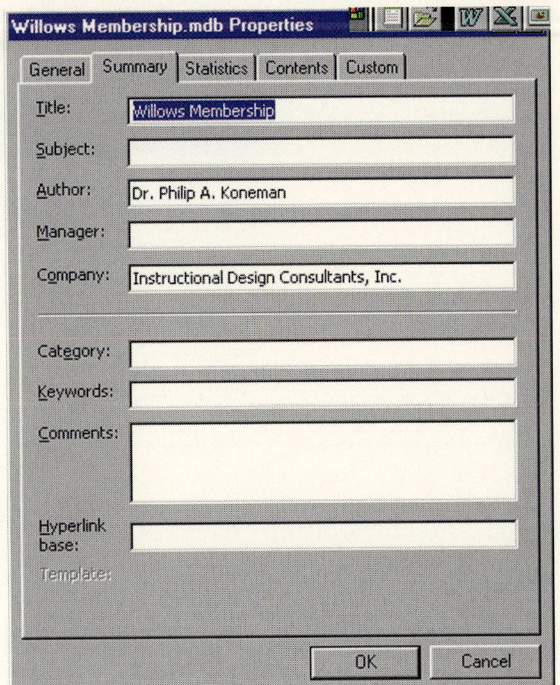

3. Place the insertion point inside the Subject: line, and type **The Willows Membership Roster**.
4. Click OK.

TASK 3: TO USE THE DATABASE TOOLBAR:

1. Click the New Database icon, as shown below.

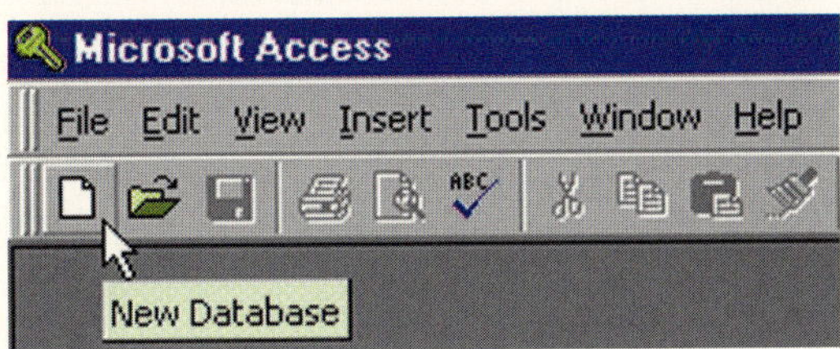

The New dialog box appears.

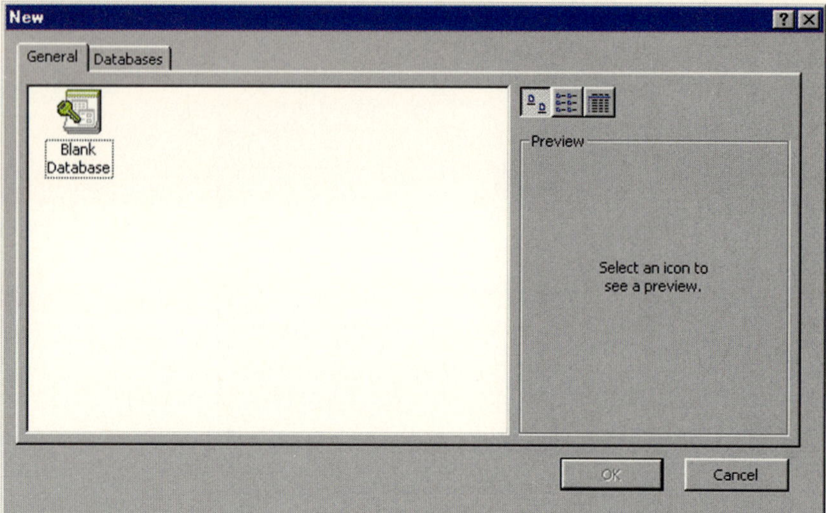

2 Click the Databases tab. The dialog box now displays the available database templates.

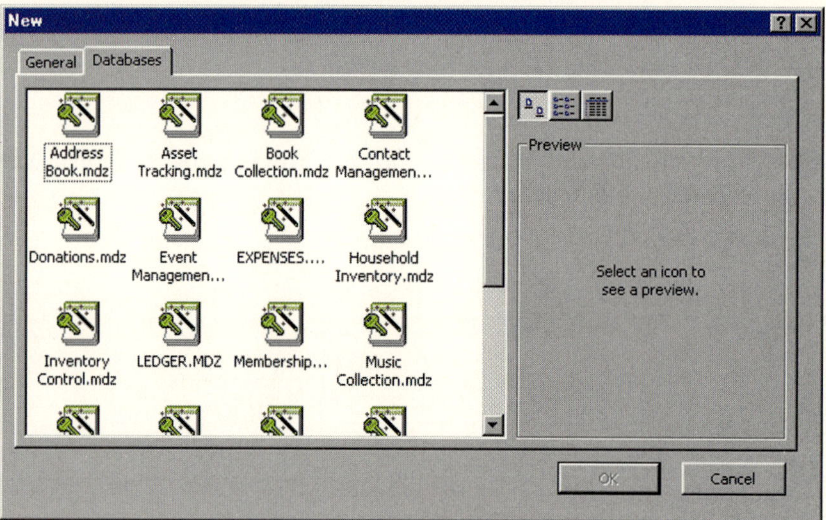

Troubleshooting If the database templates do not appear as shown in the figure above, check to make sure the Large Icons option is active by clicking the Large Icons button.

3 Click the *Address Book.mdz* icon. A graphic depicting the structure of the database should display in the Preview window shown on the next page.

Tip The *mdz* file extension identifies this file as an Access Wizard template.

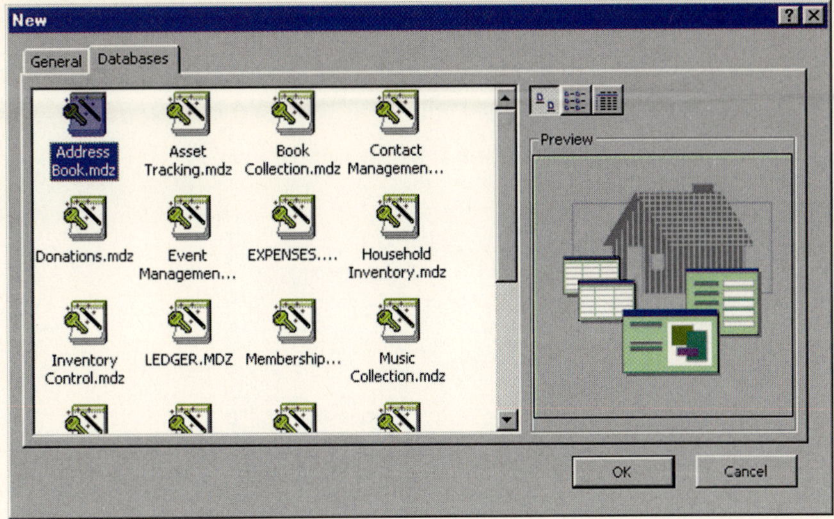

4 Click Cancel to return to the Database window.

Getting Help

Microsoft Access provides numerous options for getting help online as you work. To get help, select Help from the Access menu. Access includes four ways of obtaining help:

- Office Assistant
- Contents and Index
- What's This?
- Microsoft on the Web

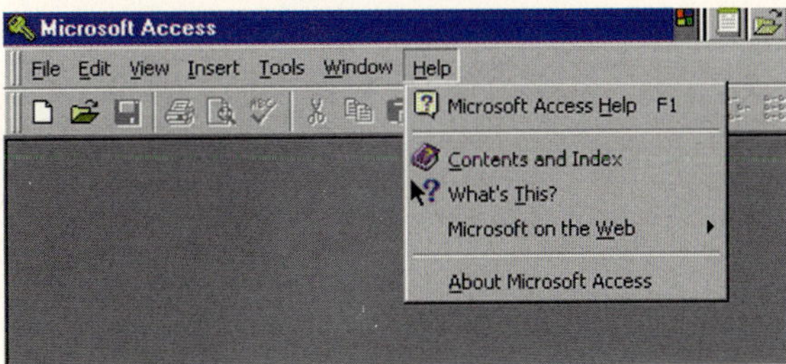

The Office Assistant

The Office Assistant can answer your questions, offer tips, and provide Help for a variety of features specific to Access. To open the Office Assistant, select Microsoft Access Help from the menu. When using the Office Assistant, you can either select an option from the list or type a word or phrase to display new options.

TASK 4: TO USE THE OFFICE ASSISTANT:

1. Select Microsoft Access Help from the Help menu.
2. The Office Assistant opens, as shown below.

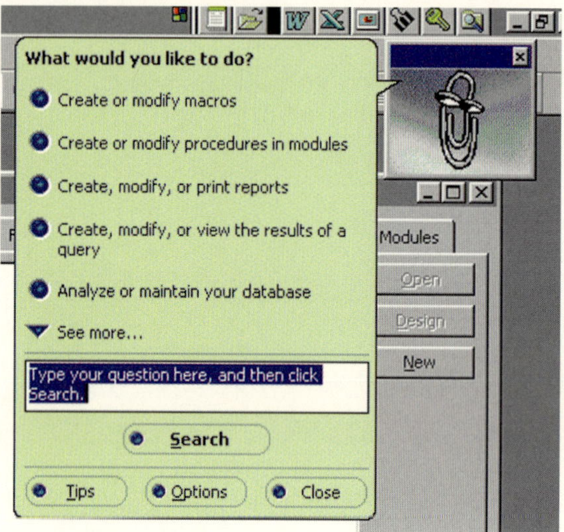

3. Type **Tables** as a search term in the text box.

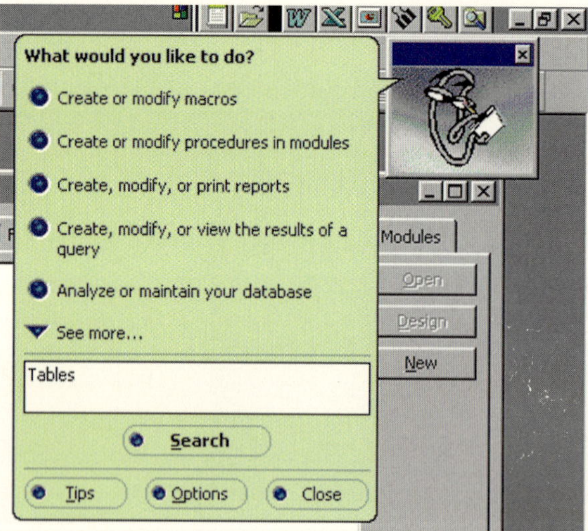

4. Click the Search button. The topics in the list change.
5. Click the first option, *Create a table*. The Help system displays the topic shown on the next page.

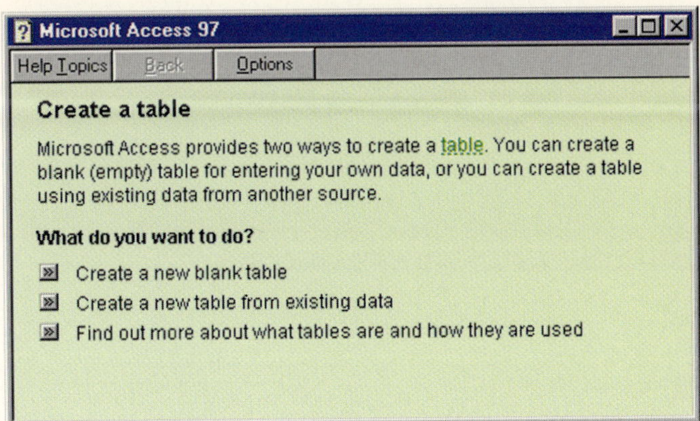

6 Use the Close button in the upper right-hand corner of the Help Topics window to close it.

Obtaining Help Using Contents and Index

Contents and Index is the familiar Help system that has been available in all Microsoft applications. Select Contents and Index from the Help menu. When using this option, Access displays the standard Windows Help system interface.

TASK 5: TO USE CONTENTS AND INDEX:

1 Select Contents and Index from the Help menu. The Help Topics dialog box appears.

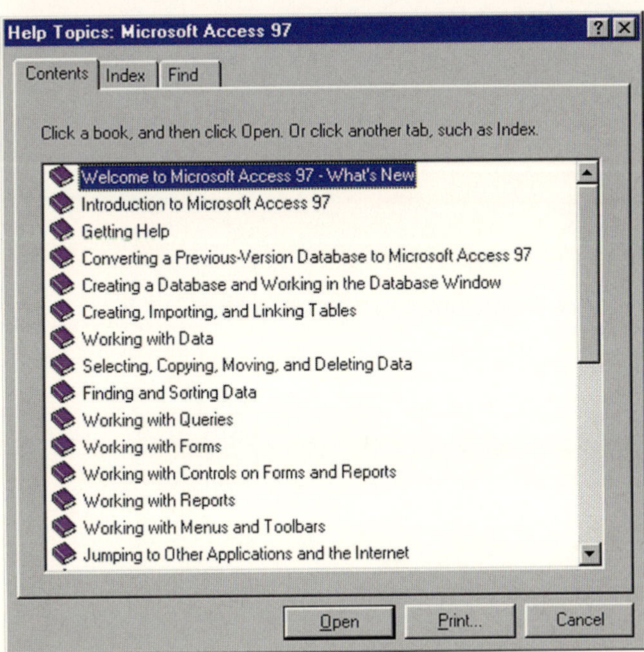

2 Click the Index tab and type **queries** in the list.

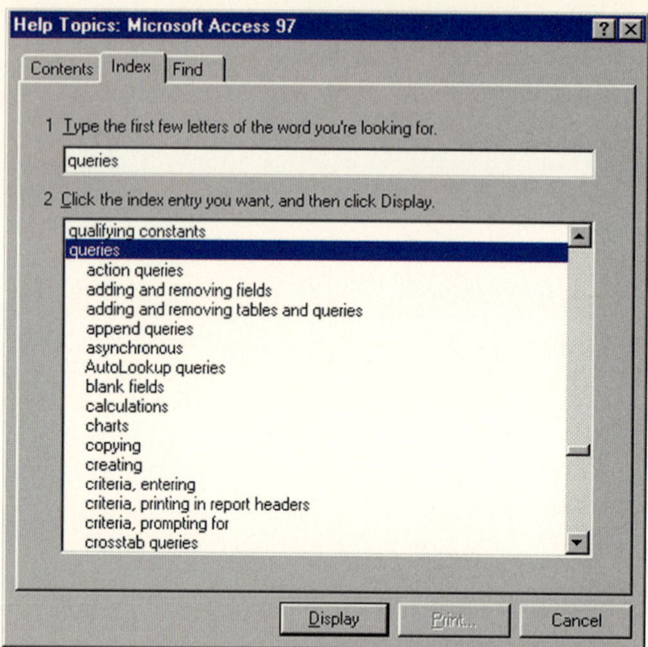

3 Select the *creating* index entry and then click the Display button, as shown below.

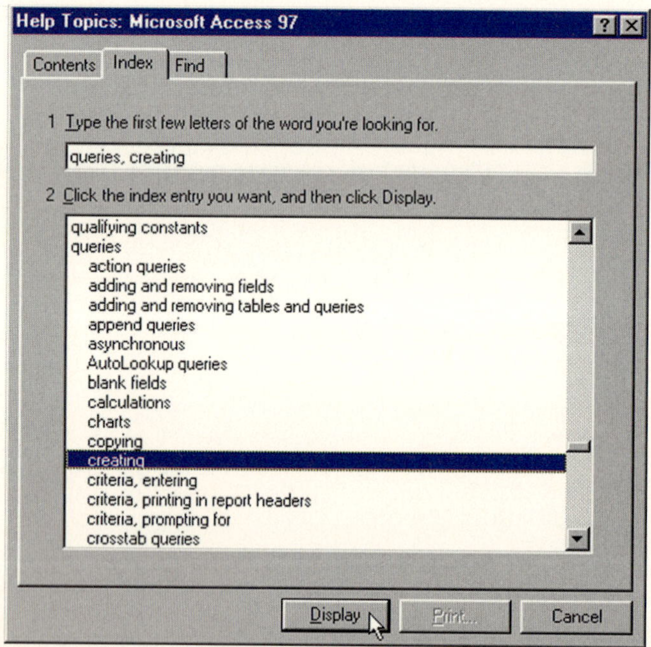

4 In the Topics Found dialog box shown in the figure on the next page, select the *Create a query* topic and then click the Display button.

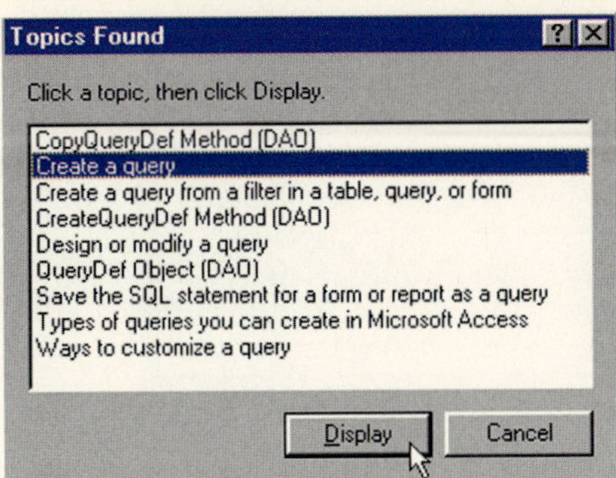

The Create a query topic appears.

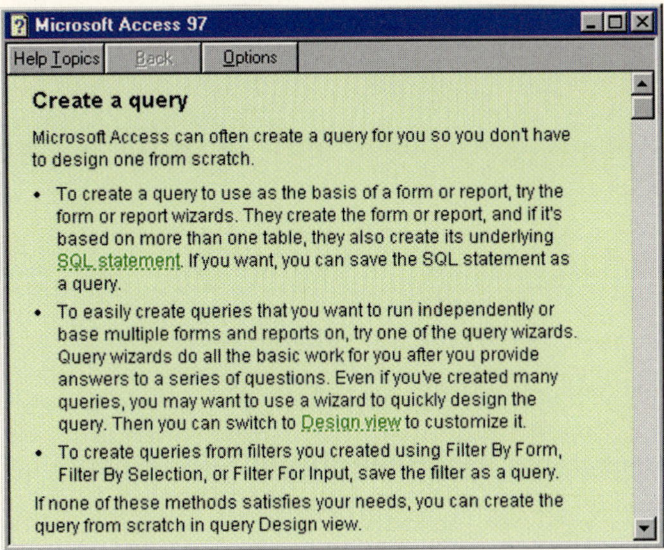

5. Click the Close button in the Help Topics window to close it.

Getting Help Using What's This?

You can easily view tips on menu commands, toolbar buttons, and other screen items using What's This?. When you select What's This? from the Help menu, the Office What's This icon is displayed. You can obtain help on any screen element by simply clicking this icon.

TASK 6: TO USE WHAT'S THIS?:

1. Select ***What's This?*** from the Help menu. The mouse pointer icon changes to indicate that What's This? is active.
2. Place the mouse pointer directly over the title bar of the Database window, and click the left mouse button.

   Information about the Database Window appears onscreen, as shown on the next page.

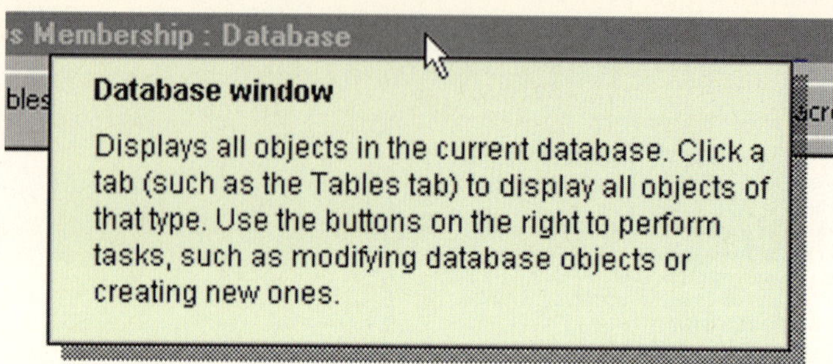

3 Click the left mouse button to close the information window.

Obtaining Help Using Microsoft on the Web

Extensive help is available online through Microsoft on the Web. This help option enables you to link to the Microsoft Web site for the latest information about using Access. To use this feature, you must have access to the Internet and a Web browser such as Internet Explorer or Netscape Navigator.

TASK 7: GETTING HELP FROM THE MICROSOFT WEB SITE:

1 Select Microsoft on the Web from the Help menu.

2 Choose Online Support from the cascading menu.

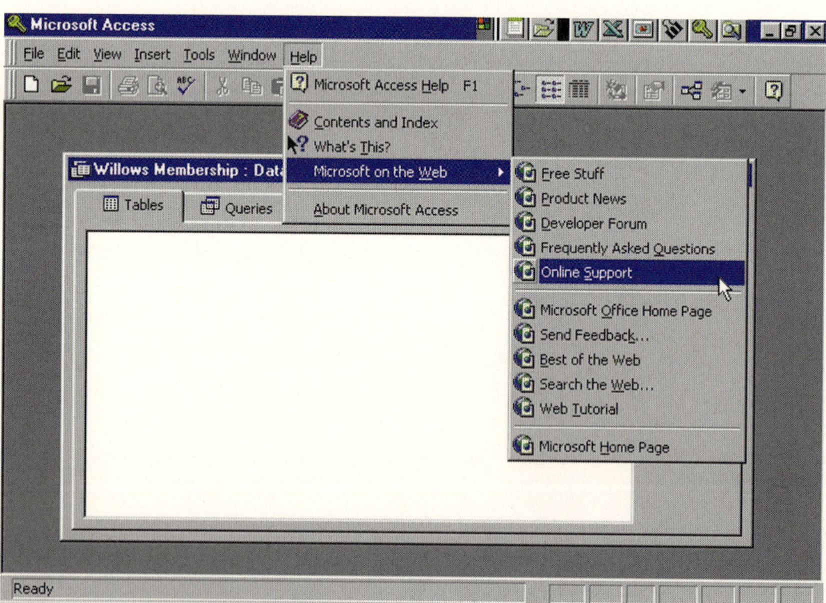

3 A Web page similar to the one displayed in the figure on the next page appears. You can use this resource to search for any topic in Access.

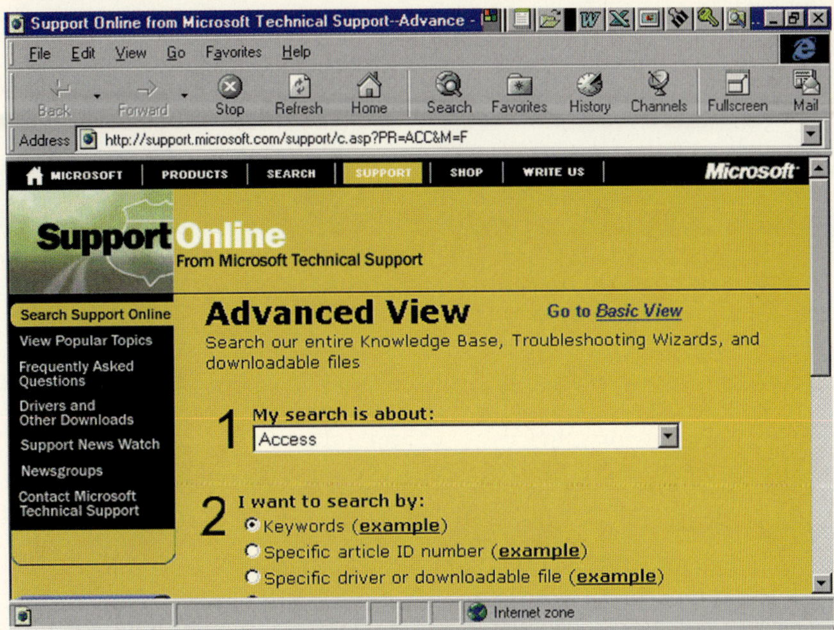

4 When you are finished using Microsoft's Web help system, close your Web browser by clicking the Close button.

Closing Your Database File and Exiting Microsoft Access

You are finished with your database for the present, so you can close it and exit Microsoft Access. You have not yet created any database objects, so you have nothing to update in the file.

> **Tip** Any time you close a database that you have modified, it is updated automatically.

TASK 8: TO CLOSE YOUR DATABASE FILE AND EXIT MICROSOFT ACCESS:

1 Click the Close button of the Database window to close the open database file.

2 Select Exit from the File menu, or click the Close button in the Application window to exit Microsoft Access.

Summary and Exercises

Summary

- Microsoft Access is a relational database management system (RDBMS).
- A database is a collection of information related to a common purpose.
- When launching Access, you must specify whether you want to open an existing database or create a new one.
- Access includes two methods for creating a new database: opening a blank database or using the database wizard.
- An Access database file contains multiple objects, including tables, queries, forms, reports, macros, and modules.
- Tables are the primary kind of database object in Access.
- Only one database can be open at a time.
- The Database window provides a graphical interface for designing and opening database objects.
- You can obtain online help in Access in four ways: the Office Assistant, Contents and Index, What's This?, and Microsoft on the Web. All types can be accessed through the Help menu.

Key Terms and Operations

Key Terms

class
database
database management system (DBMS)
database object
field
form
macro
module
query
record
relational database management system (RDBMS)
report
table

Operations

close a database file and exit Microsoft Access
display and change database properties
launch Access and create a new database
obtain online help using the Contents and Index option
use the Access File and Help menus
use the Office Assistant in Access to search for online help
use the What's This? help feature
view the available New Database templates
use Microsoft on the Web to search the World Wide Web

Study Questions

Multiple Choice

1. Which Access object is considered primary?
   - **a.** table
   - **b.** query
   - **c.** form
   - **d.** report

2. Which screen element is used to easily design or open the objects within a database?
   - **a.** Close button
   - **b.** Status bar
   - **c.** Database toolbar
   - **d.** Database window

3. Which online help option requires Internet access?
   - **a.** What's This?
   - **b.** Microsoft on the Web
   - **c.** Contents
   - **d.** Index

4. How many database files can be open simultaneously?
   - **a.** one
   - **b.** two
   - **c.** three
   - **d.** four

5. Which of the following terms describes all the data for one entity in a table?
   - **a.** record
   - **b.** file
   - **c.** field
   - **d.** query

6. Which database object is used to create printed output?
   - **a.** table
   - **b.** query
   - **c.** form
   - **d.** report

7. During which phase of the database design are the output specifications identified?
   - **a.** defining the purpose
   - **b.** planning the objects
   - **c.** creating and relating tables
   - **d.** creating queries

8. In a well-designed database, the end user almost never interacts directly with
   - **a.** tables
   - **b.** queries
   - **c.** forms
   - **d.** both a and b

9. A database contains the first name, last name, and phone number for a group of students. The first name is what kind of data?
   a. field
   b. record
   c. query
   d. table

10. A table object is an instance of what?
    a. a form
    b. a query
    c. a report
    d. a class

Short Answer

1. How do fields and records differ?
2. Which Access object is considered the primary object?
3. What is a relational database management system?
4. How is a query differ from a table?
5. Which Access object is used to make data in a database more visually appealing on the screen?
6. When you name a database file, on which screen element does the filename appear?
7. What is the Database window?
8. How are the Access menus and the Database toolbar related?
9. Why is it important to determine output specifications before creating a database?
10. How does the Office Assistant differ from the Contents and Index online help option?

For Discussion

1. What is the primary database object in a Microsoft Access database, and how does it differ from other Access objects?
2. What are the six classes of database objects? How is each category of object used?
3. What is required to use Microsoft on the Web to obtain help about Access?
4. What steps are required to design a database?

Review Exercises

1. Creating a new database using the New Database Wizard

One of the databases you will create for the Willows is an employee database. This database will be used to keep track of the names, addresses, phone numbers, and salary or wage information for each employee.

Using the design steps outlined in this Overview, plan a table to list employee data. Create a Microsoft Word document entitled *Employee Table Specifications.doc* that includes answers to the following questions:

1. What is the purpose of this database?
2. What are two potential input specifications?
3. What are two potential output specifications?
4. What fields would be appropriate for this table?

Save your document before exiting Microsoft Word.

2. Getting Help about Wizards

Microsoft Office 97 Professional incorporates Wizards to simplify common tasks. In an assignment for Project 1, you will use the New Database Wizard to create an employee database.

Use the online help system to obtain information about creating a database using Wizards. Follow these steps:

1. Select Microsoft Access Help from the Help menu.
2. Type **What is the database wizard** in the question box, and then click the Search button.
3. Select the Create a Database topic. In the Microsoft Access 97 help dialog box, select *Create a database using a Database Wizard* from the help topic and review the necessary steps to use this Wizard.

3. Creating a new database and exploring object windows

1. Launch Access 97 and create a new blank database named **High Point Foods xxx** (where **xxx** represents your initials).
2. Display each page of the blank database object window.
3. Display a list of toolbars available and display one of the toolbars available.
4. Close the toolbar.
5. Maximize the database window; then restore the window.
6. Close the database and exit Access.

Assignments

1. Using the Microsoft Web site to obtain help on Access

Connect to the Microsoft Access Web site, and search for information about publishing Microsoft Access data on the Web. If time permits, create a Word document explaining the process of publishing table data to a static Web page.

2. Designing a membership database

One of your tasks at the Willows is to design a database for tracking information about the current members. Using the same strategy from the Overview and Assignment 1, develop a set of specifications for a membership database. Save your specifications in a Microsoft Word document.

1

PROJECT

Building an Access Table

Now that you have created a database file, your first step in building the database itself is to create individual database objects. In this project you will build a table to hold membership information.

Objectives

After completing this project, you will be able to:

- **Open an Access database**
- **Create an Access table using Design view**
- **Define a table structure**
- **Add records to an Access table in Datasheet view**
- **Create an AutoForm**
- **Navigate among records and add records to a table using the navigation controls on a form**

The Challenge

As a member of the IT (Information Technology) department at the Willows, Mr. Gilmore has asked you to design a database containing information about current members of the club. The Willows has three membership categories, each with corresponding dues. A member can receive a discount on his or her membership based upon current age and length of membership. Mr. Gilmore wants the database to print a list of each member's current status and membership dues.

The Solution

Before creating a table, you must determine the appropriate data types for each field of information. Using Table Design view you can quickly create the table design by naming each field and selecting the appropriate data type and field size. After you add a few records to the table in Datasheet view, you can create a simple AutoForm to work with records in the database one at a time. Your completed table and a form displaying table data appears in Figure 1.1.

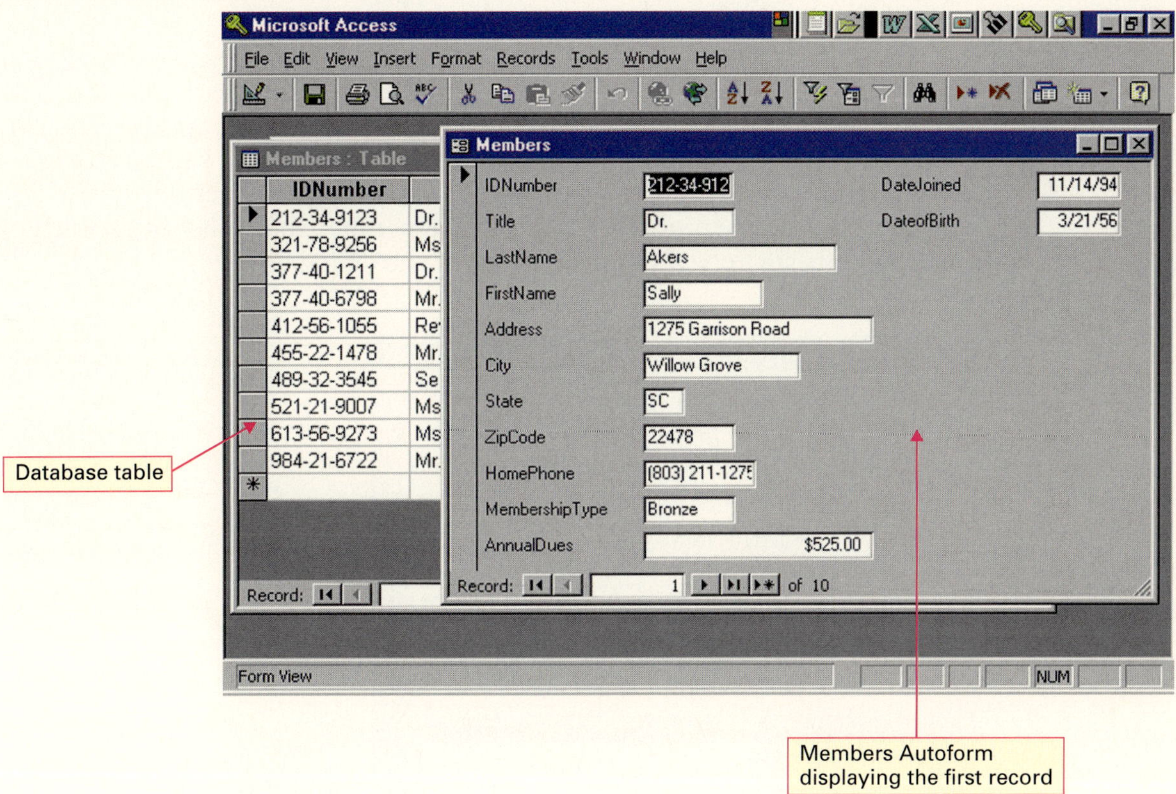

Figure 1.1

The Setup

After you launch Access and open your database, you should set up Access as shown in Table 1.1 so that your screen matches the illustrations in

Table 1.1 Access Settings

Location	Make These Settings:
View, Toolbars	Display the Database toolbar
Tools, Options	Display the Status bar

this project. The following table lists the default settings in Access, but they may have been changed on your computer.

Troubleshooting If you do not see the Database toolbar on the screen when you launch Access and open your database, choose Toolbars from the View menu. Select the Database toolbar to display it. If any additional toolbars are visible, close them. If you do not see the Status Bar at the bottom of the Application Window, choose Options from the Tools menu, click the View tab and change the Status Bar check box option.

Opening an Access Database

When you launch Access, the Microsoft Access dialog box shown in Figure 1.2 appears onscreen. This dialog box enables you to either create a new database or open an existing one. Remember that a list of recently opened databases appears at the bottom of the dialog box.

Figure 1.2

TASK 1: TO OPEN A DATABASE:

1 Launch Access.

Troubleshooting If Access is running and the Microsoft Access dialog box is not visible, select Open Database from the File menu.

2. Select the Open an Existing Database option and click OK.
3. When the Open dialog box appears, select your floppy disk drive in the Look in: drop-down list.
4. Click *Willows Membership.mdb* in the file list, as shown opposite, if it is not already selected.

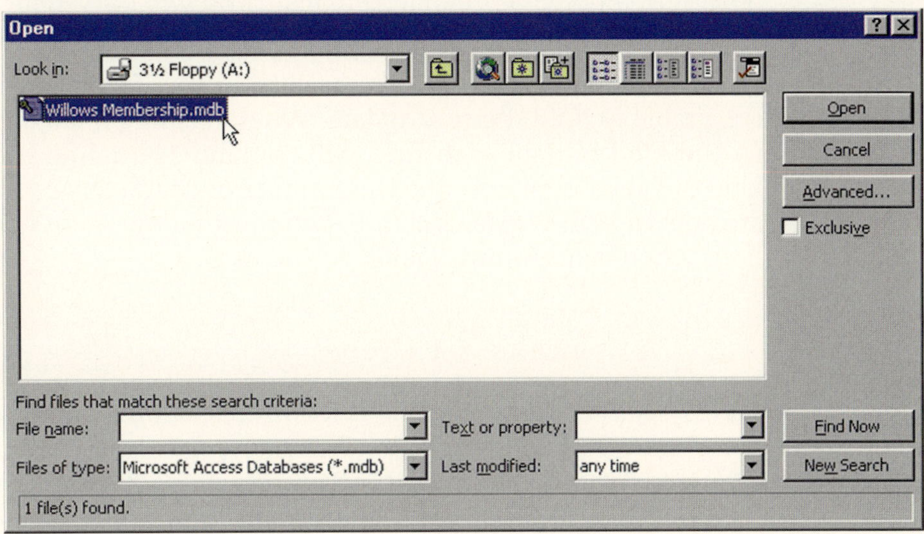

5. Click Open.
Access opens the database file, displays the name of the database in the Title bar of the Database window, and makes the Tables tab active, as shown below.

Creating a Table

As you will recall from the Overview, you must first plan a database before designing it. This database will list members and will provide a printed list of each member's current membership status, dues, and discounts. You will need at least one table and one report. To simplify the process of modifying membership data, you will also create a screen form. The discount data will be calculated using a query.

An Access table object is the primary repository for data, so you must create a table to hold the record data. When creating a table, you must specify the kind of data each field will contain. The name of each field, the kind of data it contains, and the number of characters each field can store are known as the ***table structure***. You must follow Access naming conventions when determining a table's structure.

Naming Fields and Determining Data Types

Access does not place many restrictions on naming the fields in a table. A field name can be up to 64 characters in length and can include any combination of letters, numbers, spaces, and special characters except a period (.), an exclamation point (!), an accent grave (`), and brackets ([ ]).

Tip If your database will include Visual Basic code or more complex expressions, consider omitting spaces from the field name.

To store your table data in the most efficient manner, Access supports different data types. A ***data type*** is a characteristic of how data is stored in a database. Various data types correspond to the kind of data your fields will contain. For example, a text data type is required to store name and address information. If you need to perform calculations involving monetary units, you will need to use the currency data type. Table 1.2 summarizes the 10 data types you can use for table data.

Determining an Appropriate Table Structure

Now that you know what Mr. Gilmore wants, you can design a table that stores information about the club's members. In most databases that contain name and address information, you create separate fields for first and last name, and for address, city, state, and zip code. This ensures that you can sort the data in different ways, such as by last name, by state of residence, or by zip code.

Your table will contain text, currency, and data/time data types. In the tasks that follow, you will create a new table with the table structure shown in Figure 1.3.

Table 1.2 Access Data Types

Data Type	Description
Text	Any combination of alphabetic and numeric characters, such as names, addresses, and phone numbers. The text data type holds a maximum of 255 characters, which is the default data type.
Memo	Used for long text entries that exceed 255 characters. Holds up to 64 kilobytes of data in a random format.
Number	Numeric values, such as inventory quantity or the number of items ordered. Numeric data can be used in calculations.
Date/Time	Date and time values for the years 100 through 9999.
Currency	Currency values and numeric data used in mathematical calculations that involve data with one to four decimal places.
AutoNumber	Access feature that assigns a unique and sequential number to records as they are created and added to a table. AutoNumber data cannot be changed, edited, or deleted.
Yes/No	This data type displays a checkbox and allows for Yes/No (Boolean) data. If the checkbox is empty, the value is No or False (0). If the checkbox is checked, the value is Yes or True (1).
OLE Object	Fields that contain embedded or linked objects, such as Microsoft Excel spreadsheet, a Microsoft Word document, graphics, or sounds.
Hyperlink	Text, or combinations of text and numbers, used as a hyperlink address. This data type is used to link to Web pages or other documents.
Lookup Wizard	A wizard that walks you through the process of defining a field that allows you to choose a value from another table or from a list of values.

Field Name	Data Type	Field Length / Format
IDNumber	Text	11
Title	Text	10
LastName	Text	25
FirstName	Text	15
Address	Text	50
City	Text	20
State	Text	2
ZipCode	Text	10
HomePhone	Text	14
MembershipType	Text	10
AnnualDues	Currency	
DateJoined	Date/Time	Short Date
DateofBirth	Date/Time	Short Date

Figure 1.3

TASK 2: TO CREATE FIELDS IN A TABLE WITH A TEXT DATA TYPE:

1. With the Tables tab active, click the New button in the Database window.
2. In the New Table dialog box, select Design view and click OK.

The Table Design window will appear.

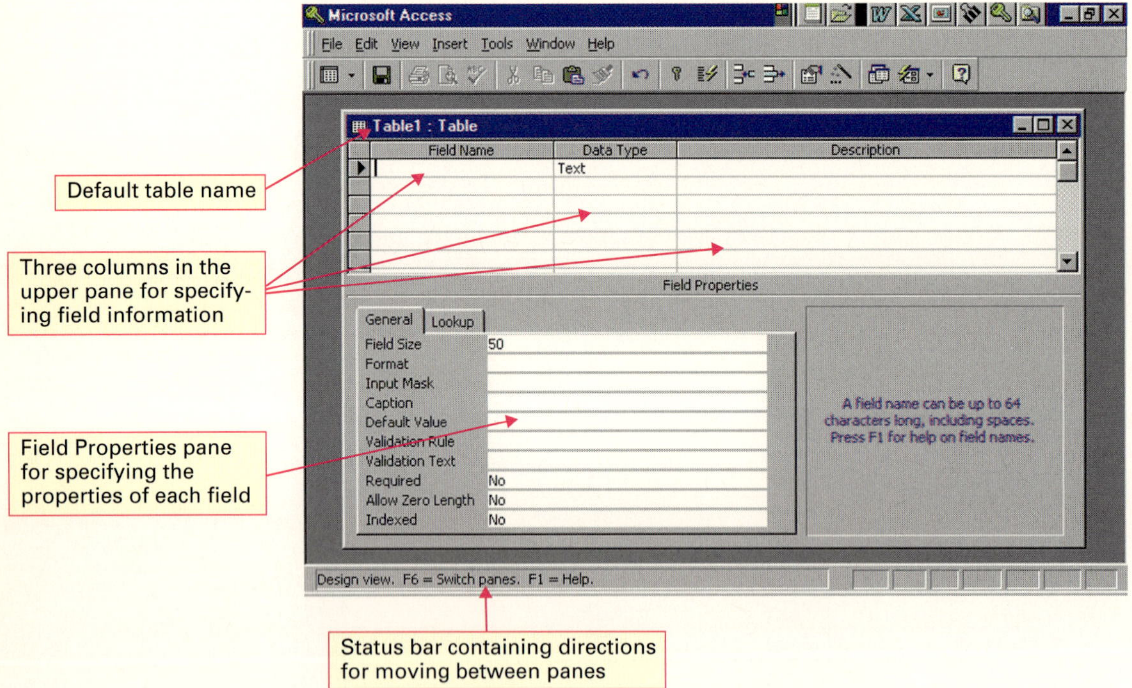

The ***Table Design window*** is a visual workspace in which you can enter information about each field in your table. ***Table Design view*** always displays this window.

3. The insertion point appears in the left column of the first row of the upper pane. Type **IDNumber** in the left column of the first row, as shown on the following page.

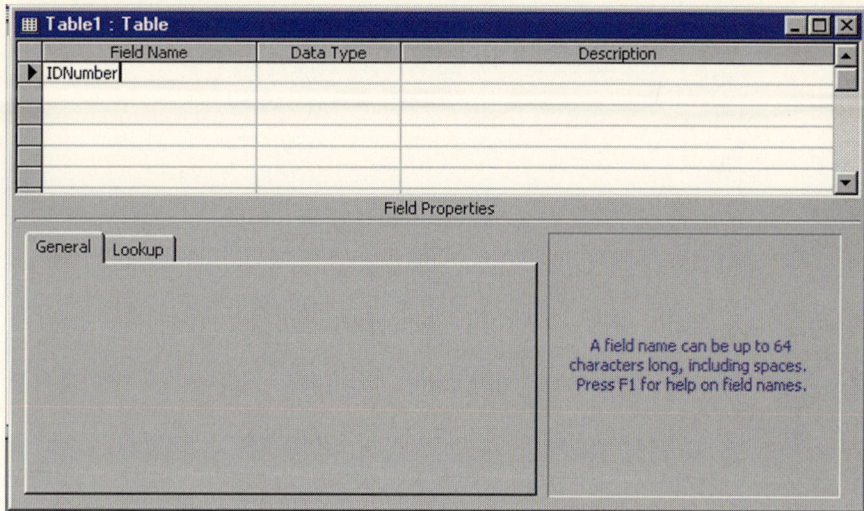

4. Press (F6) once to activate the Properties pane (the lower half of the window) for the current field. You will notice that the data type is set to text by default, and that the default field size entry is selected.
5. Type **11** as the field size for the IDNumber field.
6. Press (F6) to move back to the upper pane.
7. Click the Primary Key button on the toolbar, as shown.

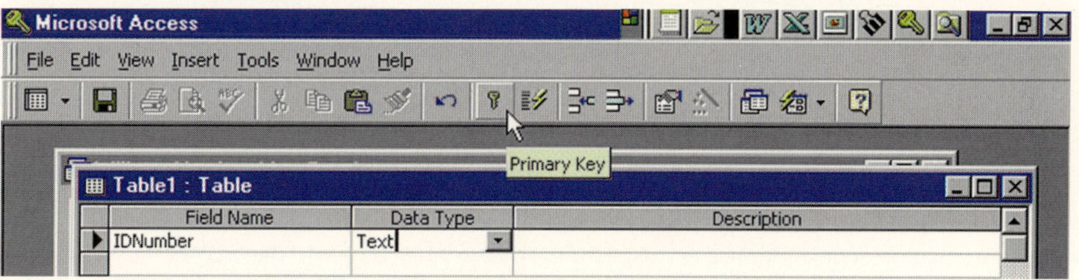

Tip The power of a relational database system such as Access comes from its ability to quickly find and bring together information stored in separate tables. In order to do this, each table should include a field or set of fields that uniquely identify each record in the table. This information is called the primary key of the table. Once you designate a primary key for a table, to ensure uniqueness, Microsoft Access will prevent any duplicate or Null values from being entered in the primary key fields.

An icon representing this field as the primary key appears in the upper pane, as shown on the next page.

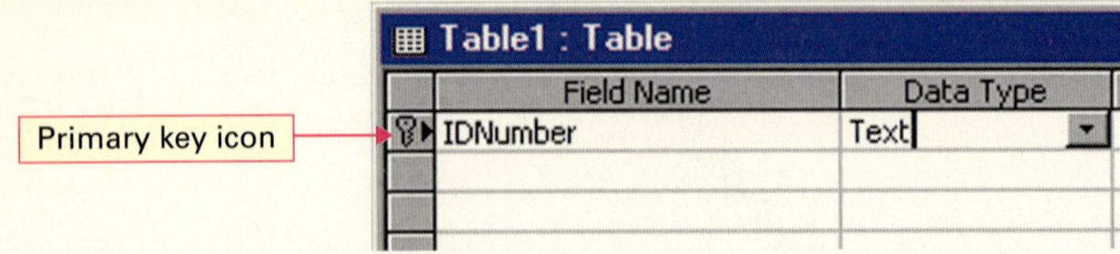

8 Using the specifications listed in Figure 1.3, add field names and change the default field size for all fields through MembershipType. When you are finished, your Table Definition window will look similar to the figure shown below.

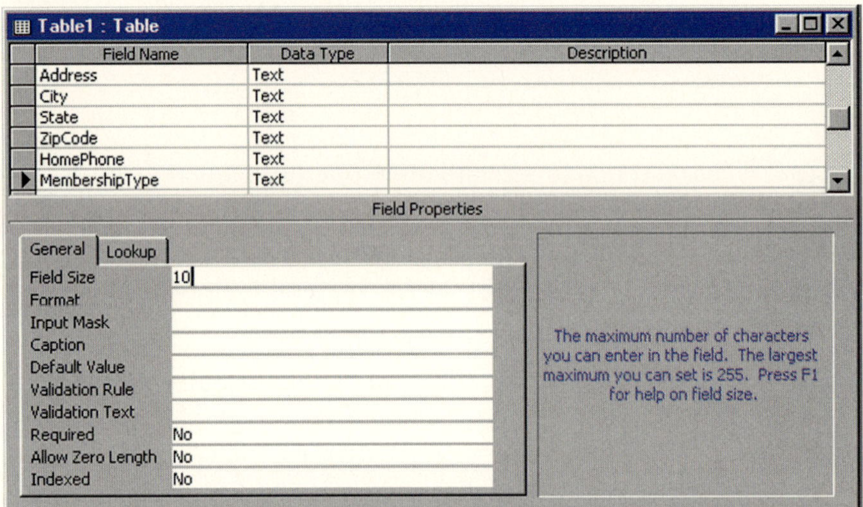

Troubleshooting If you make a mistake while defining one or more fields, use the scroll bar in the upper pane and place the insertion point into the appropriate cell in the upper pane or the row in the lower pane that must be corrected. After a table is saved, you can always return to the Table Design window to modify its structure.

9 Click the Save icon on the toolbar.
The Save As dialog box shown below appears. Notice that the default table name Table1 is highlighted.

10 Type **Members** as the table name, and click OK. The name of the table changes in the Table Title bar.

Name of table displayed in Title bar

Members : Table

Field Name	Data Type
Address	Text
City	Text
State	Text
ZipCode	Text
HomePhone	Text
MembershipType	Text

TASK 3: DEFINING FIELDS WITH CURRENCY AND DATE/TIME DATA TYPES:

1. Type **AnnualDues** as the field name in the next available row in the upper pane. Press the TAB key once to activate the Data Type column.

2. Click the drop-down list button next in the Data Type column, and select Currency as the data type.

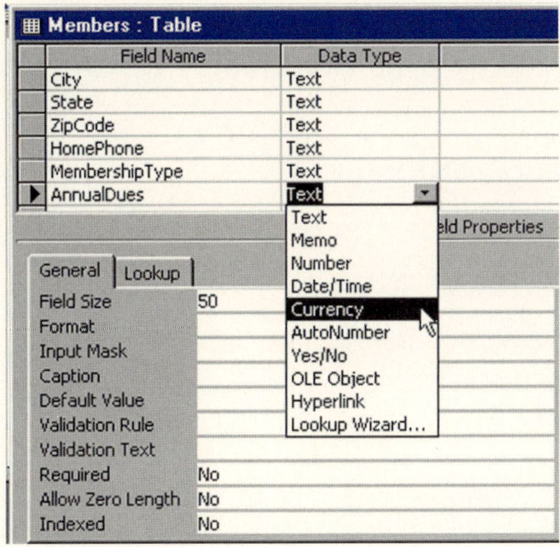

You will notice that the available properties for this field change in the lower pane.

3. Press the TAB key twice until the insertion point appears in the "Field Name" column of the next row. Then type **DateJoined** as the next field name, and set its data type to Date/Time. The data field appears, as shown on the next page.

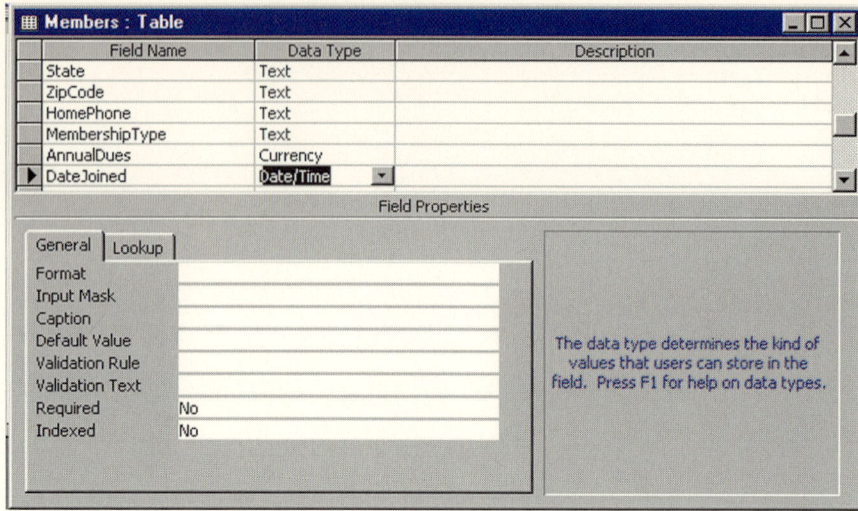

4. Type **DateofBirth** as the name of the last field. Set the data type to Date/Time.
5. Save the changes to your table design.
6. Select Datasheet view from the View menu.

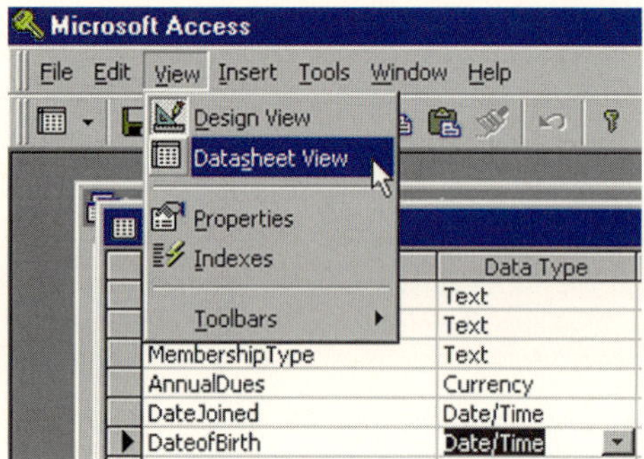

The table is now displayed in Datasheet view, as shown on the next page. ***Datasheet view*** is a display format in which field data appears in columns and record data appears in rows. Notice that the name of each field appears above the columns near the top of the window. A horizontal scroll bar appears along the bottom of the window. You can use this scrollbar to reveal the remaining fields in the table.

Tip You can also use the Up and Down directional arrow keys to move among records.

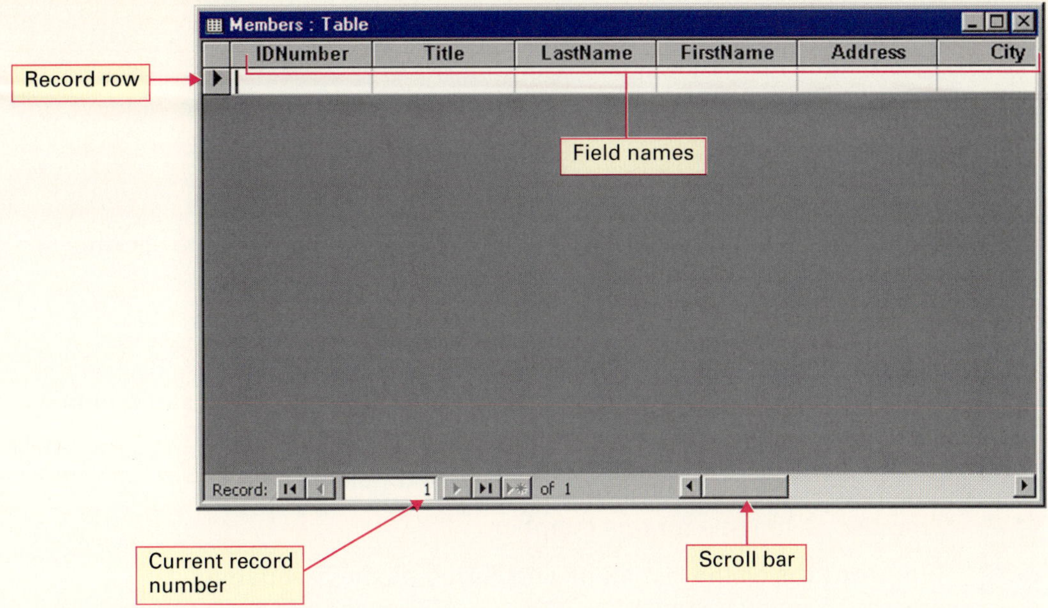

7 Use the Close button in the upper right-hand corner of the Table window to close the table and return to the Database window.

Adding Records to a Table Using Datasheet View

Now that you have successfully created a table, you can easily add records about specific members using Datasheet view. Notice that the Database window shown below displays an icon representing the table you just created. In addition, the Open and Design buttons are now enabled.

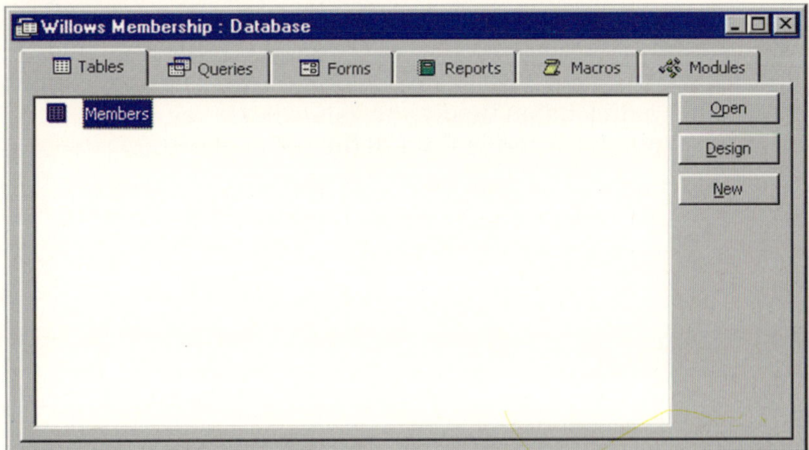

Remember that every Access object has at least two views: one for creating or editing the object's design, and one for viewing record data by the object. You will use Datasheet view to add records to the table.

TASK 4: TO ADD RECORDS TO A TABLE USING DATASHEET VIEW:

1. Highlight the *Members* table in the Tables tab of the Database window, and click the Open button.

> **Tip** You can also open a table in Datasheet view by double-clicking the table's icon in the Database window.

2. Type **455-22-1478** as the membership ID number for the first member's record.
3. Press the TAB key once to move to the next field.
4. Type **Mr.** as the title for this member.
5. Type **Jenkins** as the last name and **Adley** as the first name.

> **Troubleshooting** If you inadvertently move to the next field, you can use the SHIFT+TAB combination to move to the previous field in the datasheet. You can also click the mouse in any field to edit its contents.

6. Type **250 Windjammer Drive**, **Almont**, **SC**, **22217**, and **(803) 551-2770** respectively, as the address and phone information for this member. (Remember that you don't type in the commas.)
7. Type **Charter** as the membership type, **775** as his annual dues, **1/25/87** as the date this member joined the Willows, and **10/16/31** as this member's date of birth.

> **Troubleshooting** When adding currency data, you do not need to enter a dollar sign before the value. If the value is an integer, Access adds two zeros to the right of the decimal place.
>
> When entering dates, place a forward slash character (/) or a hyphen (-) between the month, day, and year values. If you use the hyphen character, Access will convert it to a forward slash character when you move out of the field.

8. Press the TAB key. The insertion point moves to the first field of the second record.

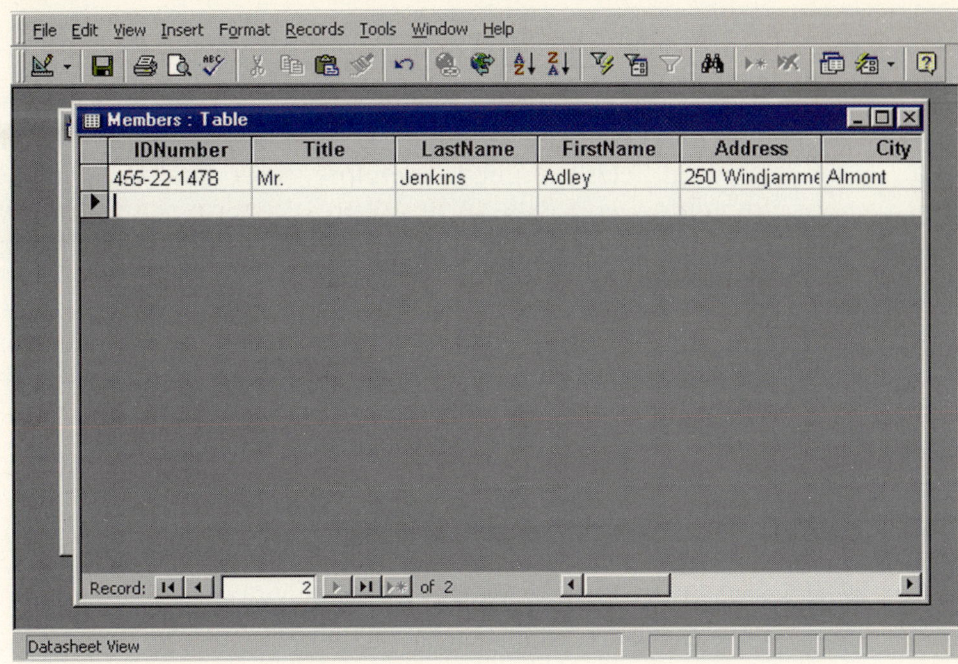

9 Using the data shown in the figure below, add four additional records to the database by following the same process as in Steps 1–8.

Record	ID Number	Title	Last Name	First Name	Address	City	State
2	212-34-9123	Dr.	Akers	Sally	1275 Garrison Road	Willow Grove	SC
3	521-21-9007	Ms.	Bock	Anita	14563 Greenridge	James Way	SC
4	412-56-1055	Reverend	Barclay	William	9007 Leesburg Pike	Smithfield	SC
5	321-78-9256	Ms.	Williams	Sandy	14419 Brooke Street	James Way	SC

Record	Zip Code	Home Phone	Membership Type	Annual Dues	Date Joined	Date of Birth
2	22478	(803) 211-1275	Bronze	$525.00	11/14/94	3/21/56
3	24382	(803) 555-1212	Gold	$650.00	2/1/64	5/3/35
4	24491	(803) 744-7611	Silver	$575.00	1/9/97	7/14/65
5	24381	(803) 555-8272	Charter	$775.00	6/29/82	4/15/30

After you add four more records, the Datasheet will appear as shown below.

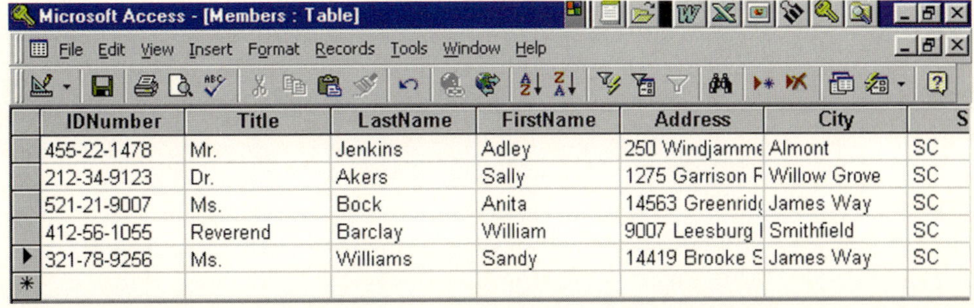

10 Close the table.

Creating an AutoForm

As you can see, working with records in Datasheet view is tedious. Not only do you have to scroll back and forth to see all fields, but navigation between fields is limited. Therefore, most databases include screen forms for editing table data. In this context, a form is a visual representation of record and field data that usually displays only one record on the screen at a time. Just as with tables, forms include multiple views.

It is not difficult to create a form in Access. In fact the ***AutoForm*** option for new forms can create a form for you after you specify the form layout you want and which table to use as the source for your form.

TASK 5: TO CREATE AN AUTOFORM:

1. Click the Forms tab in the Database window.
2. Click the New button.
3. In the New Forms dialog box, select the AutoForm: Columnar option, as shown below.

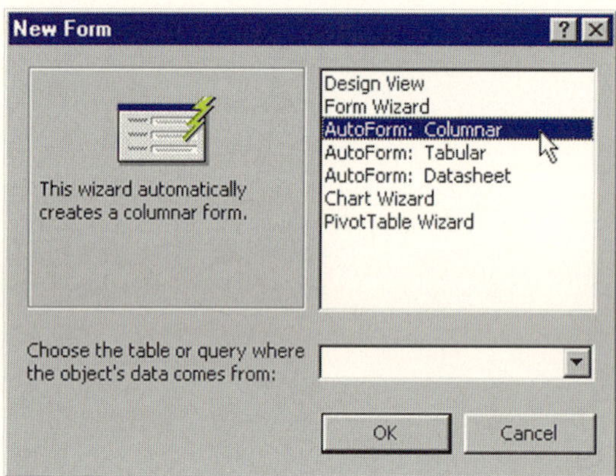

4. In the lower portion of the form, click the drop-down list button to specify a table or query.

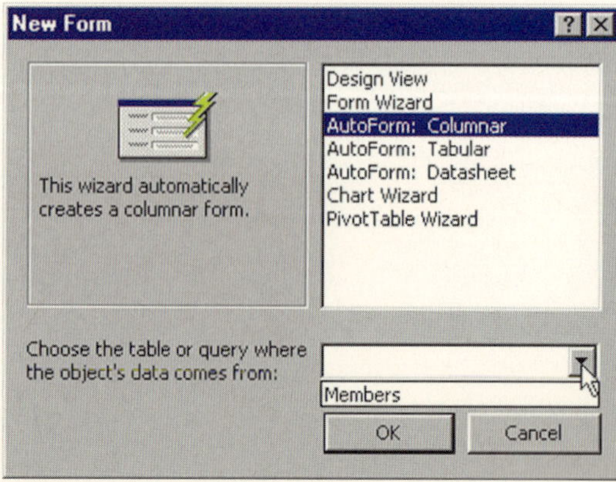

5 Because the Members table is the only object in your database that you can use as the source for an AutoForm, select Members in the list of available tables and queries. Members should now appear in the listbox, as shown below.

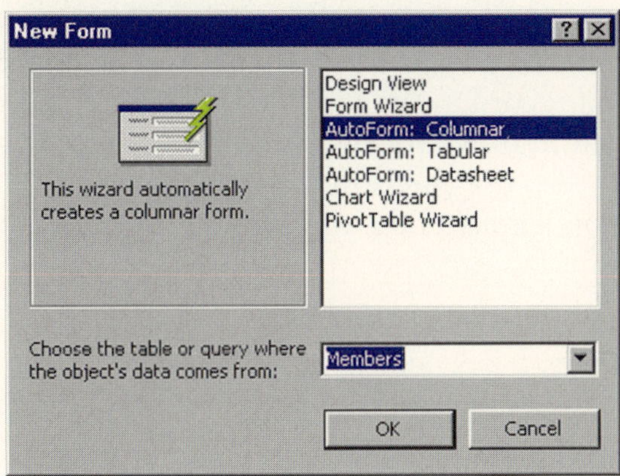

6 Click OK. AutoForm generates a form that looks similar to the one shown below.

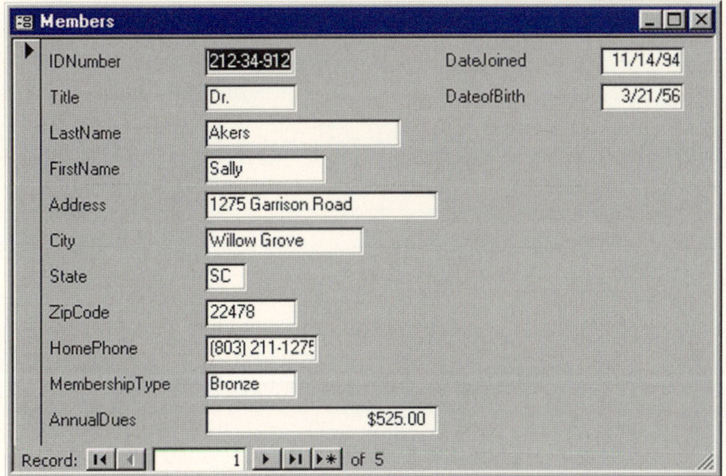

Troubleshooting Depending upon how Access is configured on your computer, your form may contain a background image or display different colors. In addition, some of the fields may not display completely.

7 Click the Save button on the toolbar to save your form. The Save As dialog box appears.

8 Accept the default name by clicking OK.

Navigating Among Records and Adding Records to a Table Using the Navigation Controls on a Form

The form you created in the last task includes navigation buttons for moving among records in the underlying Members table. To ***navigate*** among records is to move from one record to another in a table. By default, the form displays the first record in the table when it is created or opened. You can use these controls to move to the first, previous, next, and last records in the table. You can also use the New Record button to add records to the table. The figure below explains the navigation buttons that appear on the Members form.

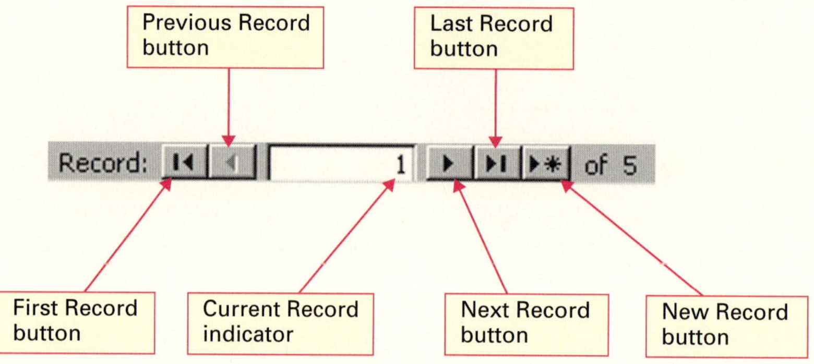

TASK 6: TO NAVIGATE AMONG RECORDS IN A TABLE USING A FORM:

1. Click the Last Record button on the Members form. Record 5 appears in the form.

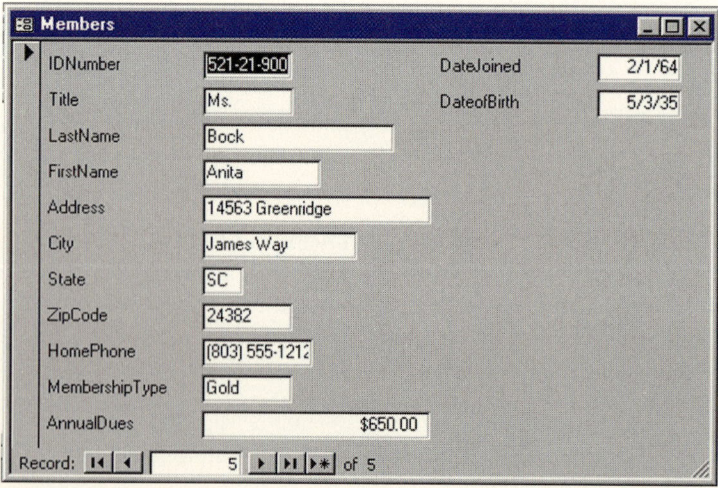

2. Click the Previous Record button. The form displays record number 4.

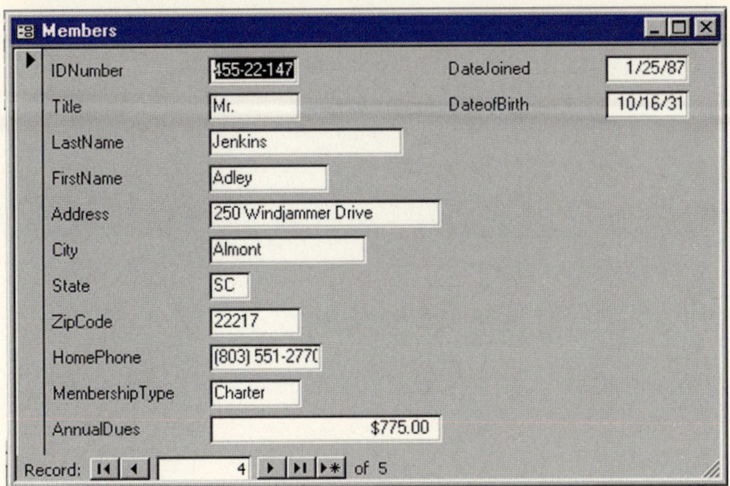

3 Select the number 4 inside the text box displaying the current record, and type **2**. When you press ENTER, the form displays the second record in the table.

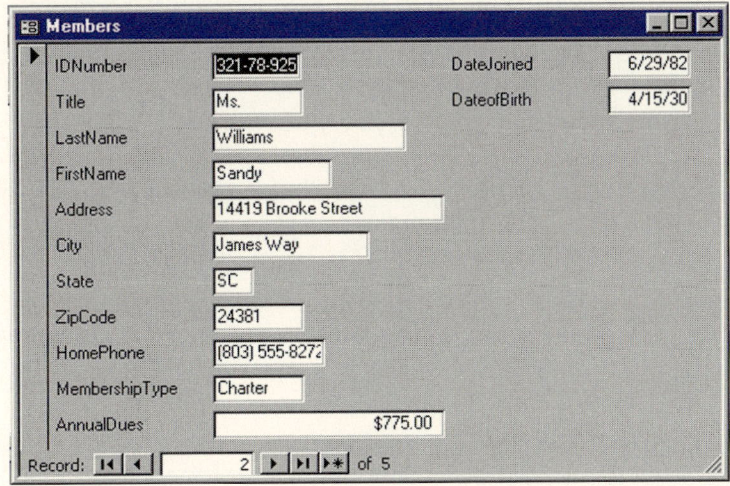

Troubleshooting As you navigate through the table the record numbers will not correspond to the order in which you entered the records. This is because the records are ordered according to the primary key.

TASK 7: TO ADD RECORDS TO THE TABLE USING THE NEW RECORD BUTTON ON THE FORM:

1 Click the New Record button on the form. A blank form appears.

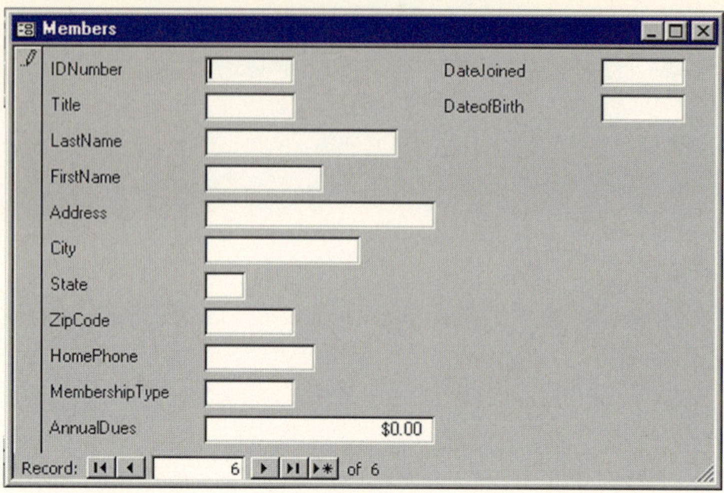

Notice that the insertion point appears inside the IDNumber field, and that the current record is record 6.

2. Type **377-40-6798** as the ID Number for the sixth member in the table.
3. Press the TAB key to move to the next field on the form.
4. Using the data shown below, complete the sixth record and add four additional records to the Members table.

Record	ID Number	Title	Last Name	First Name	Address	City	State
6	377-40-6798	Mr.	Gill	Samuel	9575 Kingsley Road	Altamont	SC
7	984-21-6722	Mr.	Thomas	Michael	15065 Knicker Drive	Fordham	SC
8	489-32-3545	Senator	Lilley	William	13411 Reardon Lane	Adamsville	SC
9	377-40-1211	Dr.	Bolts	Raymond	5622 Forest Glen	Freeman	NC
10	613-56-9273	Ms.	Adams	Jennifer	14419 Brook Street	Willow Grove	SC

Record	Zip Code	Home Phone	Membership Type	Annual Dues	Date Joined	Date of Birth
6	24122	(803) 343-2100	Bronze	$525.00	9/6/92	6/5/55
7	22786	(803) 555-2190	Gold	$650.00	1/21/96	12/11/71
8	24112	(803) 788-2131	Charter	$775.00	4/10/69	3/25/45
9	29120	(802) 522-9011	Silver	$575.00	9/27/66	7/18/32
10	22512	(803) 525-2341	Bronze	$525.00	4/21/78	5/19/56

Tip After you complete a record entry in Access, the record is automatically saved to the database file when you move to a new or a different record.

5. When you are finished, your table should look like the datasheet shown on the next page.

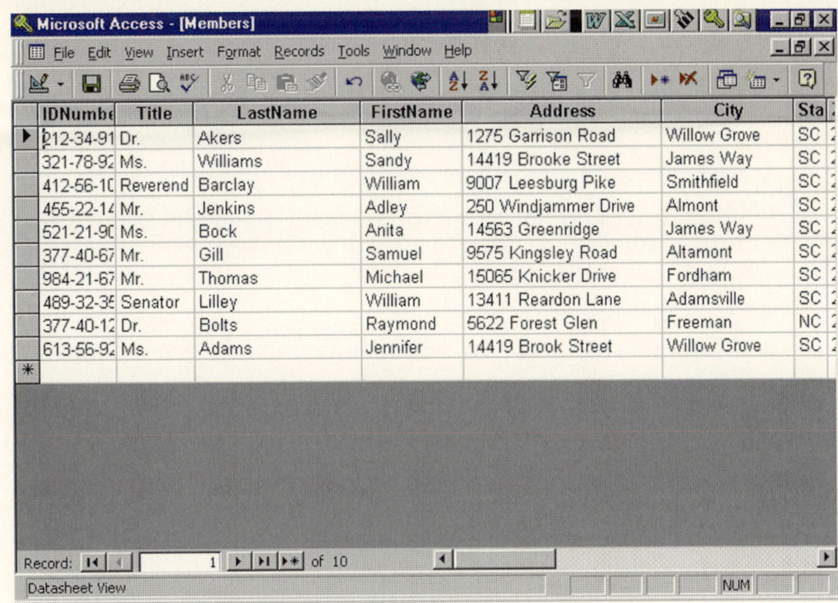

6 Close the *Members* form.

7 Close the *Willows Membership.mdb* database.

The Conclusion

In this project, you learned how to create a table using Design view, and you then learned how to enter records directly into the table. You created an AutoForm based upon the table to assist with data entry. Finally, you learned how to navigate among records and add new records to the table using the controls on a form.

Summary and Exercises

Summary

- Tables are the primary repositories for data in an Access database.
- Table structure includes field names, data types, field lengths, and field formats.
- Access supports 10 data types.
- Tables are created using Design view, and the record data is edited or displayed in Datasheet view.
- Forms are often used to display and edit database records.
- An AutoForm is an automatically generated form based upon a table (or tables).
- Forms contain controls for navigating among records and adding new records to a table.

Key Terms and Operations

Key Terms

AutoForm
controls
currency
data type
date/time
Datasheet view
Design view
hyperlink
memo
navigate
numeric
OLE
table
Table Design view
Table Design window
table structure
text
yes/no

Operations

open a database
create a table using Design view
add text data fields to a table
add currency and date/time fields to a table
add records to a table using Datasheet view
create an AutoForm
use form controls to navigate among records
use form controls to add new records to a table

Study Questions

Multiple Choice

1. Which data type is used to store long text entries?

a. text
b. memo
c. numeric
d. OLE

2. The upper pane in the Table Design Screen is used to enter:
   a. field names
   b. field data types
   c. field properties
   d. both a and b

3. Which of the following statements is false?
   a. When you open an Access database, the Database window normally is displayed.
   b. To create tables, you must first open an existing database file or create a new one.
   c. All Access database objects are contained in one file.
   d. When you open a database file, a new table is automatically created.

4. What field type uses a checkbox to store field data?
   a. text
   b. number
   c. date/time
   d. yes/no

5. Which of the following data types enables you to specify a field size?
   a. text
   b. number
   c. date/time
   d. currency

6. You are designing a table containing name and address information. How many characters should you reserve for the Last Name field, which is a text data type?
   a. 255
   b. 100
   c. 15
   d. 5

7. You have been commissioned to create a database for a hardware store. The table listing inventory items must display the current quantity in stock. Which data type will you use for this field?
   a. text
   b. currency
   c. numeric
   d. memo

8. Your database contains a form created using the Columnar AutoForm option. Which statement is false concerning this form?
   a. The form displays only one record in the form.
   b. You can use the New Record button in the navigation controls to add a record to the underlying table.
   c. The form displays the records from the underlying table as a datasheet.
   d. The form contains a text box displaying the current record number.

9. Which of the following controls does not appear on a Columnar AutoForm?
   a. First Record
   b. Delete Record
   c. Last Record
   d. Previous Record

10. When navigating among records in a table using a form, which control displays any record you specify by record number?
    - a. the Add New Record button
    - b. the Current Record text box
    - c. the First Record button
    - d. the Previous Record button

Short Answer

1. How does a table differ from a database?
2. How does a table differ from a form?
3. What is the default data type listed in the Table Design window?
4. Where do you change the properties of a field in a table?
5. Which option do you select to create an AutoForm?
6. How do you create a table in Access?
7. What is displayed onscreen when you open an Access database file?
8. Where in the Database window are forms displayed?
9. When displaying records in a form, if there are 10 records and you are positioned at record 2 and want to move to record 5, how do you display this record?
10. How do you add a new record to a table using a form?

For Discussion

1. How do text and memo data types differ? When is each appropriate?
2. Why does a form require a table?
3. What additional fields might you want to include in the Members table, and why?
4. Could the Willows Membership database include any additional tables? What data might an additional table contain?

Review Exercises

1. Creating a database per design specifications

In Review Exercise 1 from the Overview, you listed the specifications for an Employee database. Create the database and use the Table Wizard to create a table.

1. Launch Access if it is not currently running. Create a blank database named Willows Employees, and save it to your floppy diskette.
2. Make sure the Tables tab is selected in the Database window. Click the New button.
3. Select Table Wizard in the New Table dialog box and click OK, as shown on the next page.

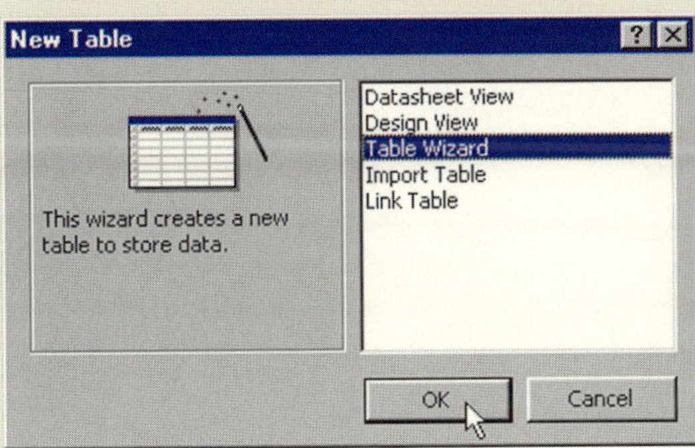

4. In the Table Wizard dialog box, select Employees from the Sample Tables: list, and check the option button for Business. You now must specify which fields to add to the table. Select SocialSecurityNumber from the Sample Fields: list, and click the single arrow button to add this field to the Fields in my New Table: list.

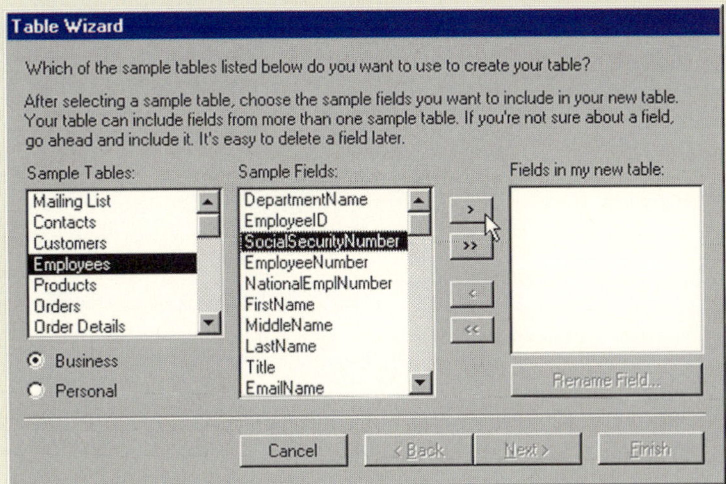

5. Add the following additional fields to your table, in the order specified: Title, LastName, FirstName, Address, City, StateOrProvince, PostalCode, and Salary. The Table Wizard dialog box should now appear.

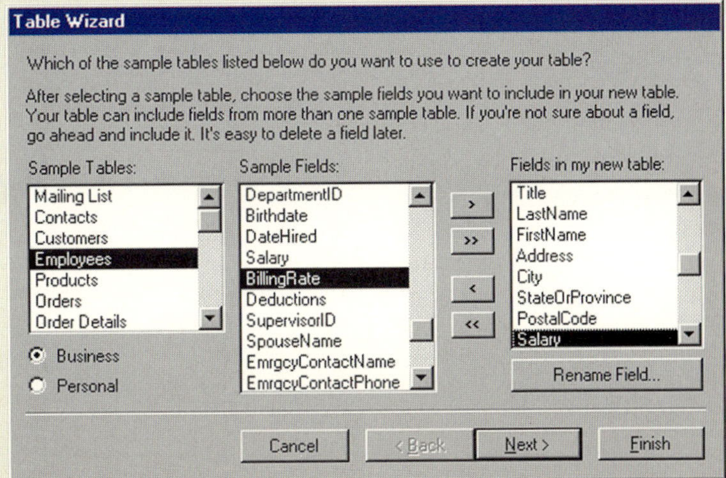

6. Click the Next button. In this step of the Table Wizard, specify Employees as the name for the table, and select the option to set your own primary key. Click Next.

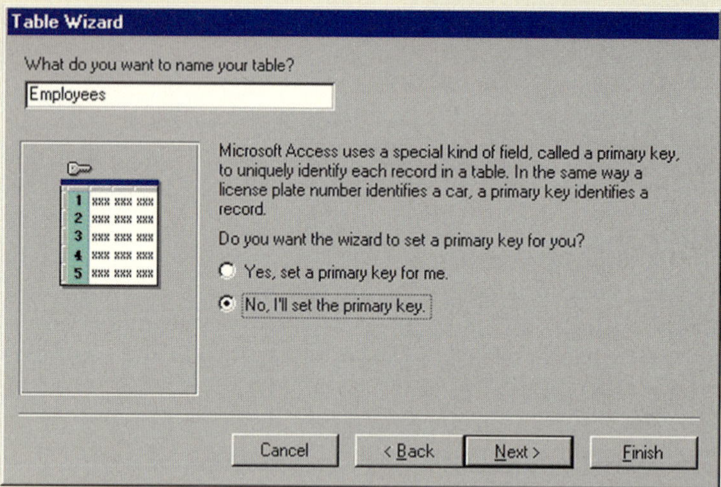

7. By default, the Table Wizard should specify SocialSecurityNumber as the primary key field since it was the first field entered. Select the last option button for the kind of data the field will contain, and click Next.

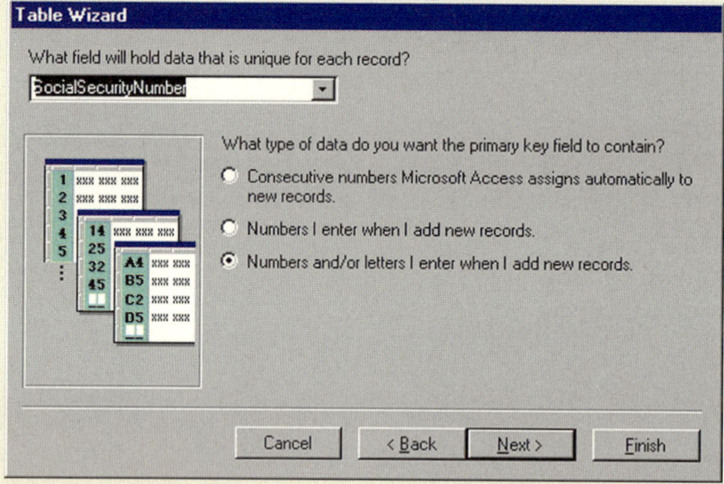

8. In the last step of the Table Wizard, select the option to enter data via a form the Wizard will create. Click the Finish button.

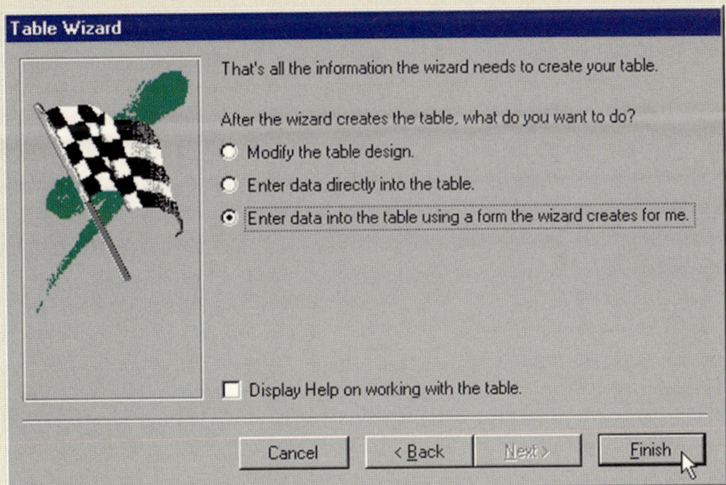

The Wizard automatically creates a table and the data entry form shown here.

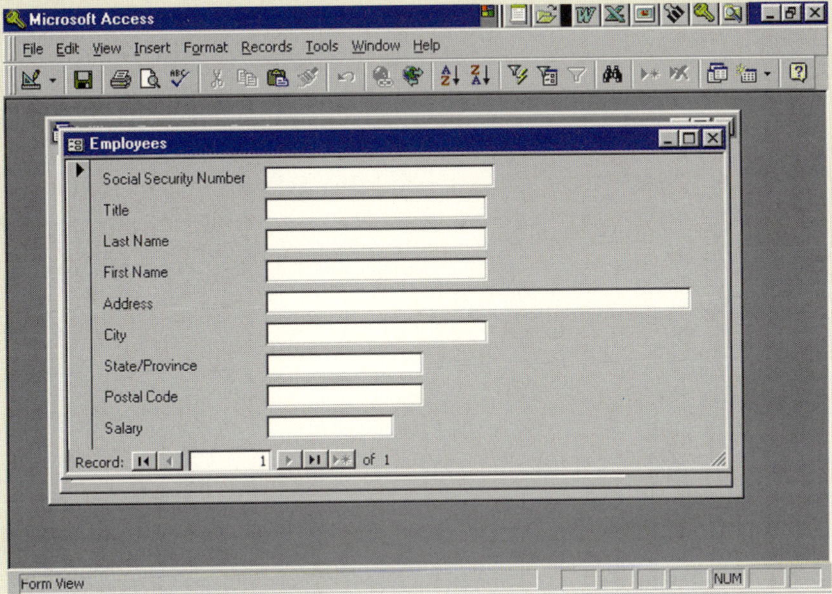

9. Close the form, and accept **Employees** as the name when you are prompted to save changes to the form.
10. Close the Willows Employees database.

2. Adding Records to a table using a form

Open the *Willows Employees.mdb* database file you created in the previous exercise. Complete the following steps to add records for five employees.

1. Click the Forms tab in the Database window.
2. Click the Open button to open the *Employees* form.

3. Using the procedures you learned in this project, add records for five employees into the table using this form.

Tip Notice that as you add records, you do not need to add hyphens in each employee's Social Security Number. You will learn how to create an input mask like this in Project 3.

4. Close the form.
5. Close the database.

3. Creating a new table, adding records, and creating an AutoForm for the table

1. Launch Access 97, if necessary, and open the database *High Point Foods xxx.mdb* (where *xxx* represents your initials).

Note If you do not have a database named *High Point Foods xxx.mdb*, ask your instructor for a copy of the file you should use to complete this exercise.

2. Create a new table containing fields and field descriptions displayed as follows:

Field Name	Data Type	Description
CategoryID	AutoNumber	Number automatically assigned to a new category
CategoryName	Text	Name of food category
Description	Memo	

3. Save the table using the table name *Food Categories* with no primary key defined.

ID	Category Name	Description
1	Beverages	Soft drinks, coffees, teas, beers, and ales
2	Condiments	Sweet and savory sauces, relishes, spreads, and seasonings
3	Confections	Desserts, candies, and sweetbreads
4	Dairy Products	Cheeses
5	Grains/Cereals	Breads, crackers, pasta, and cereal
6	Meat/Poultry	Prepared meats
7	Produce	Dried fruit and bean curd
8	Seafood	Seaweed and fish

5. Spell check the table and make the necessary corrections.
6. Create an AutoForm for the table and save the form using the form name *Food Categories*.

7. Print a copy of the *Food Categories* table and the *Food Categories* form.
8. Close the database and exit Access.

Assignments

1. Creating a database using the hyperlink data type

The hyperLink data type is new in Access 97. In this assignment, you will create a new database that incorporates this data type. Create a new database with the name *Web Sites.mdb*. Create a table named **Sites** with the following structure:

Field Name	Data Type	Size
Company	Text	50
Primary Product	Text	50
Company URL	Hyperlink	N/A

When you save the table, allow Access to create a primary key. Access will add an AutoNumber field for the primary key data. As you add records to the table, tab through this field, since Access will supply a value automatically. Close the database when you are finished.

2. Creating an AutoForm and adding records to a table

In this assignment, you will modify the database you created in Assignment 1 for this project. Open the database, and create a Columnar AutoForm based upon the Sites table. Name the form **Sites**. Add the following three records to the table using the Sites form:

Company	Primary Product	Company URL
Microsoft	Software	http://www.microsoft.com
Adobe	Graphics software	http://www.adobe.com
Fidelity	Financial services	http://www.fidelity.com

After you have added these records, use the navigation controls on the form to move to the first record. If you can access the World Wide Web from your lab or computer, click the company URL field for Microsoft. When you are finished, close your Web browser and the database.

2

PROJECT

Manipulating and Maintaining Tables

After you have created database tables and added records to them, you frequently need to edit the record data or view it in different ways. In this project, you will learn how to manipulate and maintain table data.

Objectives

After completing this project, you will be able to:

- **Use the Find feature to locate a specific record**
- **Update records in a table**
- **Use the Replace feature**
- **Sort table data**
- **Filter records by selection**
- **Filter records by form**
- **Compact the database**

The Challenge

As the database developer at the Willows, you are responsible for implementing and maintaining the database of the club's members. As with any database, Mr. Gilmore will expect you to be able to customize the database as the need for information in new formats arises. For instance, just this week two members reported a change of address. The board of directors also just voted to raise the membership fees. Finally, Mr. Gilmore has requested that the data in the *Members* table display Charter members alphabetized by last name.

The Solution

Although well-designed databases shield users from having to interact with records at the table level, Access includes a number of features that make manipulating records a straightforward task. For example, you can use the Search feature to find records for members with an address change, and you can use the search and replace feature to change fee structures. Finally, you can filter the table either by selection or by form to display the records by type of membership. Figure 2.1 shows how the *Members* table datasheet appears when the table has been filtered and sorted by charter membership and then last name.

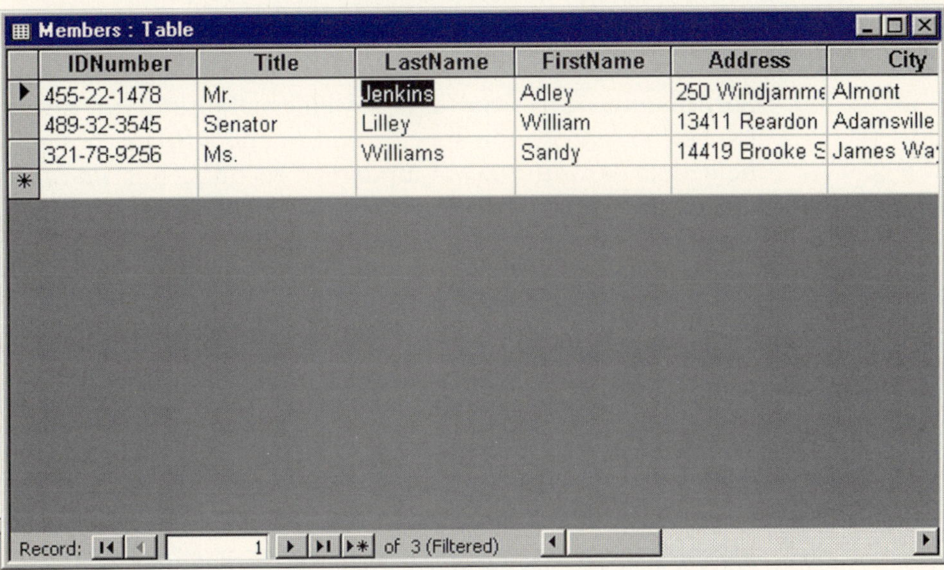

Figure 2.1

The Setup

After you launch Access and open your database, you should make sure the Database toolbar and the Status toolbar are displayed. These are the default settings in Access, but they may have been changed on your computer. (If you have forgotten how to do this, refer to Table 1.1 in Project 1.)

Troubleshooting If you do not see the Database toolbar on the screen when you launch Access and open your database, choose Toolbars from the View menu. Select the Database toolbar to display it. If any additional toolbars are visible, close them. If you do not see the Status bar at the bottom of the Application window, choose Options from the Tools menu, click the View Page tab, and change the Status bar check box option.

Using the procedures you learned in Task 1 of Project 1, open the *Willows Membership.mdb* file from your disk.

Searching a Table for a Specific Record

As with many databases, record data changes over time. This is particularly true for database tables containing address information. Although it is not difficult to find a specific record in a table that contains a small number of records, this method becomes impractical when a table contains hundreds or thousands of records.

Fortunately, Access contains search capabilities. You can use the ***Find*** dialog box to search for a specific record and ***edit***, or change, its data. Editing field data is one way of updating records, but ***updating*** also includes adding and deleting records. You will need to update the *Members* table by changing the address for Reverend Barclay and Ms. Adams.

TASK 1: TO SEARCH A TABLE FOR A SPECIFIC RECORD:

1. From the Database window, click the Forms tab to make it active.
2. Double-click the *Members* form to display the first record in the underlying table.

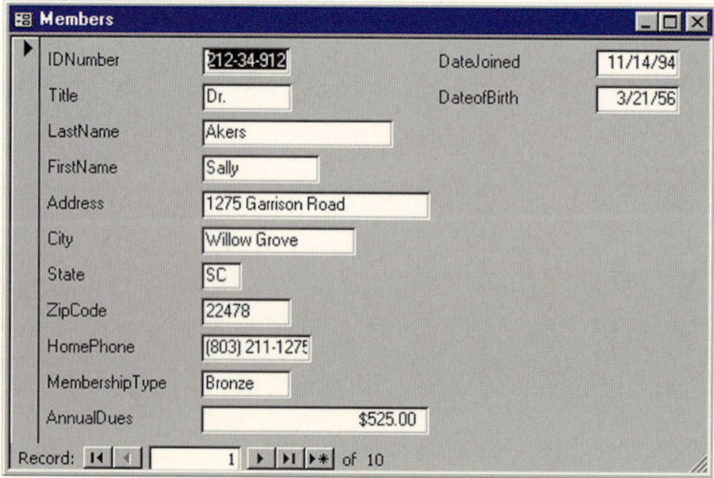

3. Click inside the LastName field on the form, to make it active.

4. Click the Find button on the Form View toolbar as shown below.

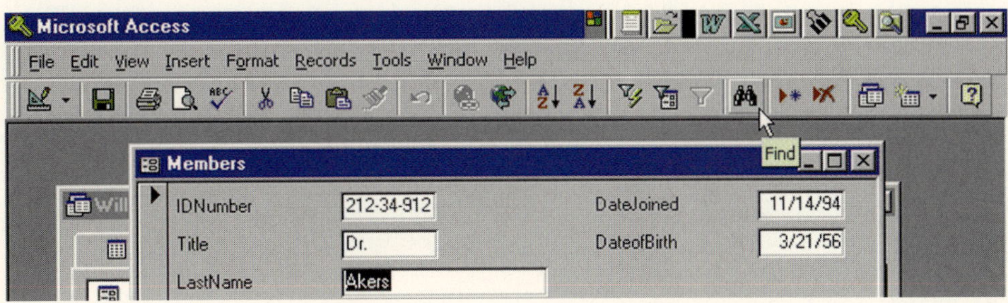

Tip You can also use the CTRL +F keyboard shortcut to open the Find dialog box.

5. Type **Barclay** as your search term in the Find What: textbox.

Tip The other two check box options allow you to find records with a specific upper and lower case combination, or to find data based upon its display format (date or currency, for example).

6. Accept the default settings in the Find dialog box. When your screen matches the figure on the next page, click the Find First button.

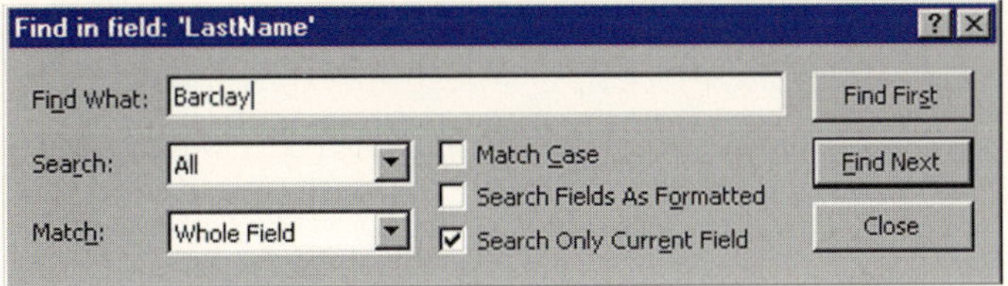

Tip Notice that you can find multiple records for your search term, if more than one record matches the search term. You can review any additional matches by clicking on the Find Next button.

7. Record 5 should now be displayed in the *Members* form. Click the Close button.

Updating Records in a Table

After you find a record using the Find option, you can edit it in the same way you edit any record displayed in a form. By moving the insertion point to the appropriate text box for a specific field, you can replace the text with a new entry.

Tip Whenever you replace the data in a field using either a table's datasheet or the Form View for a form, the changes you make to the data are stored to disk as soon as you either move to another record or close the datasheet or the form.

TASK 2: TO UPDATE RECORDS IN A TABLE:

1. Select the current address, and type **4001 Cactus Circle** as the new address for this member.
2. Click the Find button again and type **Adams** as the search term.
3. Deselect the option to search the current field only, as below. By doing so, you can search for the address even if another field has the focus.

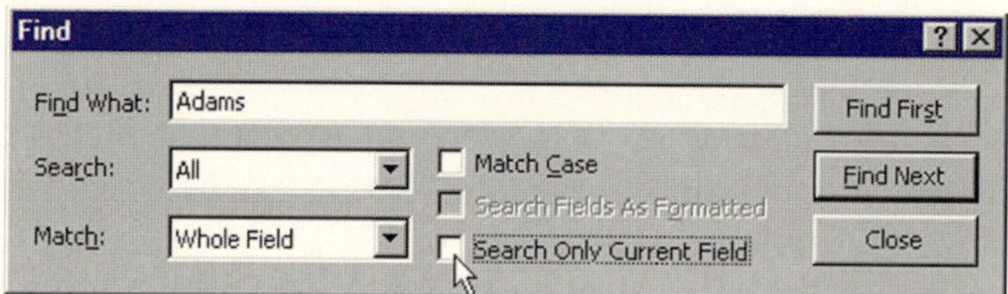

4. Click the Find First button.
5. When the form displays record 9, change the address, city, state, zip code, and phone data.

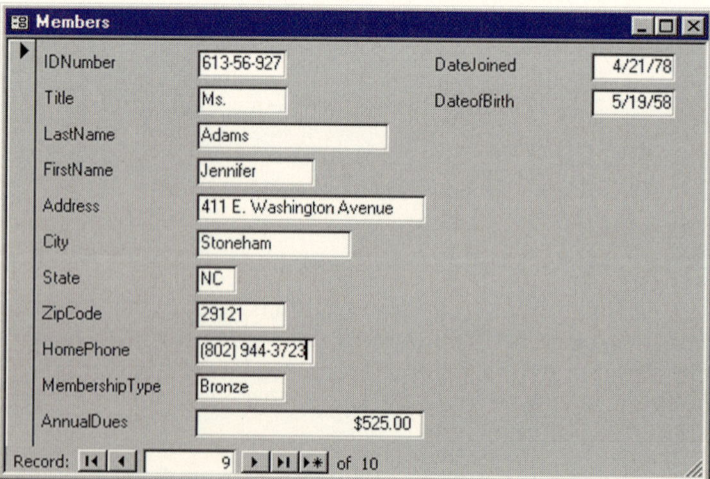

6. Close the form when you are finished.

Using the Replace Feature

As you can see, the Find feature provides a simple method for changing specific records. But what if you need to change data that occurs more frequently in the table? Consider the work it would take to change the area code for 1,500 customers if the local phone company added a new area code. Obviously, you need a method for changing all fields that contain a specific value.

Fortunately, Access utilizes the same Find and Replace feature found in the other Office applications. Consider Mr. Gilmore's request, that you change the annual membership fees. The new annual membership fees for Charter, Gold, Silver, and Bronze memberships cost $800, $675, $600, and $550, respectively. By using the ***replace*** feature, you can globally replace one value with another.

Tip Both the Find and Replace features can be used with tables and forms.

TASK 3: TO REPLACE THE CURRENT MEMBERSHIP FEES WITH NEW VALUES:

1. Click the Tables tab in the Database window.
2. Double-click the *Members* table to open it in Datasheet view.
3. Select Replace from the Edit menu.

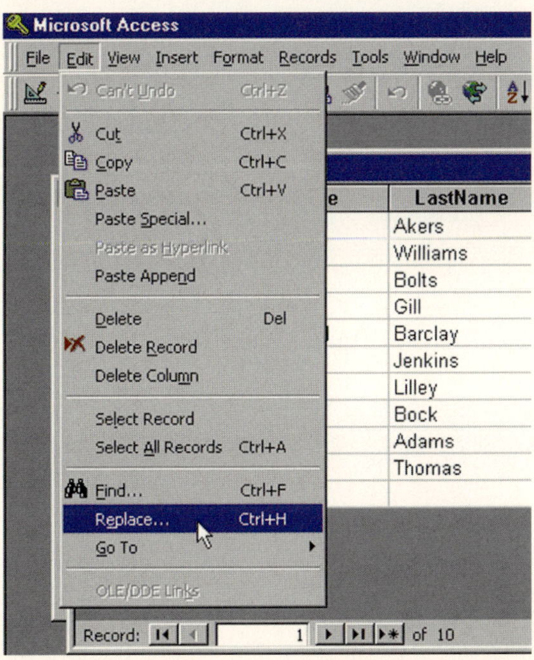

4. Type **$775.00** as the value for which to search in the Find What: text box.

Troubleshooting The Replace feature searches for a text string as it is formatted, so make sure you enter a dollar sign, a decimal point, and two zeros to the right of the decimal place when searching for a currency value.

5. Click the Find Next button. The membership value in record 2 should now be highlighted.

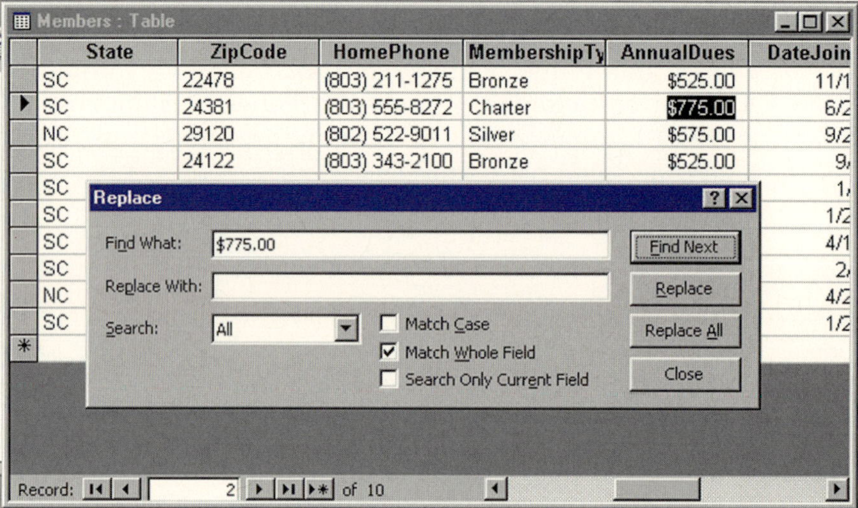

6. Type **800** in the Replace With text box. Do not add a dollar sign or decimal places, because the field is formatted to currency and Access will supply these for display. Then click on the Replace All button.

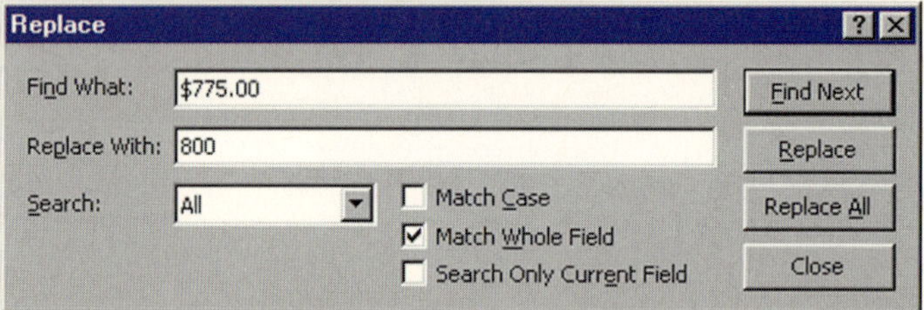

7. The warning shown below will appear. Click Yes.

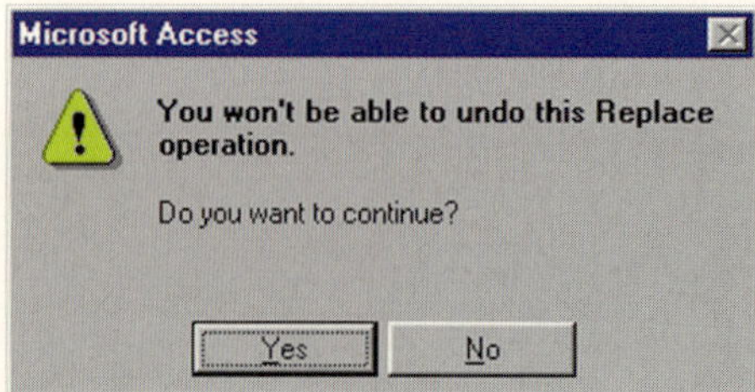

8. Verify that your datasheet looks like the one shown in the following figure. Access has replaced all instances of the value 775 in the AnnualDues field with 800.

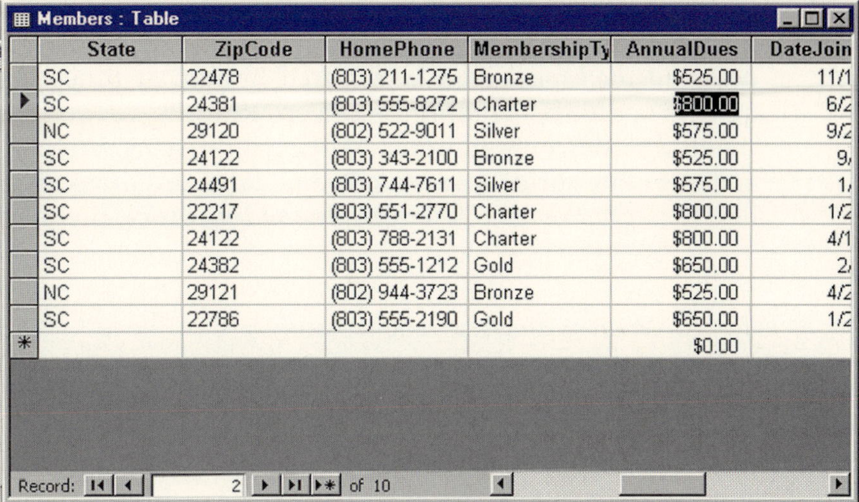
Members : Table

State	ZipCode	HomePhone	MembershipTy	AnnualDues	DateJoin
SC	22478	(803) 211-1275	Bronze	$525.00	11/1
SC	24381	(803) 555-8272	Charter	$800.00	6/2
NC	29120	(802) 522-9011	Silver	$575.00	9/2
SC	24122	(803) 343-2100	Bronze	$525.00	9/
SC	24491	(803) 744-7611	Silver	$575.00	1/
SC	22217	(803) 551-2770	Charter	$800.00	1/2
SC	24122	(803) 788-2131	Charter	$800.00	4/1
SC	24382	(803) 555-1212	Gold	$650.00	2/
NC	29121	(802) 944-3723	Bronze	$525.00	4/2
SC	22786	(803) 555-2190	Gold	$650.00	1/2
				$0.00	

Record: 2 of 10

9 Use the Replace feature to change all instances of $650.00 to 675, $575.00 to 600, and $525.00 to 550.

Troubleshooting Make sure you do not type a dollar sign or a decimal point in the Replace With text box of the Replace dialog box to search for the specified values, which are integers in this case. Although the new value will be displayed in currency format, Access will add these characters, because you specified a currency format when you created the table design.

10 Close the Replace dialog box. Your datasheet should now display the values shown below. Close the datasheet to return to the Database window.

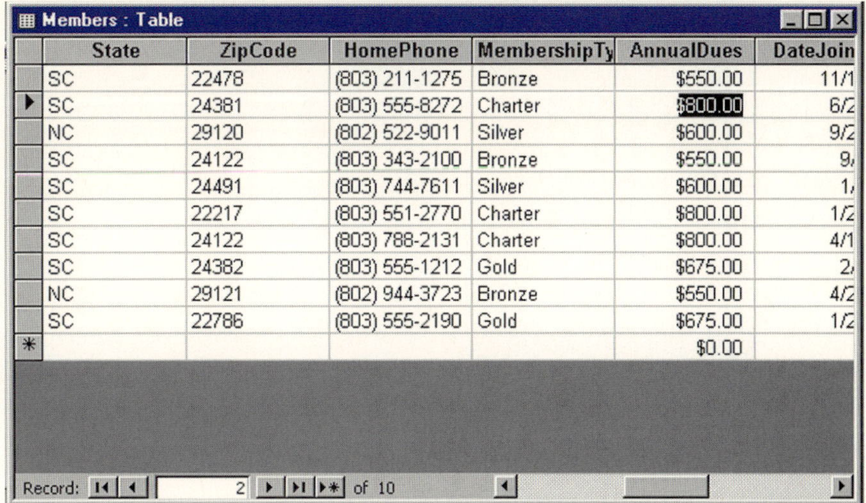
Members : Table

State	ZipCode	HomePhone	MembershipTy	AnnualDues	DateJoin
SC	22478	(803) 211-1275	Bronze	$550.00	11/1
SC	24381	(803) 555-8272	Charter	$800.00	6/2
NC	29120	(802) 522-9011	Silver	$600.00	9/2
SC	24122	(803) 343-2100	Bronze	$550.00	9/
SC	24491	(803) 744-7611	Silver	$600.00	1/
SC	22217	(803) 551-2770	Charter	$800.00	1/2
SC	24122	(803) 788-2131	Charter	$800.00	4/1
SC	24382	(803) 555-1212	Gold	$675.00	2/
NC	29121	(802) 944-3723	Bronze	$550.00	4/2
SC	22786	(803) 555-2190	Gold	$675.00	1/2
				$0.00	

Record: 2 of 10

Sorting Records

Another common database maintenance task involves sorting records. When you apply a ***sort***, you reorder the records in a table or form according to the entries in a specific field. The field you select for a sort specifies the ***sort criteria***. Although Access objects such as forms and reports can be designed to display data in a sorted format, at times you may want to quickly verify the data on the screen. Records can be sorted in either ascending or descending order. When you sort in ***ascending order***, names and terms are sorted from A to Z, and dates and times are sorted from earliest to latest. When you sort by ***descending order***, the opposite is true.

> **Tip** When sorting text, capital letters are sorted before lowercase letters.

When you sort records, Access saves the sort order when the form or datasheet is saved, and then reapplies it automatically when you reopen the object or base a new form or report on that object.

TASK 4: TO SORT RECORDS IN A TABLE:

1. Open the *Members* table in Datasheet view.
2. Click the LastName field heading to select the entire column, as shown below.

> **Tip** You can also sort on a specific field by simply placing the insertion point anywhere in the field.

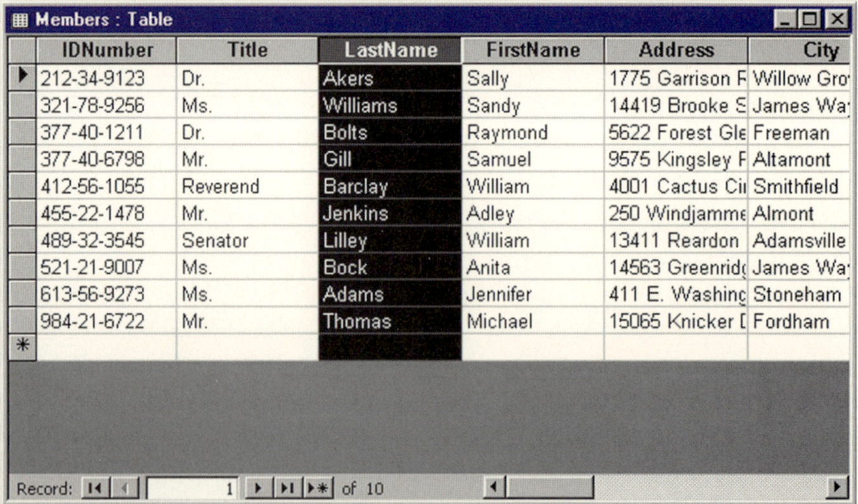

Members : Table

IDNumber	Title	LastName	FirstName	Address	City
212-34-9123	Dr.	Akers	Sally	1775 Garrison F	Willow Gro
321-78-9256	Ms.	Williams	Sandy	14419 Brooke S	James Wa
377-40-1211	Dr.	Bolts	Raymond	5622 Forest Gle	Freeman
377-40-6798	Mr.	Gill	Samuel	9575 Kingsley F	Altamont
412-56-1055	Reverend	Barclay	William	4001 Cactus Ci	Smithfield
455-22-1478	Mr.	Jenkins	Adley	250 Windjamme	Almont
489-32-3545	Senator	Lilley	William	13411 Reardon	Adamsville
521-21-9007	Ms.	Bock	Anita	14563 Greenrid	James Wa
613-56-9273	Ms.	Adams	Jennifer	411 E. Washinc	Stoneham
984-21-6722	Mr.	Thomas	Michael	15065 Knicker [	Fordham

Record: 1 of 10

3. Click the Sort Ascending button on the Table Datasheet toolbar.
4. The records are now sorted in ascending order by last name, as shown on the next page. Close the table.

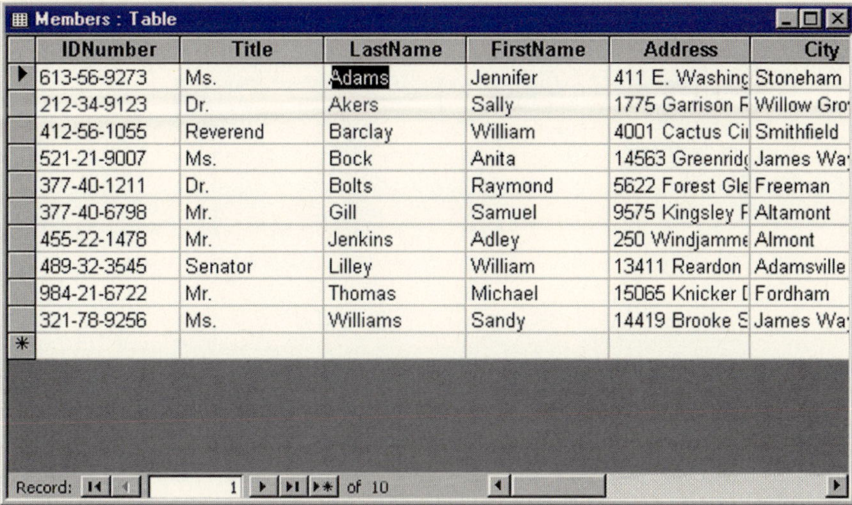
Members : Table

IDNumber	Title	LastName	FirstName	Address	City
613-56-9273	Ms.	Adams	Jennifer	411 E. Washinç	Stoneham
212-34-9123	Dr.	Akers	Sally	1775 Garrison F	Willow Gro
412-56-1055	Reverend	Barclay	William	4001 Cactus Ci	Smithfield
521-21-9007	Ms.	Bock	Anita	14563 Greenrid	James Wa
377-40-1211	Dr.	Bolts	Raymond	5622 Forest Gle	Freeman
377-40-6798	Mr.	Gill	Samuel	9575 Kingsley F	Altamont
455-22-1478	Mr.	Jenkins	Adley	250 Windjamme	Almont
489-32-3545	Senator	Lilley	William	13411 Reardon	Adamsville
984-21-6722	Mr.	Thomas	Michael	15065 Knicker [	Fordham
321-78-9256	Ms.	Williams	Sandy	14419 Brooke S	James Wa

Record: 1 of 10

5 The Microsoft Access dialog box shown in the next figure appears. You do want the table design to be modified, so click Yes.

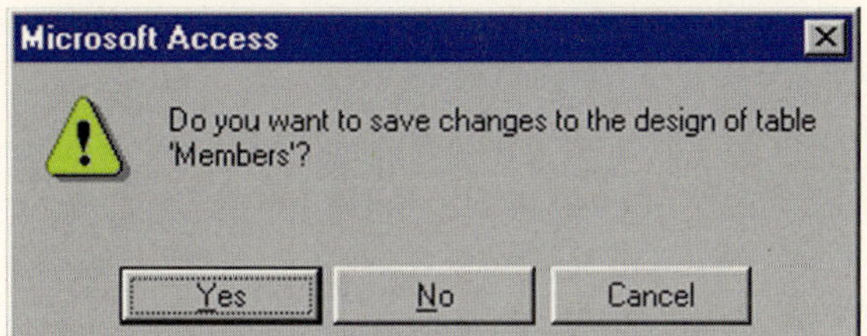

Any time you open the table, the data will now appear in alphabetical order by last name. This is because you modified the table structure by specifying a sort property for the table. A ***property*** is some characteristic of a database object. In the event that you want to change this property, you need to know where to change it.

TASK 5: TO VIEW THE TABLE PROPERTIES:

1 Click the Tables tab in the Database window.

2 Click the Design button.

3 In the Table Design window, place the insertion point inside the title bar, and click the right mouse button. The context menu shown below appears.

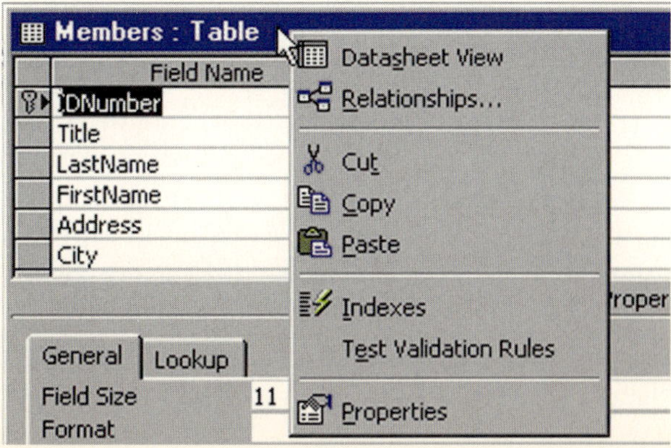

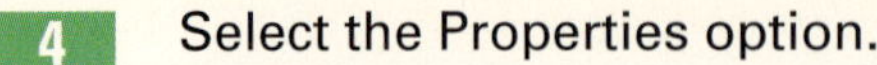

4 Select the Properties option.

The Table Properties dialog box shown below appears. Notice the setting for the Order By row. To remove or change the sort specifications, delete this entry or select another field name.

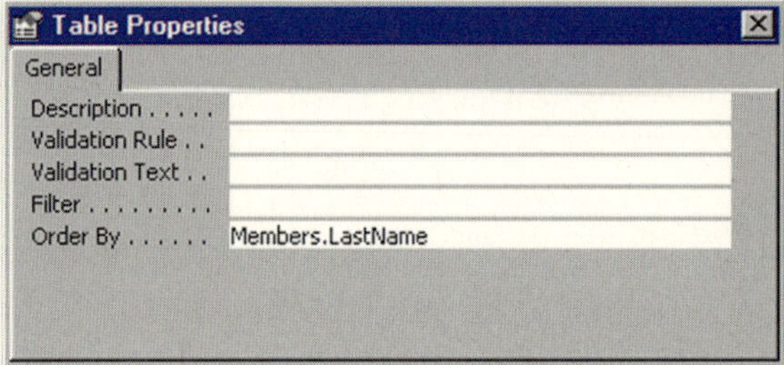

5 Close the Table Properties dialog box without making any changes.

6 Close the form.

> **Tip** To sort on more than one field, you must use either the Advanced Filter option, construct a query, or create a report, as you will do in Project 6.

Filtering Records

Sometimes you need to retrieve a subset of records from an underlying table, such as when Mr. Gilmore requests a list of charter members. With a ***filter***, you can temporarily view or edit a subset of records while you're viewing a form or datasheet. Access supports two methods for quickly filtering records. With ***Filter By Selection***, you select all or part of a value, and then click the Filter by Selection button on the toolbar to find all records with the selected value. If you would rather specify a value you're searching for by typing it or picking it from a list in the field, you can use the ***Filter By Form*** option. This option also enables you to specify multiple criteria for a filter.

When you are finished viewing the filtered data, you remove the filter to restore the datasheet or form to its previous order.

TASK 6: TO USE FILTER BY SELECTION TO DISPLAY ALL CHARTER MEMBERS:

1. Click the Tables tab in the Database window.
2. Click the Open button to open the *Members* table in Datasheet view.
3. Use the horizontal scrollbar to display the MembershipType field.
4. Select the word Charter in the seventh record.

Members : Table

ZipCode	HomePhone	MembershipTy	AnnualDues	DateJoined	DateofBi
29121	(802) 944-3723	Bronze	$550.00	4/21/78	5/1
22478	(803) 211-1275	Bronze	$550.00	11/14/94	3/2
24491	(803) 744-7611	Silver	$600.00	1/9/97	7/1
24382	(803) 555-1212	Gold	$675.00	2/1/64	5/
29120	(802) 522-9011	Silver	$600.00	9/27/66	7/1
24122	(803) 343-2100	Bronze	$550.00	9/6/92	6/
22217	(803) 551-2770	Charter	$800.00	1/25/87	10/1
24122	(803) 788-2131	Charter	$800.00	4/10/69	3/2
22786	(803) 555-2190	Gold	$675.00	1/21/96	12/1
24381	(803) 555-8272	Charter	$800.00	6/29/82	4/1
			$0.00		

Record: 7 of 10

5. Click the Filter By Selection button on the Table Datasheet toolbar. The filter is applied, as shown below. Notice that *FLTR* appears in the Status bar and the word *Filtered* appears in parentheses following the New Record button.

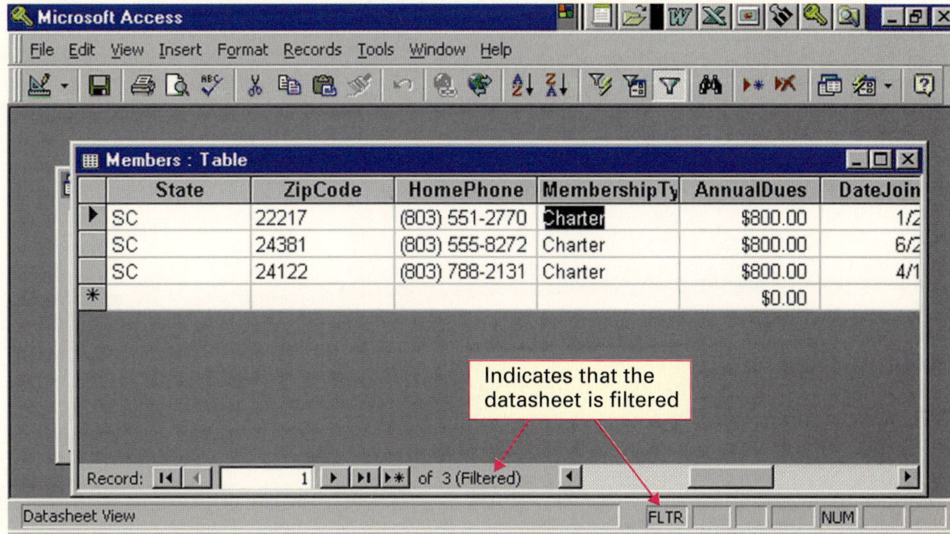

Microsoft Access

Members : Table

State	ZipCode	HomePhone	MembershipTy	AnnualDues	DateJoin
SC	22217	(803) 551-2770	Charter	$800.00	1/2
SC	24381	(803) 555-8272	Charter	$800.00	6/2
SC	24122	(803) 788-2131	Charter	$800.00	4/1
				$0.00	

Record: 1 of 3 (Filtered)

6 Click the Remove Filter button on the toolbar to remove the filter.

TASK 7: TO USE FILTER BY FORM TO DISPLAY ALL CHARTER MEMBERS IN SORTED ORDER:

1 Click the Filter By Form button on the Table Datasheet toolbar.

2 Use the Tab key or the mouse to select the MembershipType field.

3 Click the button that appears in the field.

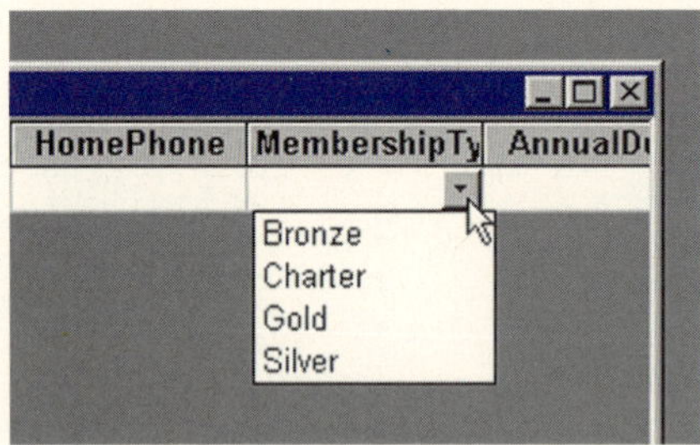

4 Select Charter in the list.

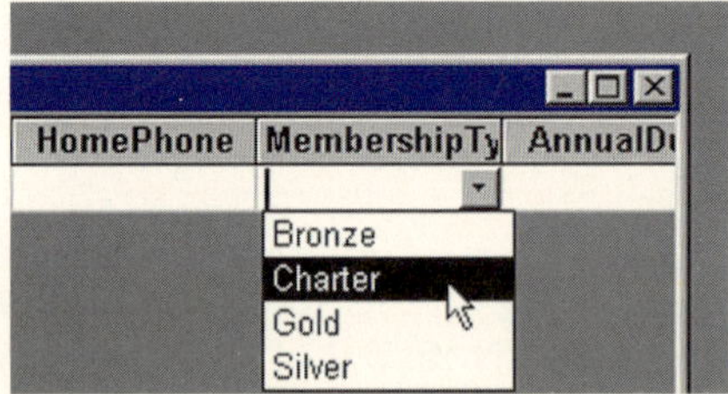

The word Charter now appears in quotes in the field.

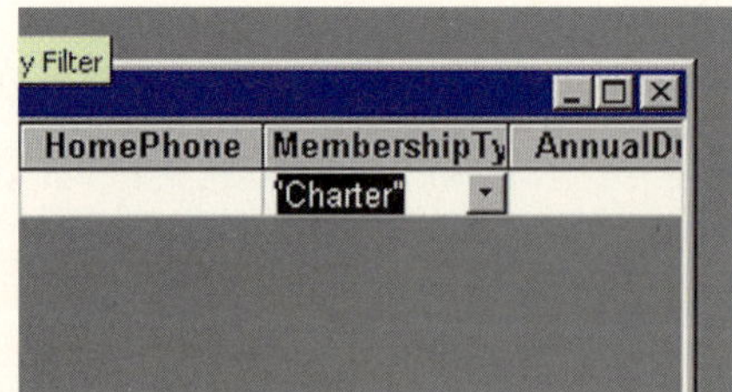

5 Click the Apply Filter button on the Table Datasheet toolbar. Once again, the datasheet displays records for charter members only.

6 Use the horizontal scrollbar to display the LastName field.
The three filtered records are now displayed in ascending order.

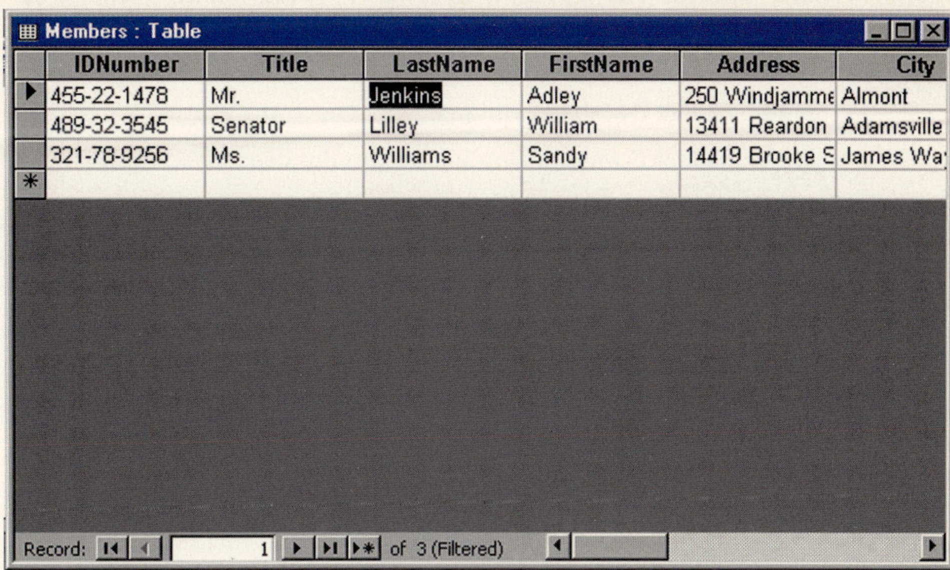

7 Close the datasheet. When the Microsoft Access dialog box shown in the next figure appears, click the No button.

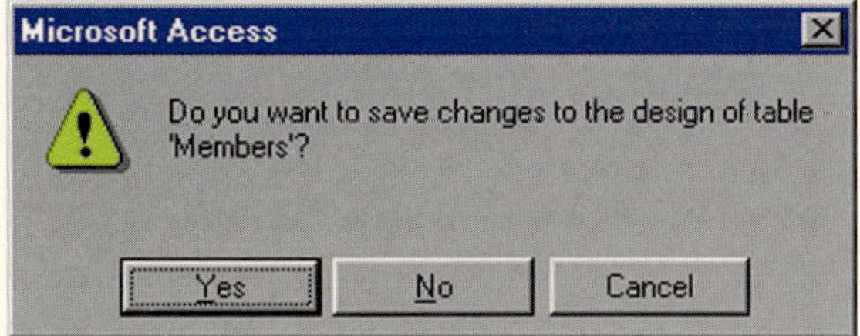

Tip Had you clicked the Yes button, the filter and sort information would have been stored with the table design. Whenever you apply sort or filter criteria and then update a table, these properties can always be edited or deleted at a later time.

Using the Database Utilities to Compact a Database

Whenever you modify your database objects, the database file contains empty space and grows in size. If you open your database from a disk, it is a good idea to periodically compact it, which will remove the empty space and reduce the file size. By keeping the file size as small as possible, you can locate and manipulate records more quickly.

TASK 8: TO COMPACT THE DATABASE:

1. Select Database Utilities from the Tools menu.
2. Select Compact Database from the cascading menu.

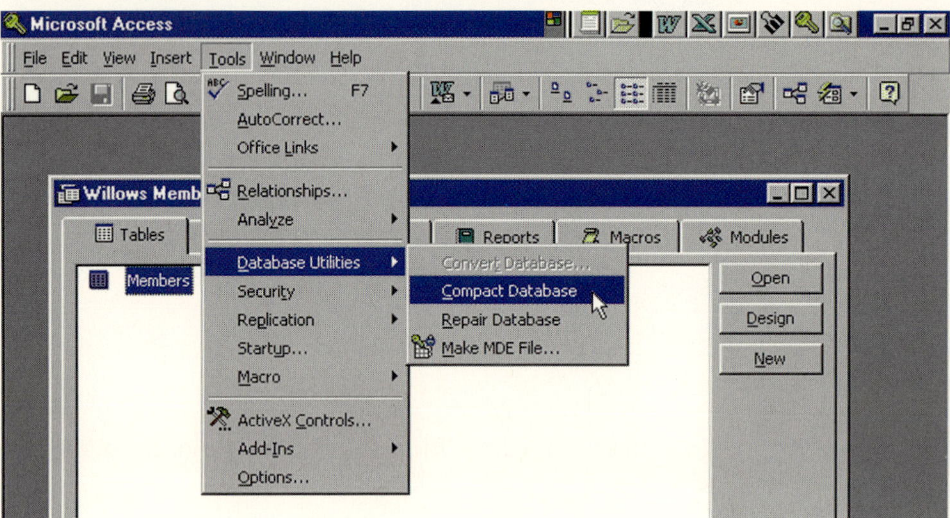

As the database is compacting, the mouse pointer displays an hourglass icon; during this time various messages appear in the Status bar.

3. When control returns to the Database window, the database has been compacted. Close the database file.

The Conclusion

As you can see, Access offers you several methods for manipulating database tables and maintaining the entire database. Although you can accomplish much when working with tables, most databases are designed so that the typical user never has to interact with a table object directly. In the projects that follow, you will learn how to create additional database objects that also support some of the tasks you learned here for manipulating records.

Summary and Exercises

Summary

- You can use the Find dialog box to locate one or more records displayed in a table or form. You will often use this feature to update a record.
- You can use the Replace dialog box to replace information in one or more records displayed in a table or form. You will often use this feature in order to update a record.
- If you select the Replace All button in the Replace dialog box, all occurrences of a text string (any combination of letters, numbers, and symbols) or numeric value are replaced with another string or value.
- You can easily sort records by a specific criterion. Records can be sorted in ascending or descending order according to the letters, dates, or numbers occurring in a field.
- By applying a filter, you can view a specific subset of a table's records. The two easiest methods for applying a filter are Filter By Selection and Filter By Form.
- As you work with Access database objects, the database file grows in size. You can compact the database file using one of the Access database utilities.

Key Terms and Operations

Key Terms

ascending order
descending order
edit
filter
find
property
replace
sort
sort criteria
update

Operations

locate and update a table or form using the Find feature
locate and update a table or form using the Replace feature
organize a table or form using the Sort Ascending feature
organize a table or form using the Sort Descending feature
organize a table or form using the Filter By Selection feature
organize a table or form using the Filter By Form
optimize your database file by compacting it using a database utility

Study Questions

Multiple Choice

1. To quickly locate a record in a table or form, use the
   - **a.** Find dialog box.
   - **b.** Replace All button.
   - **c.** Table Datasheet view.
   - **d.** Apply Filter button.

2. Updating records in a table includes all of the following except
   - **a.** changing an employee's address.
   - **b.** creating a new table.
   - **c.** inserting records.
   - **d.** deleting records.

3. The easiest way of making a global change in a database is by using the
   a. Replace All feature.
   b. Sort Ascending button.
   c. Remove Filter button.
   d. Compact Database option in the Database utilities.

4. Which of the following is not true concerning the sort feature in Access?
   a. Records can be sorted in ascending or descending order according to the values in a specific field.
   b. Information about the sort can be saved with the table design properties.
   c. Dates are sorted from most recent to least recent when using the sort-descending feature.
   d. The case of text entries does not matter when sorting records.

5. The filter option that enables you to select records that match multiple criteria is the
   a. Apply filter.
   b. Filter By Form.
   c. Remove Filter.
   d. Filter By Selection.

6. The filter feature that enables you to select records containing the same text or value as one highlighted in a specific field is the
   a. Apply filter.
   b. Filter By Form.
   c. Remove Filter.
   d. Filter By Selection.

7. If a database file grows in size, what should you do to remedy this situation?
   a. Create a new table.
   b. Split the database into two files.
   c. Create a new database and copy all the records into it.
   d. Compact the database.

8. To identify the field you want to use for sorting records, you should
   a. click the Sort Ascending button.
   b. select the entire table.
   c. position the insertion point somewhere in the desired field.
   d. click the Sort Descending button.

9. Which feature enables you to select criteria for viewing records by using a drop-down list?
   a. Sort Ascending
   b. Filter By Selection
   c. Sort Descending
   d. Filter By Form

10. Which feature enables you to use a selected entry in a field to specify which records in the table to display?
    a. Sort Ascending
    b. Filter By Selection
    c. Sort Descending
    d. Filter By Form

Short Answer

1. What is the difference between finding and replacing data?
2. How does sorting records differ from applying a filter?
3. How does the case of a text entry affect the sort order?
4. How many criteria can you specify when using the Filter By Selection option?
5. Does the Replace All feature conduct a global search and replace?
6. What is an easy method for locating records to update?
7. Which option should you use to view a record in a table that meets a specific criterion?
8. How can you reduce the size of a database file without deleting any data?
9. Can you include multiple criteria when using the Filter By Form option?
10. How do date values appear if a database is sorted in descending order?

For Discussion

1. When should you consider using Filter By Form rather than Filter By Selection?
2. How does the data type of a field affect how the records are ordered when you sort a table?
3. What happens to a database file as you modify its objects and what can you do to remedy any potential problems?
4. Explain how editing, filtering, and sorting records differ.

Review Exercises

1. Deleting Records from a Table

Deleting records from a table is a common database maintenance task. In this exercise you will learn how to delete records from a table in Datasheet view. Complete the following tasks:

1. Open the *Willows Employees.mdb* file from your disk.
2. Click the Tables tab, and open the *Employees* table in Datasheet view.
3. Place the insertion point in the record selector for the third record, as shown below.

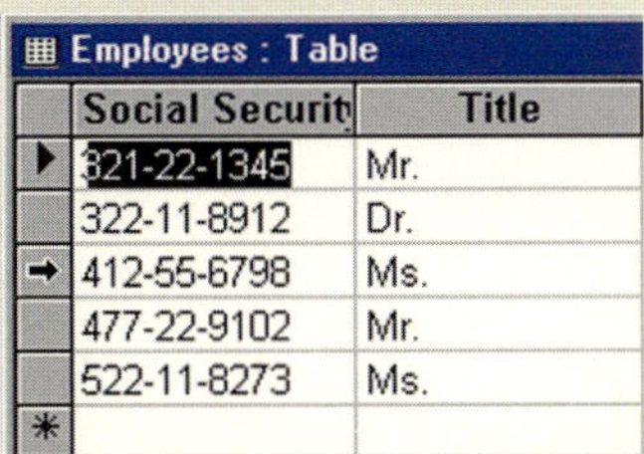

Tip The Record Selector allows you to easily select an entire record. Depending upon the current task, the Record Selector will display an icon indicating the current record, a record currently being edited, or a new record.

4. Click the Record Selector. The entire record is now selected, as shown below.

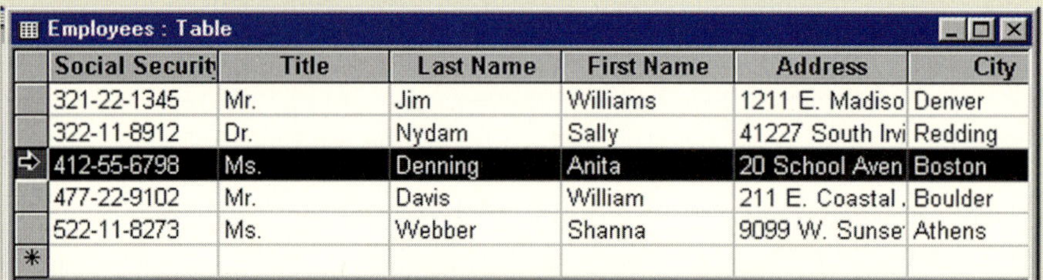

Employees : Table

Social Securit	Title	Last Name	First Name	Address	City
321-22-1345	Mr.	Jim	Williams	1211 E. Madiso	Denver
322-11-8912	Dr.	Nydam	Sally	41227 South Irvi	Redding
412-55-6798	Ms.	Denning	Anita	20 School Aven	Boston
477-22-9102	Mr.	Davis	William	211 E. Coastal .	Boulder
522-11-8273	Ms.	Webber	Shanna	9099 W. Sunse	Athens

5. Click the Delete Record button on the Table Datasheet toolbar.
6. The Microsoft Access dialog box appears. Click Yes to delete the record.

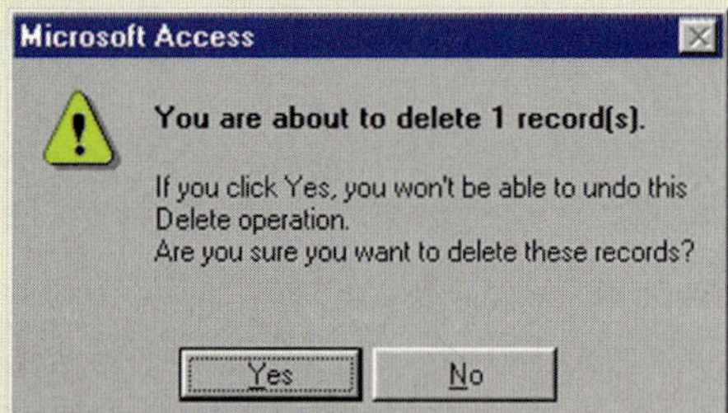

7. Select Database utilities from the Tools menu, and then select Compact Database from the cascading menu. This action closes the table.

2. Filtering a Table by Multiple Criteria

As you may guess, at times you may need to filter a table by multiple criteria. In this exercise, you use the Filter By Form method to filter a table by two criteria.

1. Open the *Employees* table in the *Willows Employees.mdb* database in Datasheet view.
2. Click the Filter By Form button on the Table Datasheet toolbar.
3. Select Mr. in the Title field.
4. Select CO in the State/Province field.
5. Click the Apply Filter button on the Table Datasheet toolbar. The database now displays records that meet the criteria you specified.
6. Click Yes in the Microsoft Access dialog box to save the filter information with the table. Now whenever you open the table this filter will be available. To apply the filter, simply click the Apply Filter button.
7. Close the *Willows Employees.mdb* database.

3. Sorting and filtering records in a table

1. Launch Access 97 and open *High Point Foods xxx.mdb* (where *xxx* represents your initials).

> **Note** If you do not have a workbook named *High Point Foods xxx.mdb*, ask your instructor for a copy of the file you should use to complete this exercise.

2. Make the following change using the *Food Categories* form:
   - Find the record for *Seafood* and add *Shellfish* to the Description field.
3. Print a copy of the *Food Categories* table.
4. Sort the *Food Categories* table in reverse alphabetical order based on the Category Name field and print a copy of the table.
5. Close the table without saving the changes.
6. Filter the records in the table to locate all records containing the word *bread* in the Description field and print a copy of the filtered table.
7. Remove the filter and close the table without saving the changes.
8. Close the database and exit Access.

Assignments

1. Adding Records to a Table and Specifying Sort Criteria

In this assignment, you will modify the Web Sites database by adding records and then sorting the datasheet according to software category. After you open the *Web Sites.mdb* database file from your disk, add the following records using either the datasheet view or the form:

Company	Primary Product	Company URL
Macromedia	Multimedia software	http://www.macromedia.com
Asymetrix	Multimedia software	http://www.asymetrix.com
E-Trade	Financial services	http://www.etrade.com

Sort the Sites table in ascending order by company name. Note that the Auto-Number record for each record does not change when the records are sorted. Save the table design when you close the table.

2. Filtering the Sites Table in the Web Sites Database

As you learned in this project, both sort and filter specifications can be saved as a part of a table's design. In this assignment you will add filter specifications to the Sites table in the Web Sites database.

Open the Sites table in datasheet view. Select Filter By Form, and specify Multimedia Software as the filter criterion. Apply the filter. Update the table design when you close the table. Reopen the table and click the Apply Filter option again. Close the database and exit Access when you are finished.

3

PROJECT

Modifying Table Design

Most database developers periodically refine their databases to improve performance, increase accuracy, or to meet the changing needs of an organization. Because tables serve as the primary storage location in Access, many database enhancements involve modifying a table's design.

Objectives

After completing this project, you will be able to:

- **Add fields to a table**
- **Delete a field**
- **Change field properties**
- **Change a table's primary key**
- **Create data input masks**
- **Add data validation rules to a table**

The Challenge

Mr. Gilmore is pleased with the progress you have made in developing a membership database for the Willows. He has made a few suggestions for improving the database after reviewing the initial design specifications. First, he wants you to add two additional fields to the database: one to assign each member a unique membership number, and one to specify the number of family members included in the membership. Second, he wants you to assign a new field as the primary key, because many organizations are moving away from using a patron's Social Security number for identification. Finally, he wants you to find a way to simplify the data entry process.

The Solution

You can easily modify the *Members* table to fulfill all of Mr. Gilmore's recommendations. You can create an AutoNumber field that will automatically assign each member a unique number, and you can create a numeric field to store the number of family members included in the membership. By setting the AutoNumber field as the primary key, you will no longer need to use Social Security number as a unique identifier. Finally, by adding validation rules and input masks to the table design, you can simplify data entry and protect against certain data entry errors. Figure 3.1 displays a new *Members* form created using the updated table.

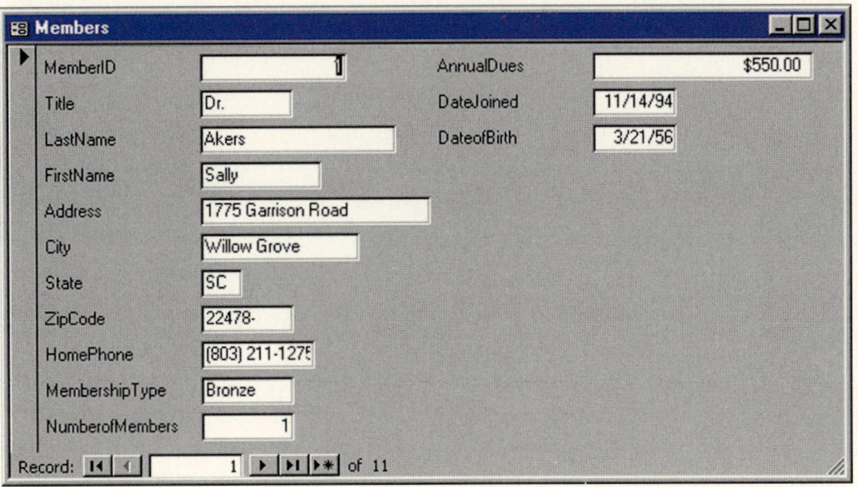

Figure 3.1

The Setup

After you launch Access and open your database, you should make sure the Database toolbar and the Status toolbar are displayed. These are the default settings in Acccss, but thcy may have been changed on your computer. (If you have forgotten how to do this, refer to Table 1.1 in Project 1.)

> **Troubleshooting** If you do not see the Database toolbar on the screen when you launch Access and open your database, choose Toolbars from the View menu. Select the Database toolbar to display it. If any additional toolbars are visible, close them. If you do not see the Status bar at the bottom of the Application window, choose Options from the Tools menu, click the View Page tab and change the Status bar check box option.

Using the procedures you learned in Task 1 of Project 1, open the *Willows Membership.mdb* file from your disk.

Modifying a Table's Design

Any enhancements you make to your database tables are table ***design modifications***. Remember that tables are where Access stores record data; all other objects—queries, forms, and reports—are based upon the table data. Therefore, any changes you make to a table's design affect the objects that derive their data from a table.

In this project you will change the *Members* table in two ways. Adding fields, deleting fields, and changing the primary key field will change the underlying ***table structure***, or how the table is physically arranged. When you add input masks and data validation, you are changing specific ***field properties***, which affect how the field data is entered and displayed.

Modifying the *Members* Table Structure

Mr. Gilmore has asked you to make three modifications to the *Members* table structure. You will add an AutoNumber field, add a numeric field, and change the primary key and delete the IDNumber field.

When you delete the IDNumber field, you lose any data that the field contains, which is the Social Security number of each member. If you will ever need this data in the future, it is a good idea to first create a copy of the *Members* table before you modify its structure.

TASK 1: TO CREATE A BACKUP OF THE *MEMBERS* TABLE:

1. Verify that the Tables tab is active and that the *Members* table is selected in the Database window.

2. Select Save As/Export from the File menu.

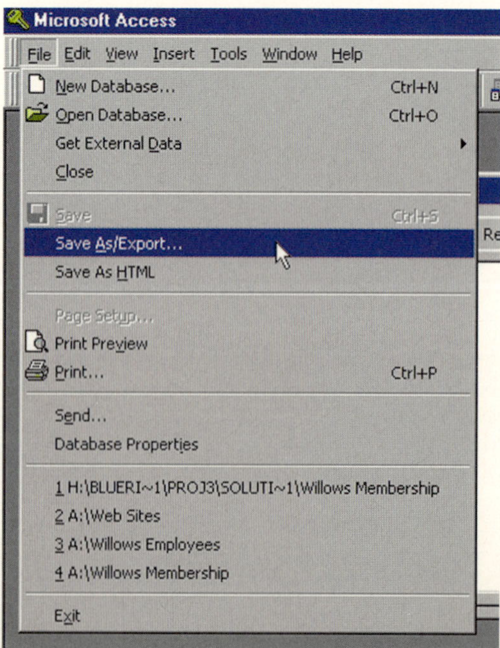

3 In the Save As dialog box, select the option button to save the *Members* table in the current database. Accept the default name shown in the figure below, and click OK.

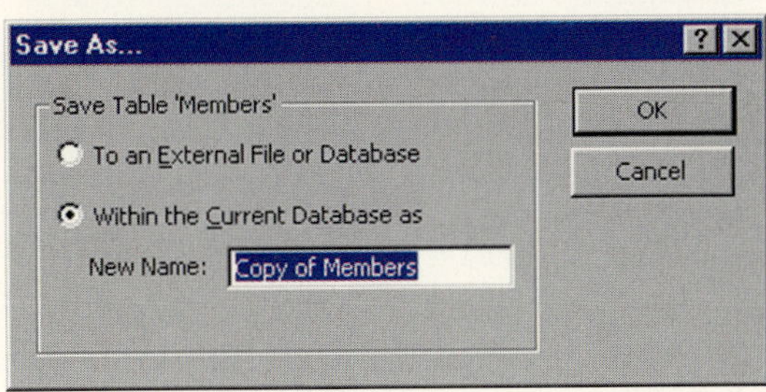

Two table objects now appear in the Database window.

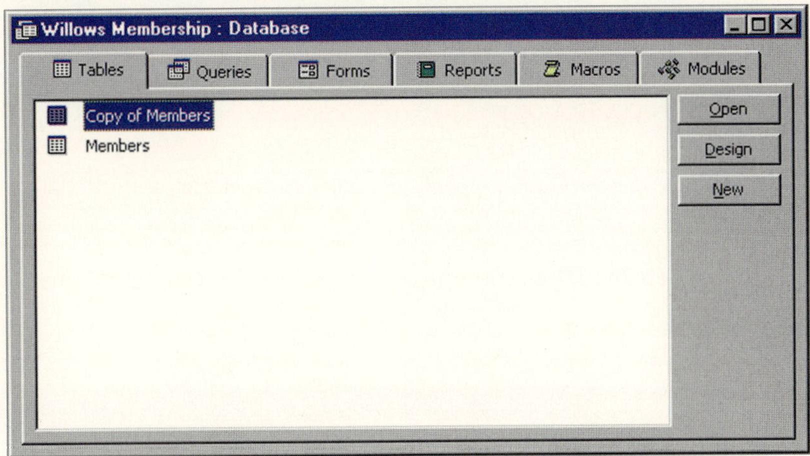

You are now ready to add fields to the *Members* table. For the rest of this project, you will modify the *Members* table, not the copy you just created.

TASK 2: TO ADD FIELDS TO THE *MEMBERS* TABLE:

1 Highlight the *Members* table in the Database window, and click the Design button to open the table in Design view.

2 Place the insertion point over the Row selector for the Title field, as shown below and click.

Members : Table

Field Name	Data Type
IDNumber	Text
Title	Text
LastName	Text
FirstName	Text
Address	Text
City	Text

The entire field should now be selected.

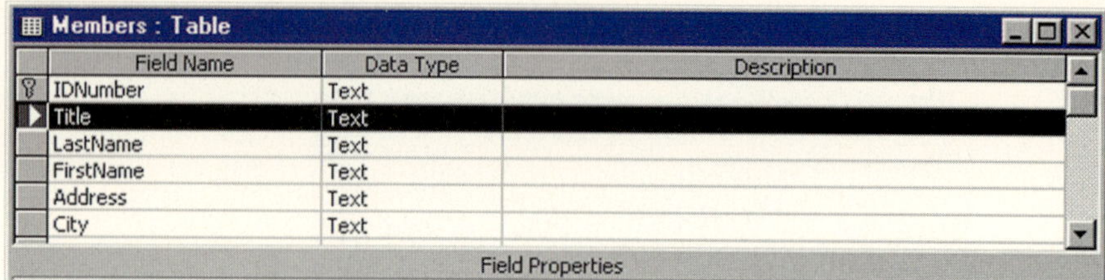

3 Click the Insert Rows button on the Table Design toolbar.
A row is inserted in the upper pane of the Table Design window above the Title field.

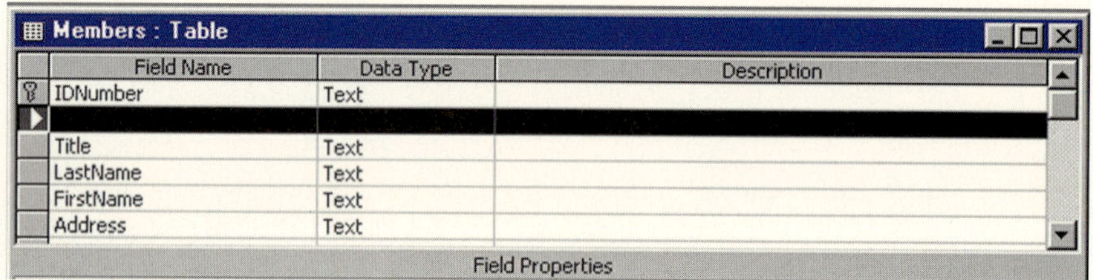

4 Type **MemberID** as the name of this field, and select AutoNumber as the data type.

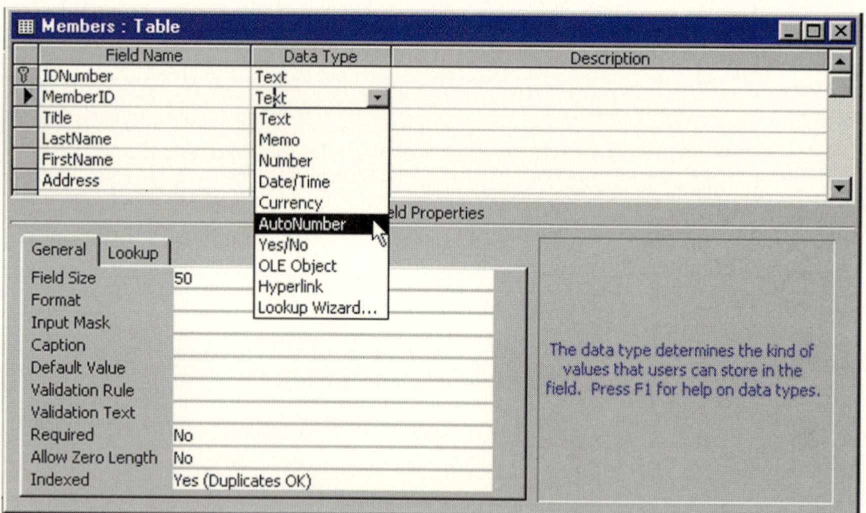

5 Use the vertical scroll bar in the upper pane of the Table Design window to display the MembershipType and Annual Dues fields.

6 Highlight the Annual Dues field and add a new row between it and the MembershipType field. The Table Design window should now look similar to the window shown in the following figure.

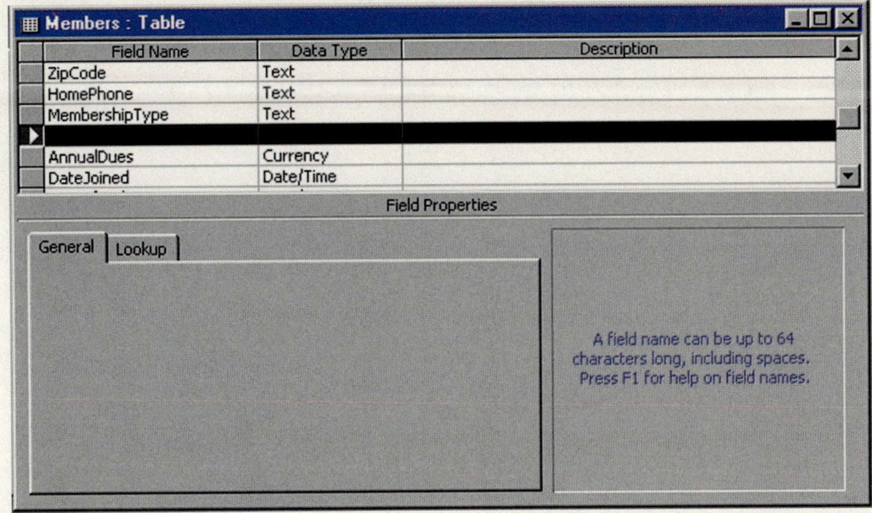

7 Type **NumberofMembers** as the name of this field, and select Number as the data type.

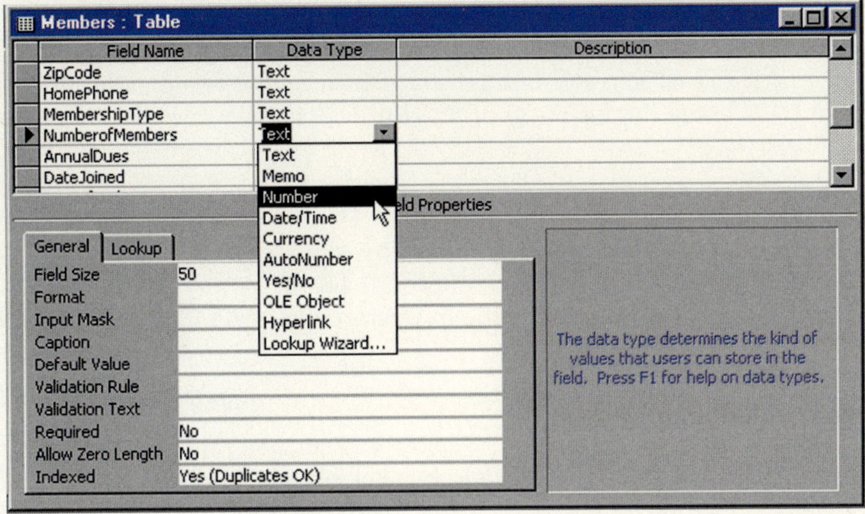

8 Click the Save button on the Table Design toolbar.
This saves the table design to your database file.

9 Click the View button on the Table Design toolbar.
This switches the view from Design view to Datasheet view. Your datasheet now appears as shown in the figure below.

Members : Table

IDNumber	MemberID	Title	LastName	FirstName	Addres
212-34-9123	1	Dr.	Akers	Sally	1775 Garris
321-78-9256	2	Ms.	Williams	Sandy	14419 Broc
377-40-1211	3	Dr.	Bolts	Raymond	5622 Fores
377-40-6798	4	Mr.	Gill	Samuel	9575 Kings
412-56-1055	5	Reverend	Barclay	William	4001 Cactu
455-22-1478	6	Mr.	Jenkins	Adley	250 Windja
489-32-3545	7	Senator	Lilley	William	13411 Rea
521-21-9007	8	Ms.	Bock	Anita	14563 Gree
613-56-9273	9	Ms.	Adams	Jennifer	411 E. Wa
984-21-6722	10	Mr.	Thomas	Michael	15065 Knic
*	(AutoNumber)				

You will notice that Access added a numeric value for each record in the table. An ***AutoNumber field*** adds a number value for each record in the database, starting with 1 and increasing by 1.

10 Close the table.

Changing the Primary Key for the *Members* Table

In many businesses and organizations, it has become common to use a patron's Social Security number as a unique identifier. This number is a logical candidate for a primary key in a database, because no two individuals can ever have the same number. Lately, however, this practice is changing because it is fairly easy to obtain confidential information, such as credit history, about a person by using this number.

Mr. Gilmore has requested a unique identification number other than the Social Security number for each member, because some members have alerted him to the problems this can create. After you designate a new field as the primary key, you will delete the IDNumber field.

Caution Remember that a primary key field cannot contain a null value (blank entry) or any duplicate values!

TASK 3: TO CHANGE THE PRIMARY KEY:

1 Open the *Members* table in Design view. The IDNumber field is now selected.

2 Click the Primary Key button on the Table Design toolbar. This removes the primary key icon from the field.

3 Select the MemberID field by clicking the Row selector.

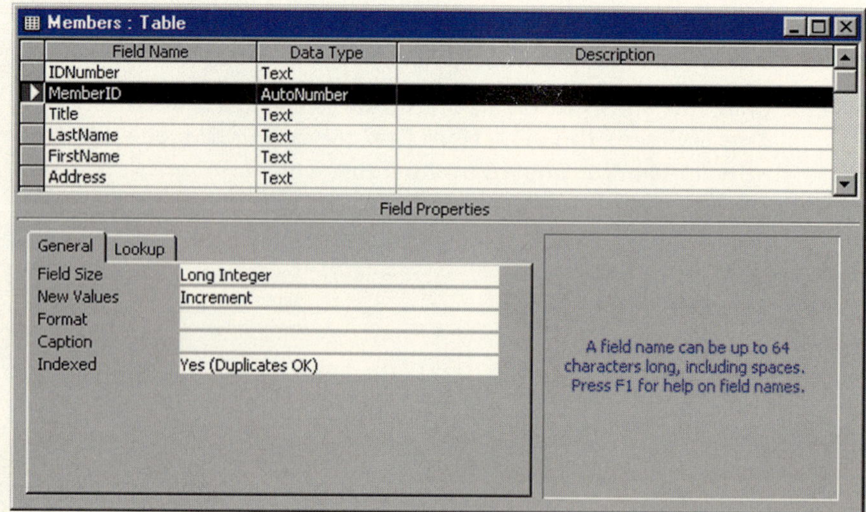

Tip In Project 2 you used the Row Selector to select a record in Datasheet view. You can also use the Row Selector to select fields in Table Design view.

4 Click the Primary Key button. The primary key is now set to the Member ID field.

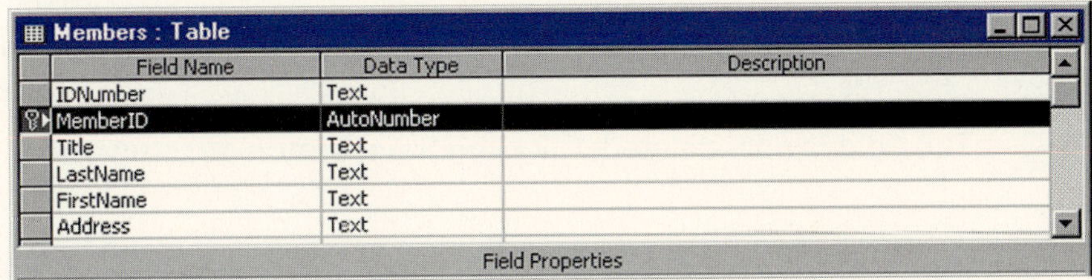

5 Click the Save button to update the table.

TASK 4: TO DELETE THE IDNUMBER FIELD:

1 Select the IDNumber field by clicking its Row Selector.

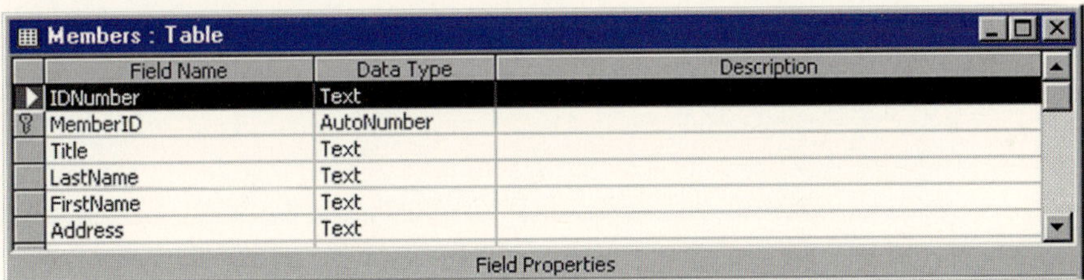

2 Click the Delete Rows button on the Table Design toolbar.

3 The dialog box shown below appears. Verify that you want to delete the field by clicking the Yes button.

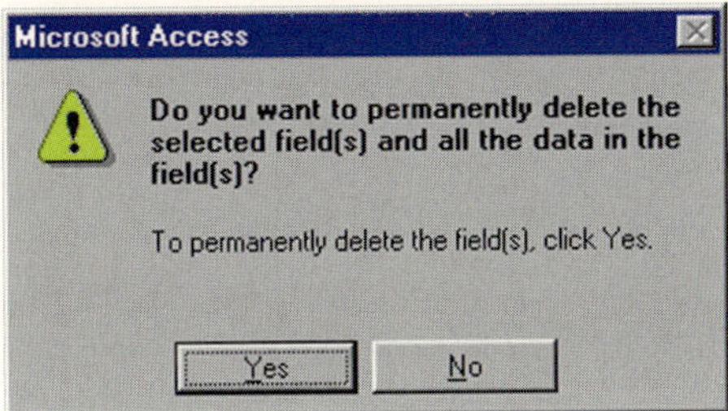

The dialog box displayed in the figure at the top of the next page appears. Because this field was previously the primary key, Access indexed the table by this field. An ***index*** is a method for speeding up record access in a table. Access uses indexes in a table as you use an index in a book: to find data, it looks up the location of the data in the index. The primary key field of a table is automatically indexed.

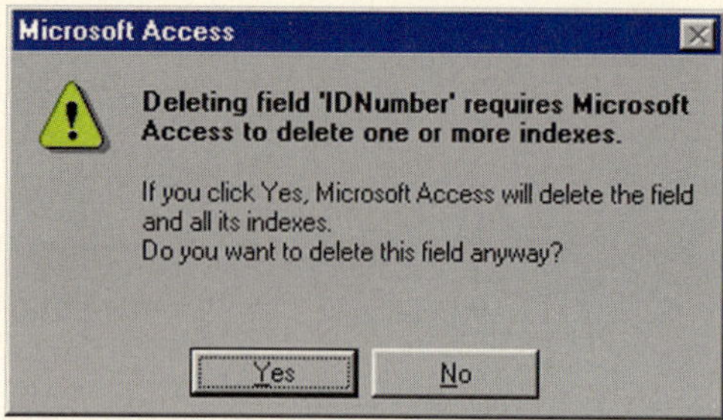

4 Click Yes.

5 The field is now deleted. Click the Save button to update the table design.

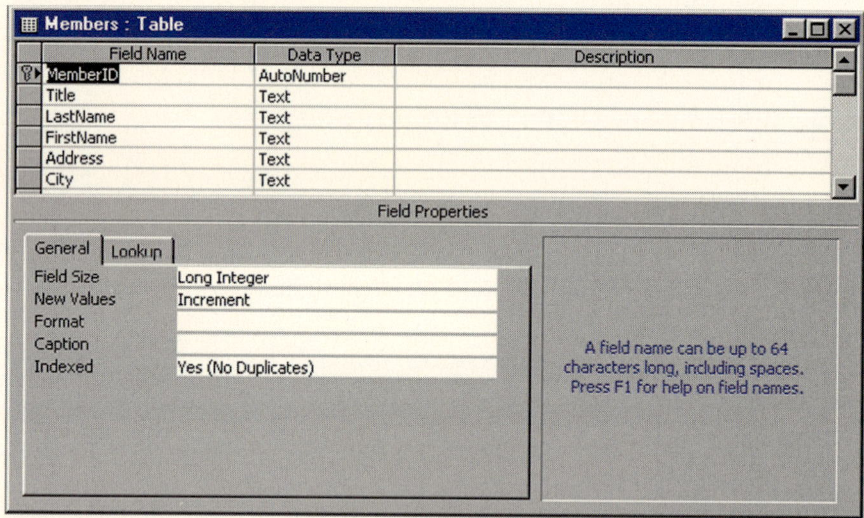

Changing Field Properties for the *Members* Table

Now you have made all the necessary changes to the structure of the *Members* table. You can think of table structure as the physical description of the table — the number of fields, data types, field sizes, indexes, and primary key designation. Sometimes you modify a table's structure by changing the field properties.

Other field properties in Access do not change the physical structure of the table, but they affect how the records are displayed in a datasheet or form, or limit the actual values that can be entered in the field. Mr. Gilmore has asked you to make data entry as simple as possible, and to minimize the chance for data entry errors. Entering data into some fields is simpler if the field contains an input mask. An ***input mask*** is a template that uses literal display characters (spaces, dots, dashes, or parentheses) to control how data is entered in a field. The ZipCode and HomePhone fields should use an input mask. Access will supply additional characters to make it easier to enter data into these fields.

Data validation is the process of checking field data as it is entered into a table or form. A ***validation rule*** is a field property that limits what the user can enter into a field. If what the user types violates the validation rule, the ***validation text*** property displays a message that explains the data entry error. The NumberofMembers, AnnualDues, DateJoined, and DateofBirth fields should all utilize a validation rule.

TASK 5: TO SPECIFY AN INPUT MASK FOR THE ZIPCODE AND HOMEPHONE FIELDS:

1. Select the ZipCode field in the upper pane of the Table Design window, and click the Input Mask property row. The Table Design window should appear similar to the window shown below.

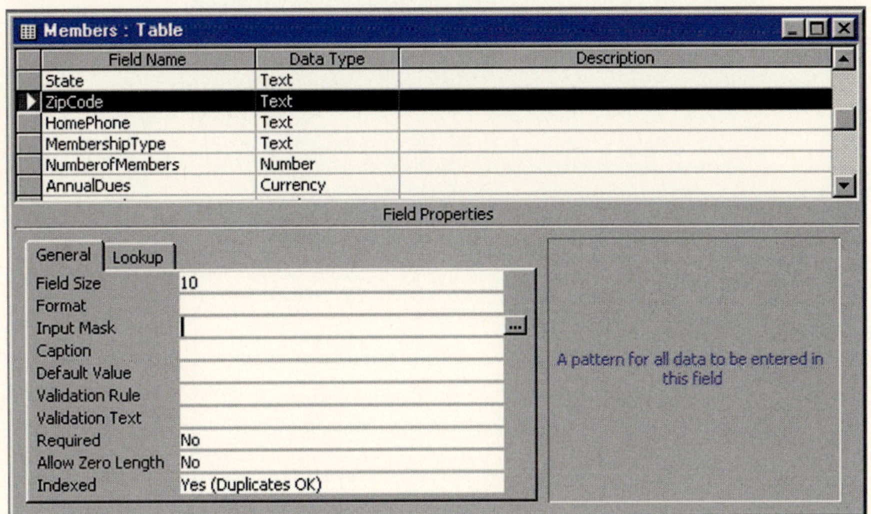

2. Click the ellipsis button ... that appears next to the Input Mask row. Access starts the Input Mask Wizard and displays the Input Mask Wizard dialog box.

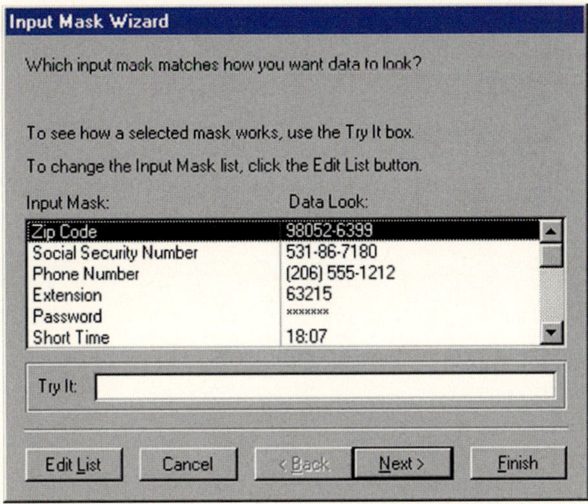

Troubleshooting If the Wizards are not installed on your computer or network, enter **00000\-9999;0;_** as the value for this property. For more information about these input mask characters, search for Input masks in the Help System, select the topic, and then select Examples of input masks from the topics found list.

3. The ZipCode field should be selected. Click Next.
4. Accept the default setting for the name, the mask, and the placeholder by clicking on the Next button.

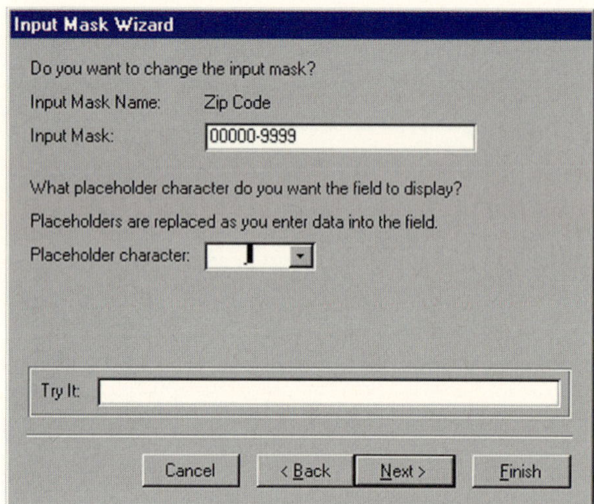

5. Select the option to store the symbols with the mask. Click Next.

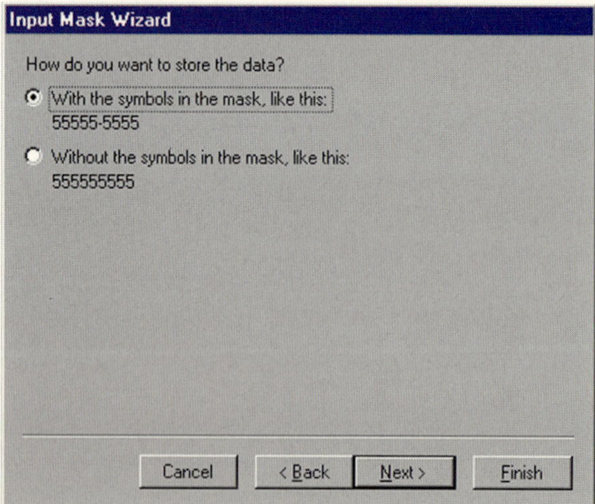

6. The last dialog box in the Input Mask Wizard appears. Click Finish.

The text string shown below has been entered as the ZipCode Input Mask property.

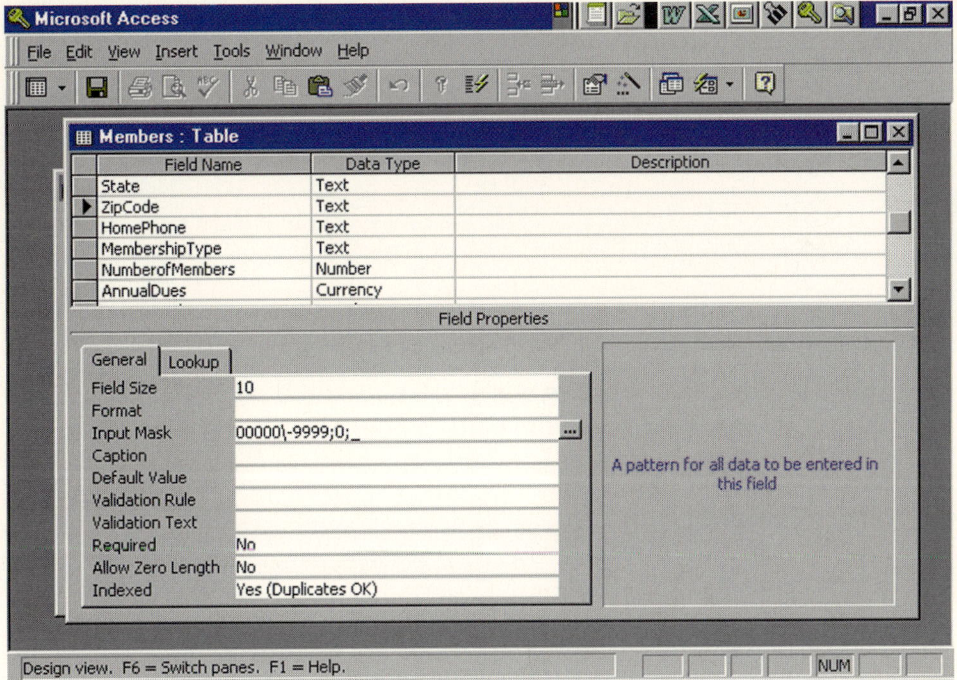

7 Select the HomePhone field in the upper pane of the Table Design window.

8 Type **!(999) 000-0000;0;_** as the input mask property for this field. The input mask should appear as shown in the following figure.

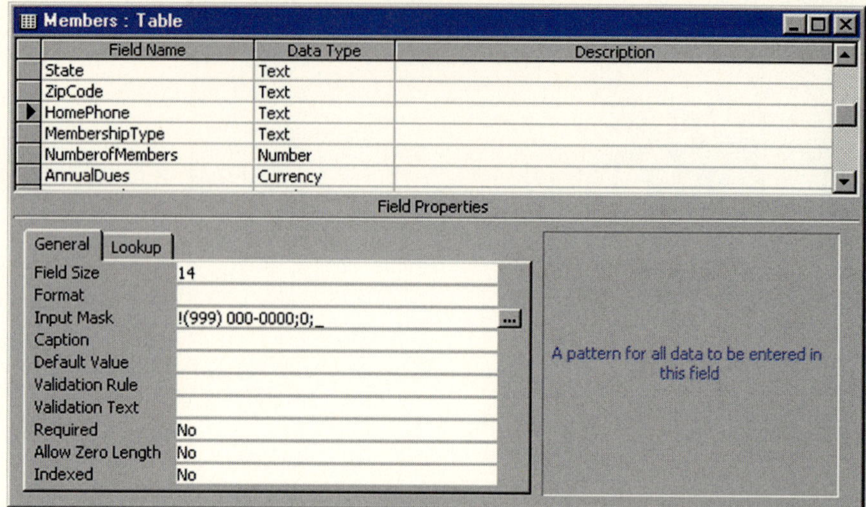

Troubleshooting Make sure you type the input mask exactly as specified, including the trailing underscore.

9 Click the Save button to update the table design.

10 Close the table.

TASK 6: TO CHANGE THE VALIDATION PROPERTIES FOR THE *MEMBERS* TABLE:

1 Open the *Members* table in Datasheet view.

2 Scroll until the NumberofMembers field is visible. For records 1 through 10, type **1**,**1**,**4**,**2**,**3**,**1**,**2**,**2**,**1**,**1**, respectively, as the value for each record. When you are finished, the table should look similar to the datasheet shown below.

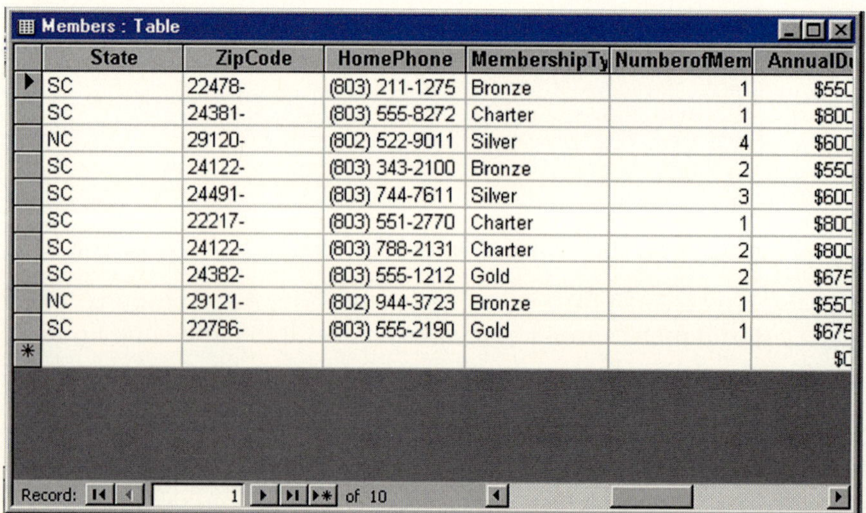

Members : Table

State	ZipCode	HomePhone	MembershipTy	NumberofMem	AnnualD
SC	22478-	(803) 211-1275	Bronze	1	$550
SC	24381-	(803) 555-8272	Charter	1	$800
NC	29120-	(802) 522-9011	Silver	4	$600
SC	24122-	(803) 343-2100	Bronze	2	$550
SC	24491-	(803) 744-7611	Silver	3	$600
SC	22217-	(803) 551-2770	Charter	1	$800
SC	24122-	(803) 788-2131	Charter	2	$800
SC	24382-	(803) 555-1212	Gold	2	$675
NC	29121-	(802) 944-3723	Bronze	1	$550
SC	22786-	(803) 555-2190	Gold	1	$675
					$0

Record: 1 of 10

3. Click the View button to switch to Design view.

4. Select the NumberofMembers fields in the upper pane of the Table Design window to activate this field's properties.

5. In the Properties pane, click the Default Value row. Type **1** as the default value. The default value must meet the conditions of the validation you create in the next step.

6. Click the Validation Rule row. Type **>0 and <7** as the validation rule.

> **Tip** This validation rule specifies that a value entered in this field for any existing or new record must be greater than zero and less than seven.

7. Click the Validation Text row. Type **Must be fewer than seven family members!** in the Validation Text row. The Field Properties pane for the NumberofMembers field should now appear as shown below.

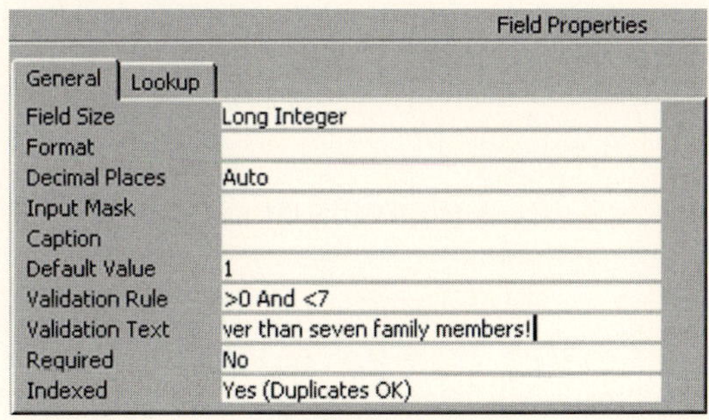

8. To specify additional validation rules, type the entries shown in Table 3.1 into the specified fields.

> **Tip** For more information about these validation rule characters, search for ValidationRule property in the Help System, select the topic, and then select ValidationRule, ValidationText Properties (Microsoft Access) in the Topics Found list.

9. When you are finished, click the Save button. The dialog box shown on the next page appears. Click Yes.

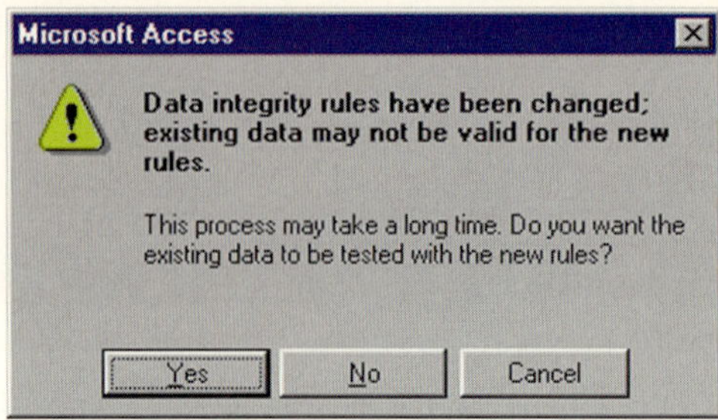

10 Close the table.

Table 3.1 Additional Validation Rules and Text

Field Name	Validation Rule	Validation Text
Annual Dues	550 or 600 or 675 or 800	Invalid Fee!
DateJoined	<=CDate(Now())	Invalid Date!
DateofBirth	>=#1/1/1910#	Invalid Date!

Testing the Validation Rules

You are now ready to test the validation rules you have set by adding a new record to the table.

TASK 7: TO ADD A NEW RECORD TO THE TABLE:

1 Open the *Members* table in Datasheet view.

2 Click the New Record button. A blank record will be selected.

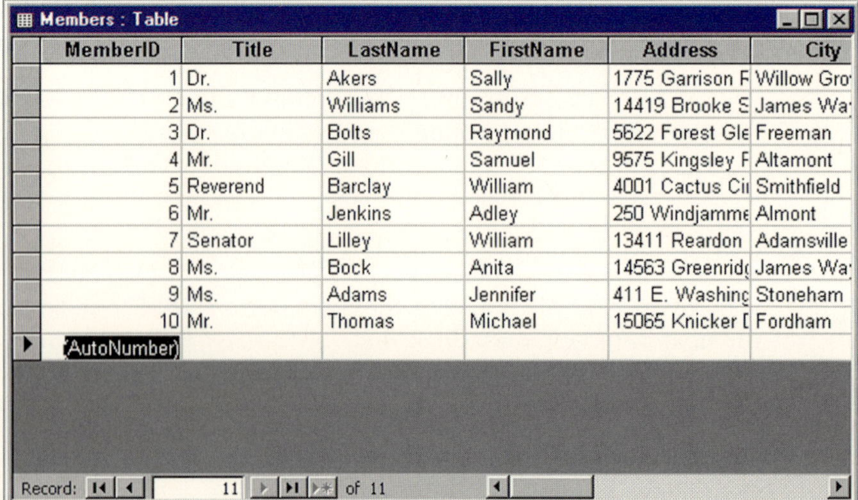
Members : Table

MemberID	Title	LastName	FirstName	Address	City
1	Dr.	Akers	Sally	1775 Garrison F	Willow Gro
2	Ms.	Williams	Sandy	14419 Brooke S	James Wa
3	Dr.	Bolts	Raymond	5622 Forest Gle	Freeman
4	Mr.	Gill	Samuel	9575 Kingsley F	Altamont
5	Reverend	Barclay	William	4001 Cactus Cii	Smithfield
6	Mr.	Jenkins	Adley	250 Windjamme	Almont
7	Senator	Lilley	William	13411 Reardon	Adamsville
8	Ms.	Bock	Anita	14563 Greenrid	James Wa
9	Ms.	Adams	Jennifer	411 E. Washing	Stoneham
10	Mr.	Thomas	Michael	15065 Knicker	Fordham
(AutoNumber)					

Record: 11 of 11

3. Press the TAB key to move the focus to the Title field. Type **Ms.** as this new member's title.
4. Using the TAB key to move to the appropriate fields, type **Hopkins** as the last name, **Jennifer** as the first name, **31101 S.E. Quail** as the address, **James Way** as the city, **SC** as the state, and **24382** as the zip code. Notice that the input mask for the zip code displays the digits and the placeholder as you type.
5. Press the TAB key. Type **8005552131** as the phone number. The input mask supplies the parentheses and the hyphen character.
6. Press TAB. Type **Silver** as the membership type.
7. Press the TAB key twice. Type **900** as the membership fee. The figure below shows the validation text that appears on the screen. Click OK.

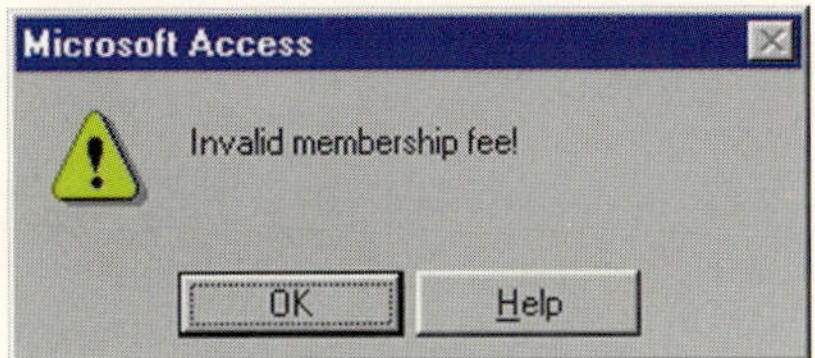

8. Change the entry to **600**, and press TAB.
9. Type today's date (in MM/DD/YY format) into the DateJoined field.
10. Press TAB. Type **6/5/68** as the date of birth for Ms. Hopkins. Close the table.

Creating an Autoform for the Updated Table

In Project 1 you created an Autoform based upon the *Members* table. If you open the *Members* form, the form will try to display an IDNumber for each member, because this field was included in the form's design. Because you have modified the table design, you must either modify the form design, or delete the form and create a new one. In this case, it will be easiest to create a new form.

TASK 8: TO CREATE AN AUTOFORM:

1. Click the Forms tab in the Database Window.
2. Select the *Members* form and press the DEL key to remove the form from the database. When the Microsoft Access dialog box shown on the next page appears, click Yes to verify that you want to remove the form from the database.

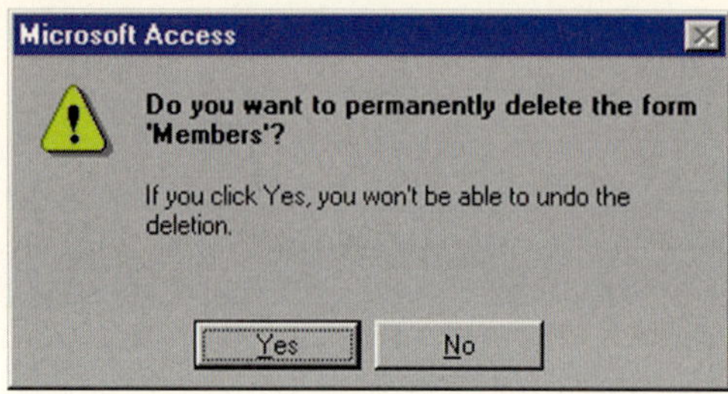

3. Click the New button to create a new form.
4. In the New Form dialog box, select Form Wizard as the form, and select the *Members* table as the source of the form's data. Your selection should match the one shown in the figure below. If it does, click OK.

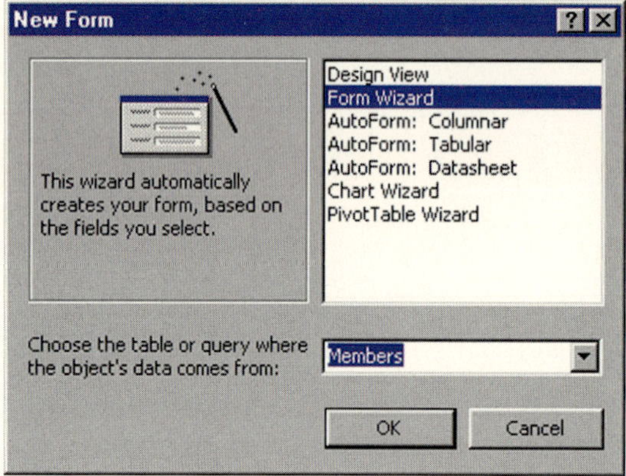

5. Add all fields in the Available Fields: list to the Select Fields: list by clicking the double-arrow button. Click Next.

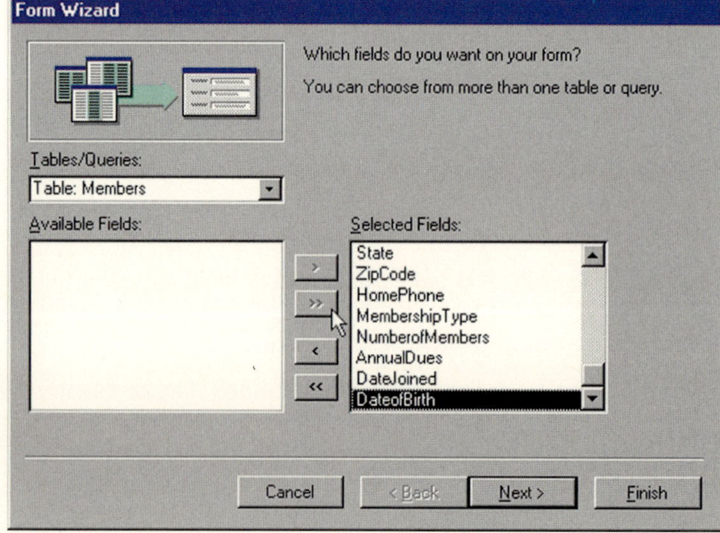

6. Select Columnar as the form type. Click Next.
7. Select Standard as the style. Click Next.
8. Accept *Members* as the name for the form, and click Finish. Your form should look similar to the one displayed below.

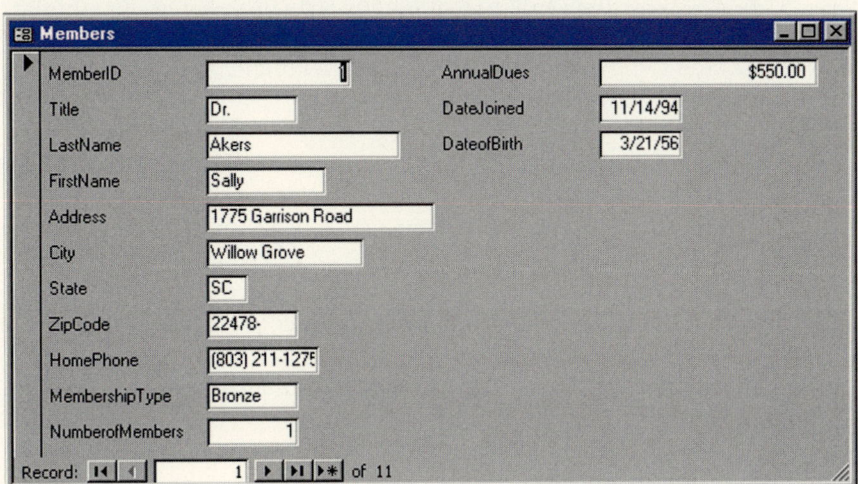

9. Close the form. Before you exit Access, select Database Utilities from the Tools menu, and select the Compact Database option. This stores the database file in the smallest size possible.

The Conclusion

Modifying a database often entails modifying the underlying tables. This might include modifying the physical structure of a table, changing the field properties, or both. Be mindful that altering a table's structure affects any database objects that use the table's data.

Summary and Exercises

Summary

- If you are planning to change the structure of a table, you may want to create a backup copy of the table first.
- Modifying a database entails both changing the physical structure of tables and altering the field properties that specify how data is entered and displayed in tables.
- Maintaining a database often requires adding fields to a table or removing fields from a table.
- You can change a table's primary key, as long as the new field does not contain any null or duplicate values.
- Input masks are used to simplify data entry and increase data accuracy.
- Validation Rules help to increase data accuracy by limiting a field entry to a specified value or range.
- A field's Validation Text property specifies the message that will appear if a validation rule is violated.

Key Terms and Operations

Key Terms

AutoNumber field
data validation
design modifications
field properties
index
input mask
table structure
validation rule
validation text

Operations

add fields to a table
change a table's primary key
create a backup copy of a table
create an AutoForm based upon the updated table
create input masks
delete a field from a table
delete an existing form
specify validation rules
test validation rules by adding a record to the table

Study Questions

Multiple Choice

1. To insert a field into a table, you must use the
   a. Datasheet view.
   b. Design view.
   c. Form view.
   d. Database window.

2. A warning appears when you
   a. insert a field.
   b. change fields.
   c. edit field data.
   d. delete a field.

3. A primary key cannot contain
   a. a numeric value.
   b. an AutoNumber value.
   c. a null value.
   d. a patron's Social Security number.

4. To add validation rules to a field, you use
   a. the upper pane of the Table Design window.
   b. the table's datasheet.
   c. the properties pane of the Table Design window.
   d. the Database window.

5. An input mask is used to
   a. limit the data that is entered into a field.
   b. supply a template for entering data into a field.
   c. limit the data entry to a specific range.
   d. both a and b.

6. Records in a table can contain how many instances of a primary key value?
   a. one
   b. two
   c. four
   d. eight

7. When you create a validation rule, it's also a good idea to include
   a. a primary key.
   b. validation text.
   c. an input mask.
   d. an AutoNumber field.

8. Which data type ensures that a primary key always contains a unique value?
   a. currency
   b. text
   c. number
   d. AutoNumber

9. When you add a field to a database, it automatically contains a value if it is which data type?
   a. currency
   b. text
   c. number
   d. AutoNumber

10. Mr. Gilmore is concerned with finding a good primary key for the *Members* table that protects each member's confidentiality. Which field is a logical candidate, but should not be used?
    a. home phone number
    b. work phone number
    c. Social Security number
    d. zip code

Short Answer

1. Which button do you use to switch between table views?
2. Does a validation rule require validation text?
3. How many records in a table can contain the same primary key value?

4. What happens if you delete a field from a table that contains data?
5. Should you consider validating numeric field data?
6. If you want to improve the accuracy of data entered into a table, which field property or properties should you modify?
7. Which data type ensures that a primary key is always unique?
8. Many organizations have used what common identifier as a primary key in their databases?
9. Which property setting supplies a template that assists in data entry?
10. Which field property specifies a range of acceptable values for the field?

For Discussion

1. What is the difference between an input mask and a validation rule?
2. When you add a field to a table, what happens to the existing records?
3. In many Access database tables, an AutoNumber field is used as the primary key. Is this a good choice, and if so, why?
4. If you add a validation rule to a field, should you add validation text as well? Explain your answer.

Review Exercises

1. Creating an additional table and relating tables

You cannot appreciate the power of a relational database such as Access until you see why being able to relate table data is so significant. In this exercise, you will copy the Willows Membership database file, create an additional table, and relate the two tables. In Project 4, you will create a query that lists data from both tables. Complete the following:

1. Using the Windows Explorer or My Computer, copy the *Willows Membership.mdb* file. Rename the copy as **Membership Payments.mdb**.
2. Select the copy of *Members* table, and press the DEL key. Then click Yes on the confirmation alert box to delete the copy.
3. Create a new table using Design view. Use the field specifications in Table 3.2, set PaymentNumber as the primary key, and save the table as **Payments**.

   When you are finished defining the table structure and naming the table, the Table Design window should appear as below.

Table 3.2 Payments Table Field Specifications

Field Name	Data Type
PaymentNumber	AutoNumber
MemberID	Number
PaymentDate	Date/Time
Amount	Currency

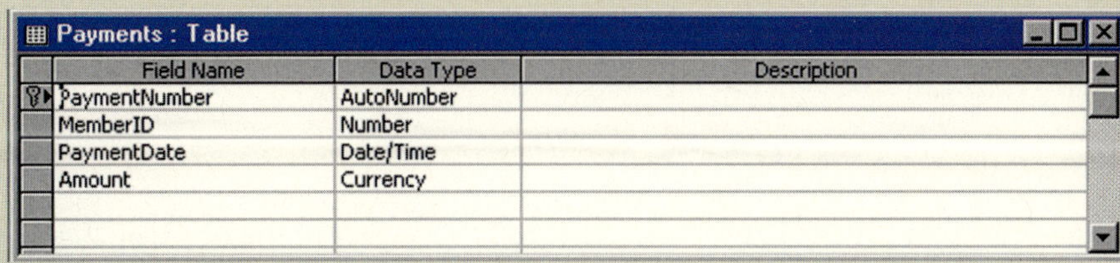

4. Close the table.
5. Click the Relationships button on the Database toolbar. The Show Table dialog box appears, and the *Members* table will be selected. Hold down the SHIFT key and click the *Payments* table to select it as well. Click the Add button.

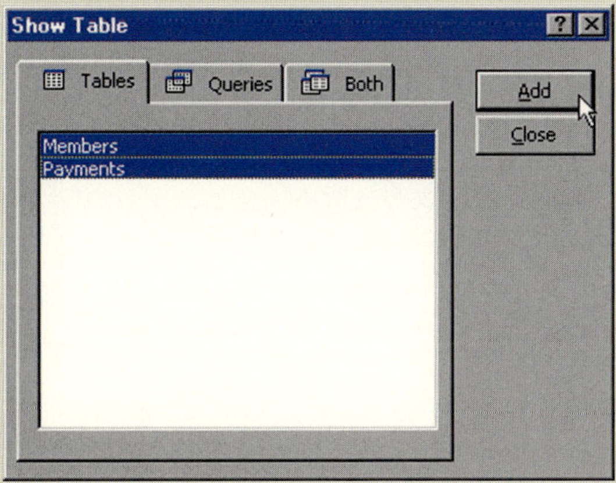

6. Click the Close button. The two tables appear in the Relationships window. Click the MemberID field in the *Members* table, hold down the left mouse button, and drag it toward the Member ID field in the Payments table. Notice the icon representing the field, shown below.

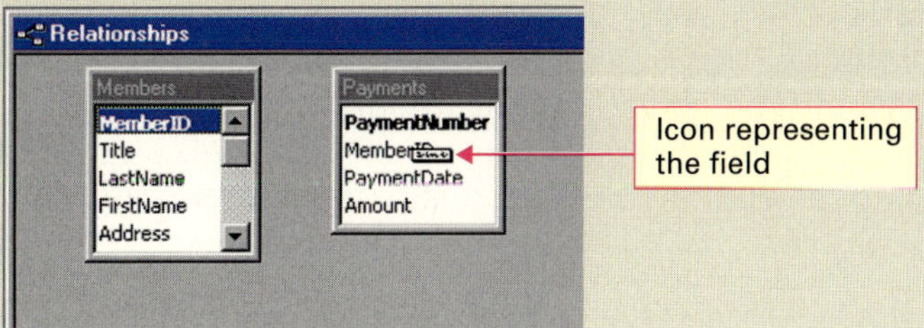

7. Release the left mouse button. Click the Create button in the Relationships dialog box.

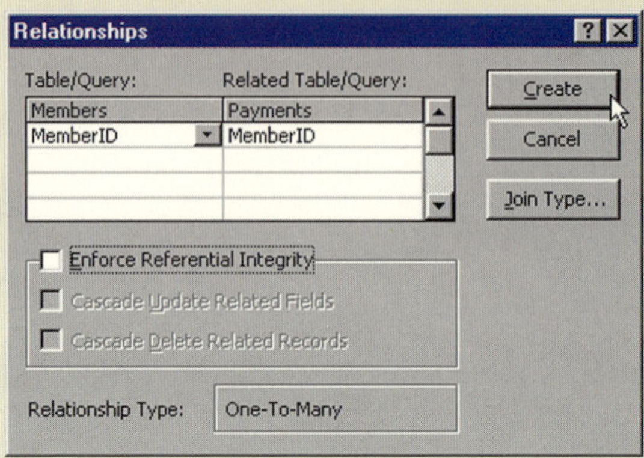

The line that extends between the fields in the two tables represents the relationship.

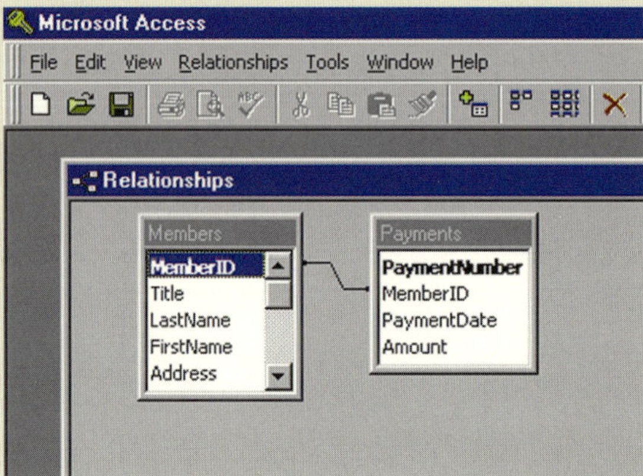

8. Close the Relationships window, and save your changes.
9. Close the table.

Comment You may have noticed a check box for maintaining referential integrity. You will learn more about this in Project 4, but in this example you may want to think about problems that could potentially arise if a data entry person entered a MemberID entry incorrectly. By enforcing referential integrity, this would never happen.

2. Adding Records to the Payments Table

The *Payments* table you created in Assignment 1 of this project does not contain any records. In this assignment, you will add records to the table that lists each member's payments toward his or her total dues. Add 10records to the table as follows:

1. Open the *Membership Payments.mdb* database if it is not currently open.
2. Open the *Payments* table in Datasheet view.
3. Add the records listed in Table 3.3 into the table. Remember that the PaymentNumber value is automatically entered, because this is an AutoNumber data type.

Table 3.3

Payment Number	MemberID	PaymentDate	Amount
1	1	1/5/98	275
2	1	6/1/98	275
3	2	1/5/98	200
4	2	4/20/98	200
5	2	6/1/98	400
6	3	1/5/98	600
7	4	1/5/98	500
8	4	3/16/98	50
9	5	1/5/98	300
10	5	6/1/98	300

4. Close the table.
5. Close the database.

3. Changing a table design and creating an AutoReport

1. Launch Access and open *High Point Foods xxx.mdb*.

Note If you do not have a database named *High Point Foods xxx.mdb*, ask your instructor for a copy of the file you should use to complete this exercise.

2. Make the following changes to the *Food Categories* table design:
   - Make CategoryID the primary key field.
   - Add a field named **Quantity Consumed** as a text field and position it at the end of the table. Include the following description for the field: **Average number of pounds of food used per month.**
3. Save the changes to the table and add the following information to the *Quantity Consumed* field:
   6391 Gallons
   50 Pounds
   500 Servings
   903 Pounds
   2548 Pounds
   8192 Pounds
   1500 Pounds
   2164 Pounds
   12495 Pounds

4. Create an AutoReport named *Food Categories* for the table and print a copy of the AutoReport.
5. Save changes to the database and exit Access.

Assignments

1. Adding Validation Rules to the Willows Employees database

The Willows Employees database contains at least one field that requires a value within a specific range. Open the database, and then open the *Employees* table in Design view. Add a validation rule to the Salary field that specifies a salary greater than or equal to 25,000 and less than 100,000. Add validation text specifying that the value entered falls outside the salary range. Save your changes to the table, and close the table.

2. Changing Field properties in the Willows Employees database

When the Database Wizard created the Employees database, it set some of the field sizes to a value that is larger than necessary. Open the Willows Employees database if it is not currently open, and then open the *Employees* table in Design view. Change the field properties for the fields specified in Table 3.4.

For the StateOrProvince field, type **>LL** as the input mask. The mask requires an entry of two letters—A through Z—and if the user enters lowercase letters, they will be displayed in uppercase. Save your changes to the table, close it, and close the database.

Table 3.4 Field Size Property Values

Field Name	Field Size Property
SocialSecurityNumber	9
Title	10
LastName	20
FirstName	15
Address	50
City	15
StateOrProvince	2
PostalCode	9

PROJECT 4

Creating Queries

Most databases contain much more information than is useful at any given time. End users need some way of viewing information from the database that meets specific conditions, such as all members who live in a specific zip code. Although filters are useful, designing and running queries offers a much more flexible and powerful way for seeing the data you need.

Objectives

After completing this project, you will be able to:

- **Create a new query using Design View**
- **Add fields to a query**
- **Add calculated fields to a query**
- **Modify the format of a calculated field**
- **Run a query**
- **Specify query criteria and conditions**
- **Sort data in a query**
- **Create a form to display the results of a query**

The Challenge

Mr. Gilmore is very pleased with the work you have done on the membership database. Now he wants to see a list of the exact fees each member will pay this year. Membership fees include a base fee that varies depending upon the type of membership, plus a surcharge for each family member. Members over 65 years of age receive a 15 percent discount of the base membership fee. Finally, Mr. Gilmore wants a separate listing of the membership fee paid by charter members who also received a qualifying discount. As usual, this information will be sorted by last name.

The Solution

Fortunately, Access has powerful database query capabilities that enable you to deliver the exact information that Mr. Gilmore has requested. You can create a query that will calculate each member's total membership fee, based upon the specifications Mr. Gilmore gave you. In addition, you can specify criteria that will return records that meet specific conditions. Figure 4.1 shows a form displaying the total membership fees for one member.

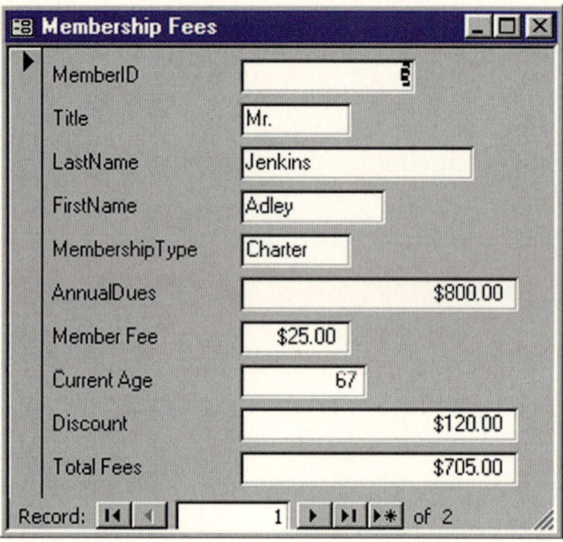

Figure 4.1

The Setup

After you launch Access and open your database, you should make sure the Database toolbar and the Status toolbar are displayed. These are the default settings in Access, but they may have been changed on your computer. (If you have forgotten how to do this, refer to Table 1.1 in Project 1.)

Troubleshooting If you do not see the Database toolbar on the screen when you launch Access and open your database, choose Toolbars from the View menu. Select the Database toolbar to display it. If any additional toolbars are visible, close them. If you do not see the Status Bar at the bottom of the Application window, choose Options from the Tools menu, click the View Page tab and change the Status Bar check box option.

Using the procedures you learned in Task 1 of Project 1, open the *Willows Membership.mdb* file from your diskette. Delete the *Copy of Members* table from the database.

Creating Queries

An Access ***query*** is a database object that you create to view, change, and analyze data in different ways. You can also use queries as the source of records for forms and reports. Sometimes you will want to see information from the database that requires a ***calculated field***—a field that displays data resulting from a calculation that you specify rather than stored data.

Think of a query as a set of specifications that returns a subset of data from one or more tables. Data returned by a query isn't stored in the query; it is stored in the tables underlying the query, and the query stores the specifications. Therefore, the query always displays the most recent data in the database. Queries can also be used to add or edit table data.

Creating a Select Query

The most common kind of query is a ***select query***—a query that retrieves data from one or more tables and displays the results in a datasheet where you can update the records.

TASK 1: TO CREATE A SELECT QUERY USING DESIGN VIEW:

1. Click the Queries tab in the Database window.
2. Click the New button.
3. In the New Query dialog box, select Design View.

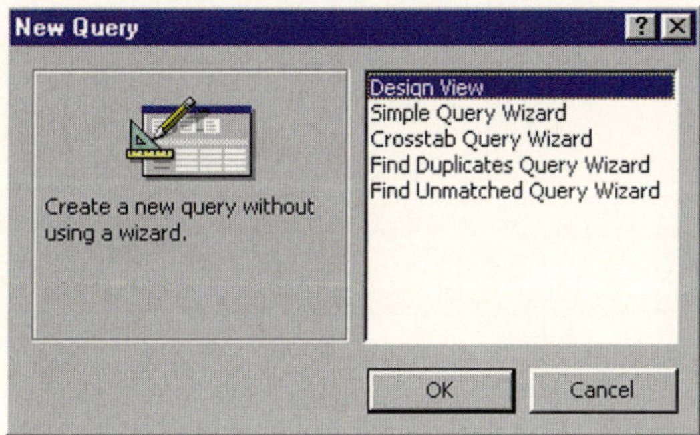

4. When the Show Table dialog box appears, click the *Members* table to select it. Then click Add. Notice that the *Members* table appears in the query window behind the Show Table dialog box.

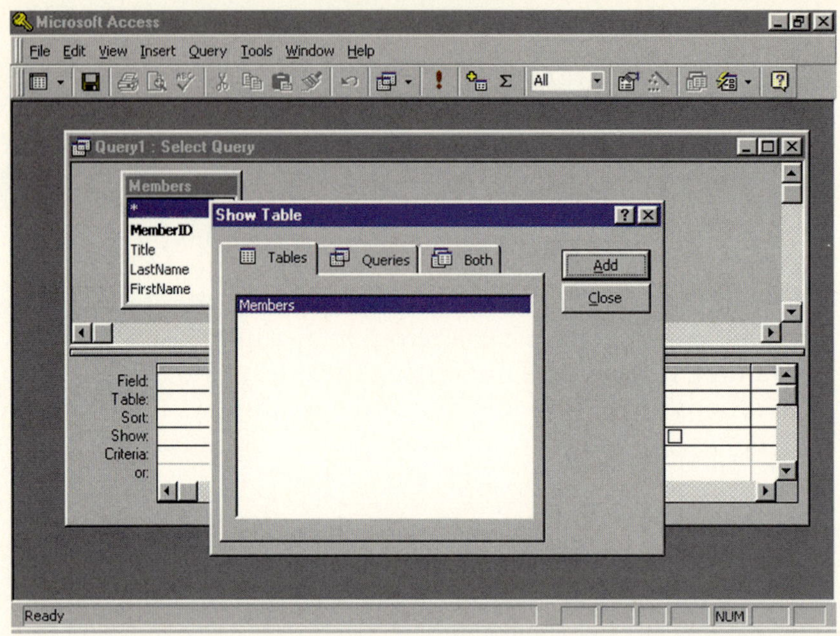

5 Click the Close button. The Query Design window should now be displayed.

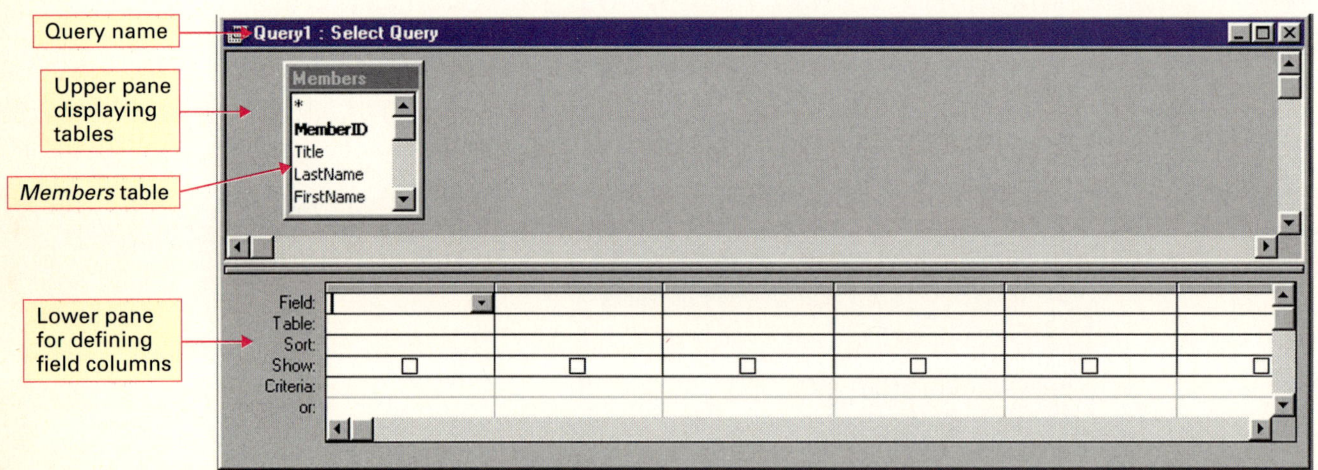

The Query Design window consists of two panes. The upper pane includes the tables containing the fields that you will use in the query. The lower pane consists of columns where you can define the fields of data the query displays. This is the ***query design grid***. This view is called the ***Query Design View***. Notice that the default name of the query is displayed in the query's title bar.

Tip You can add additional tables to the upper pane at any time by clicking the Show Table button on the toolbar.

6. Click the Save button on the Query Design toolbar.
7. Type **Membership Fees** in the Save As dialog box.
8. Click OK.

Adding Fields to a Select Query

As with a table, an Access query has multiple views. You use Query Design View to create the query specifications before you ***run*** a query, which is the process of loading your specifications and displaying the results in a query datasheet. A ***query datasheet*** appears almost identical to a table datasheet; you can use it to modify field data and add records to the underlying table or tables.

Before a query datasheet will display any records, you must specify which fields the query will return. These are then added to the query design grid. You can add fields in a variety of ways.

TASK 2: TO ADD FIELDS TO THE QUERY DESIGN GRID USING TWO DIFFERENT METHODS:

1. Click the MemberID field in the field list of the Members table in the upper pane of the Query Design window.

2. While holding down the left mouse button, drag the field name from the upper pane to the first available row and column in the lower pane.

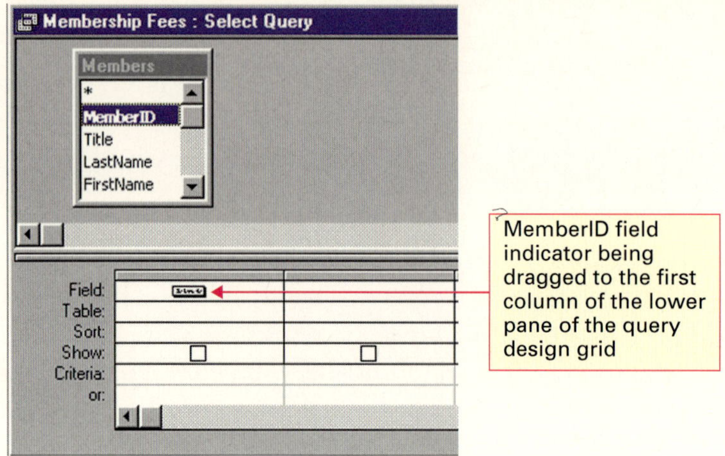

3 Release the left mouse button.
The MemberID field is now displayed in the leftmost column of the query design grid. The name of the table from which the field is referenced is listed immediately under the field name.

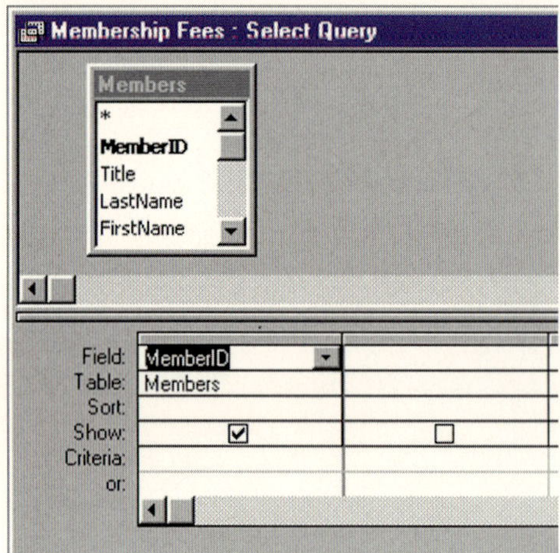

This click-and-drag method is one way you can add fields to your query design grid. Another method follows:

4 Move the mouse pointer inside the first row of the next available column in the lower pane and click the left mouse button.
A drop-down list button appears.

5 Click the drop-down list button and select the Title field.

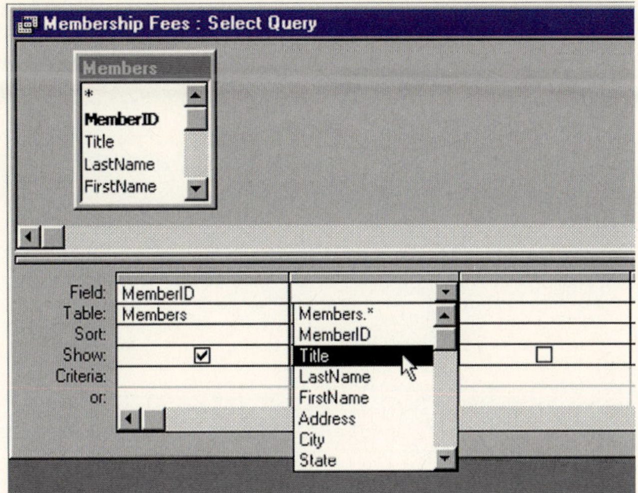

The Title field is added to the lower pane and the *Member* table is listed directly under it.

6 Using either the drag method or the drop-down list method, add the LastName, FirstName, MembershipType, and AnnualDues fields to the query design grid. When you are finished, six fields are displayed.

Tip Notice that the Show: checkbox for each field is checked. If you need to use a field for the query but do not want it to show in the query datasheet, deselect the field's Show: button.

7 Click the Save button on the Query Design toolbar to update the changes to your query.

Viewing the Results of a Query

So far you have not seen how the query datasheet will look when you run the query. One of the advantages of using a graphical query design tool such as the Query Design window is that you can run your query at any time while you are designing it to see what data it will display.

TASK 3: TO VIEW THE RESULTS OF A QUERY:

1 Click the Run button on the Query Design toolbar.
The query switches to Datasheet View. The following figure shows what your datasheet will look like after you run the query.

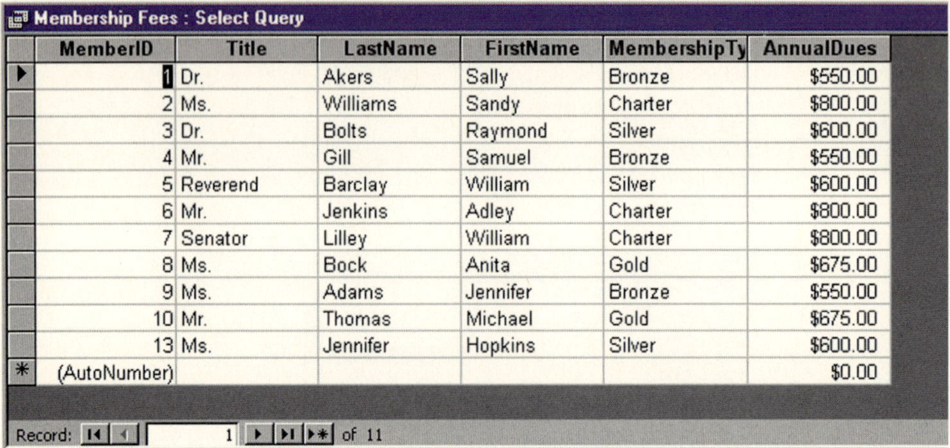

Membership Fees : Select Query

MemberID	Title	LastName	FirstName	MembershipTy	AnnualDues
1	Dr.	Akers	Sally	Bronze	$550.00
2	Ms.	Williams	Sandy	Charter	$800.00
3	Dr.	Bolts	Raymond	Silver	$600.00
4	Mr.	Gill	Samuel	Bronze	$550.00
5	Reverend	Barclay	William	Silver	$600.00
6	Mr.	Jenkins	Adley	Charter	$800.00
7	Senator	Lilley	William	Charter	$800.00
8	Ms.	Bock	Anita	Gold	$675.00
9	Ms.	Adams	Jennifer	Bronze	$550.00
10	Mr.	Thomas	Michael	Gold	$675.00
13	Ms.	Jennifer	Hopkins	Silver	$600.00
(AutoNumber)					$0.00

Record: 1 of 11

Tip You can also use the View menu or the View button on the toolbar to switch between views.

Notice that the title bar identifies the datasheet as belonging to a select query.

2. Click the View button on the Query Datasheet toolbar.
3. Close the query.
   The query object name appears in the Database window.

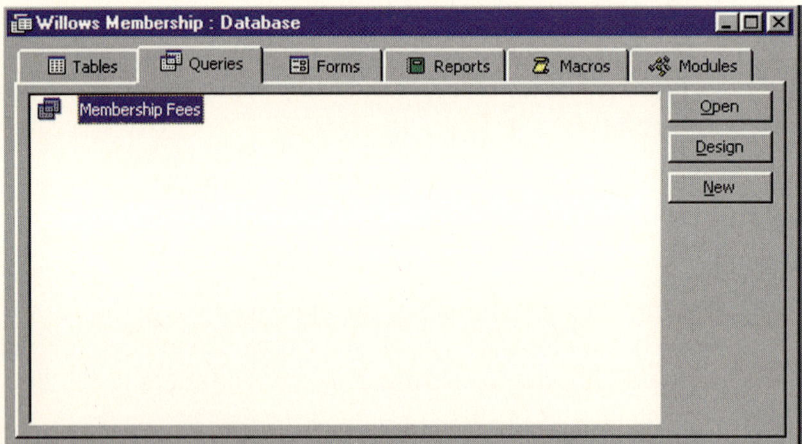

4. Click the Design button. The query again opens in Query Design View.

Adding Calculated Fields to a Query

To determine each member's total membership fee, you must first determine which members receive a discount or pay a surcharge for additional family members.

You can create calculated fields in the query design grid. You should recall that a calculated field is a field that returns data according to a certain expression. An ***expression*** is a combination of object identifiers such as table and field names, arithmetic or logical operators such as an addition sign or a less than (<) symbol, and numeric values that produce a result. Access includes an ***Expression Builder*** that is a graphical workspace you can use to create an expression.

TASK 4: TO ADD AN EXPRESSION TO CALCULATE THE MEMBER SURCHARGE:

1. Use the scroll bar in the query design grid to display additional columns in the pane.
2. Place the insertion point over the next available column and click the left mouse button.
3. Click the Build button on the Query Design toolbar. The Expression Builder appears.

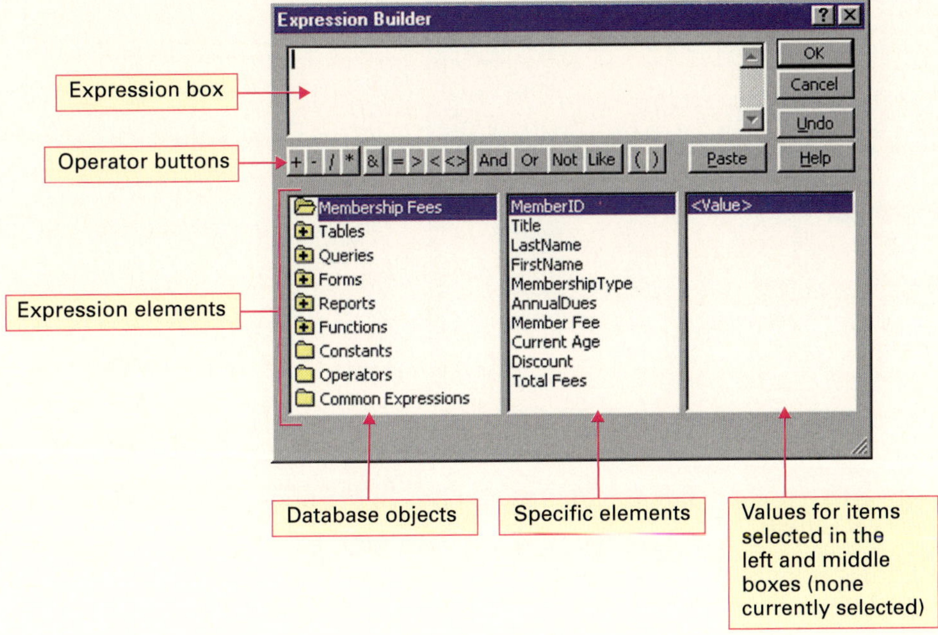

4. Double-click the Plus sign Tables on the folder immediately to the left of the Tables list in the leftmost pane of the Expression Builder.

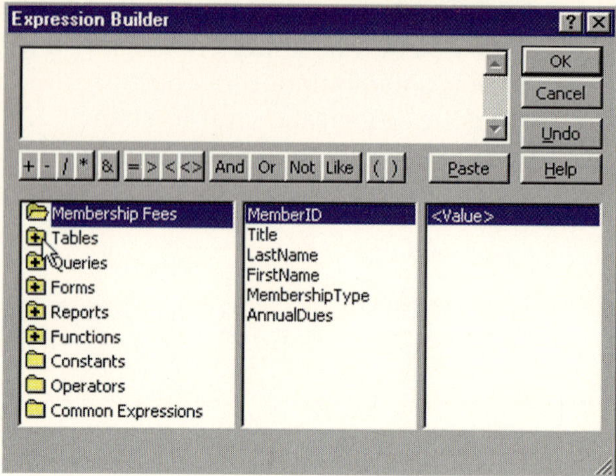

5 Click the *Members* table name. The list of fields in the table now appears in the middle pane of the Expression Builder.

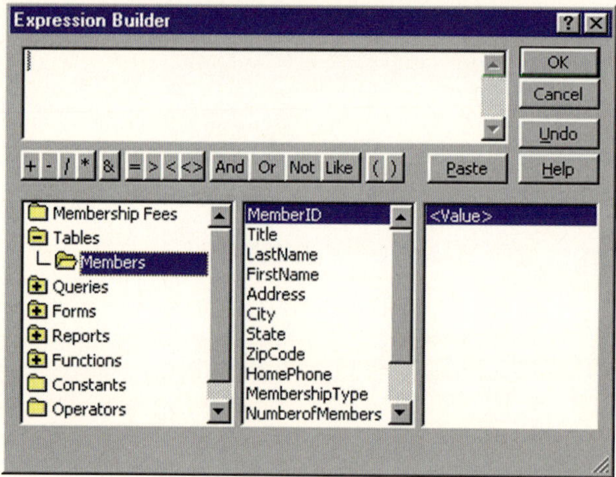

6 Place the insertion point inside the Expression box in the upper portion of the Expression Builder.

7 Click the Equals Sign button = appearing on the toolbar inside the Expression Builder. You will note that an equals sign appears in the workspace.

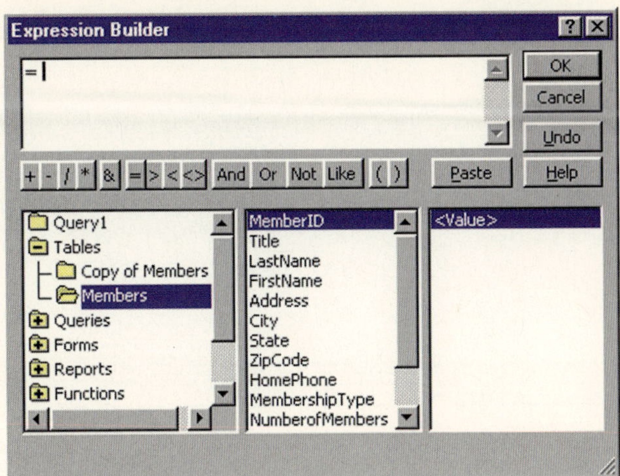

Tip For many expressions, the equals sign is optional. For more information about the Expression builder and the syntax required for specific expressions, click the Help button in the Expression Builder and select the Read more about expressions option.

8. Highlight the NumberOfMembers field name in the middle pane of the Expression Builder, and click the Paste button Paste.

9. Type ***25** at the end of the equation that is forming in the workspace. The expression displayed in the Expression Builder specifies that the value in the NumberOfMembers field will be multiplied by the value 25.

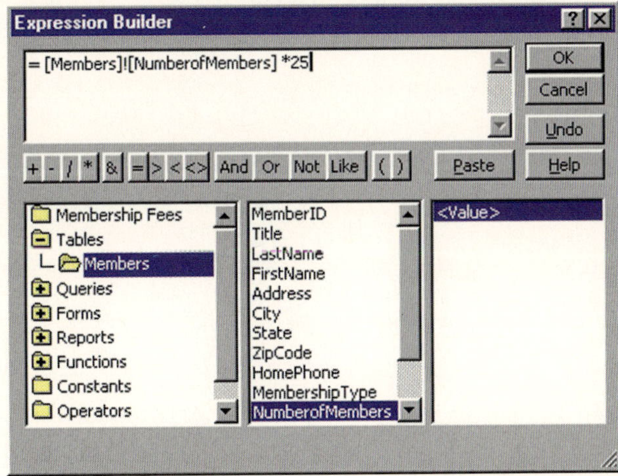

Tip In this expression, [Members]! [NumberofMembers] represents a field in the *Members* table. The ampersand character is the arithmetic operator for multiplication, and 25 is the literal value by which all field data is multiplied for each record.

10 Click OK. The expression appears in the query design grid.

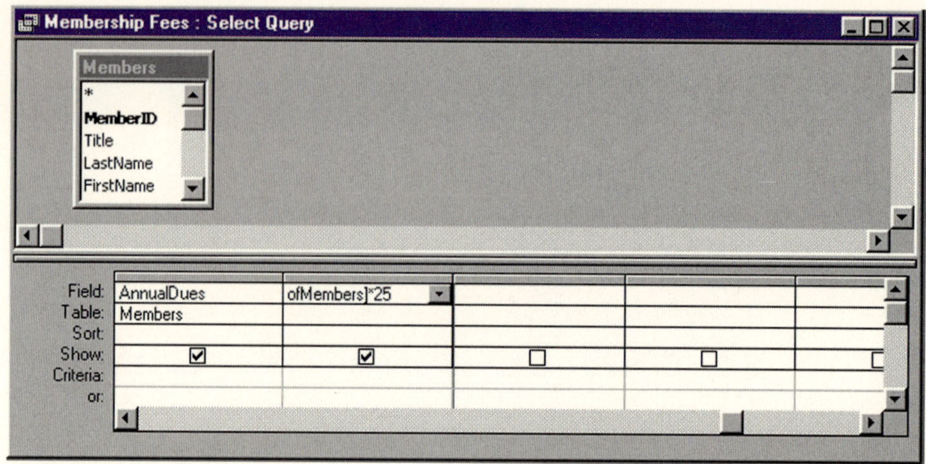

Troubleshooting The expression will appear truncated because it is too wide to appear in the current column width.

TASK 5: TO VIEW THE RESULTS OF THE EXPRESSION AND MODIFY ITS FORMAT:

1 Click the Run button on the Query Design toolbar.

2 Using the scrollbar in the datasheet, position the columns so that you can see the calculated field data. Your results should match the results shown in the figure below.

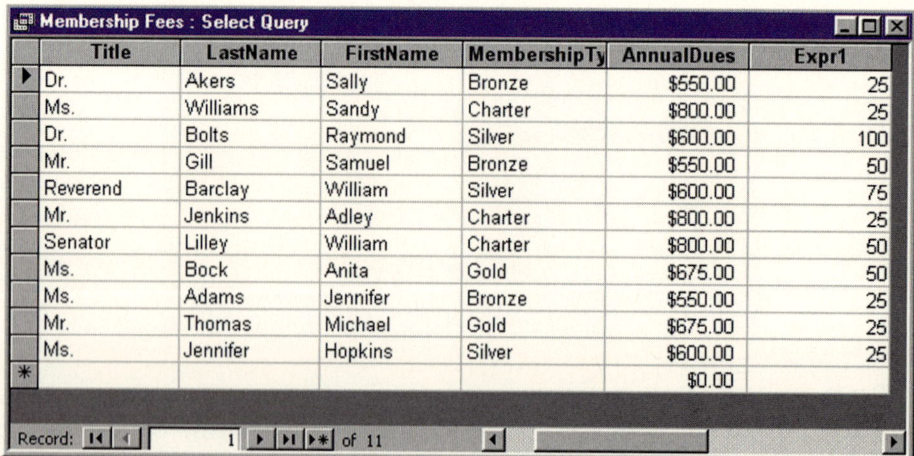
Membership Fees : Select Query

Title	LastName	FirstName	MembershipTy	AnnualDues	Expr1
Dr.	Akers	Sally	Bronze	$550.00	25
Ms.	Williams	Sandy	Charter	$800.00	25
Dr.	Bolts	Raymond	Silver	$600.00	100
Mr.	Gill	Samuel	Bronze	$550.00	50
Reverend	Barclay	William	Silver	$600.00	75
Mr.	Jenkins	Adley	Charter	$800.00	25
Senator	Lilley	William	Charter	$800.00	50
Ms.	Bock	Anita	Gold	$675.00	50
Ms.	Adams	Jennifer	Bronze	$550.00	25
Mr.	Thomas	Michael	Gold	$675.00	25
Ms.	Jennifer	Hopkins	Silver	$600.00	25
				$0.00	

Record: 1 of 11

You will notice that the calculated field has the default name of *Expr1*, and that the data does not appear in currency format.

3 Click the View button on the Query Datasheet toolbar.

4 Highlight the text *Expr1* in the first row of the column containing the calculated field expression.

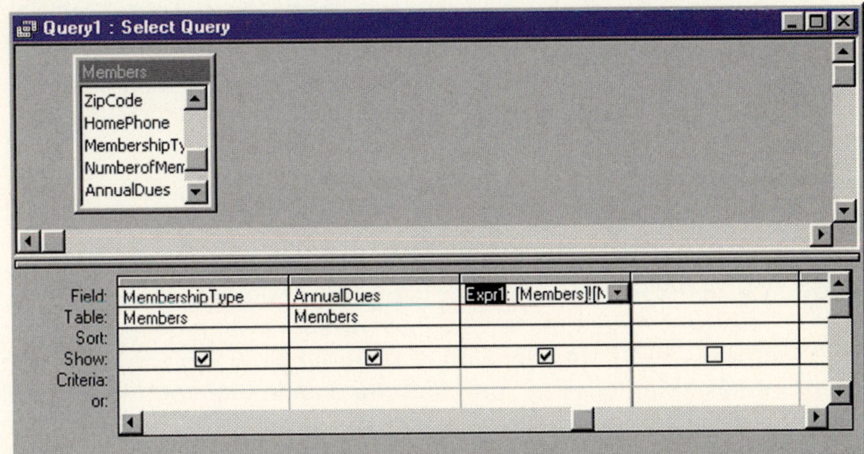

Troubleshooting Make sure you do not highlight the colon character! This character is needed to separate the name of the calculated field from its expression.

5 Type **Member Fee** in place of *Expr1*.

6 Click the Properties button on the Query Datasheet toolbar.

7 Click the Format row in the Field Properties dialog box.

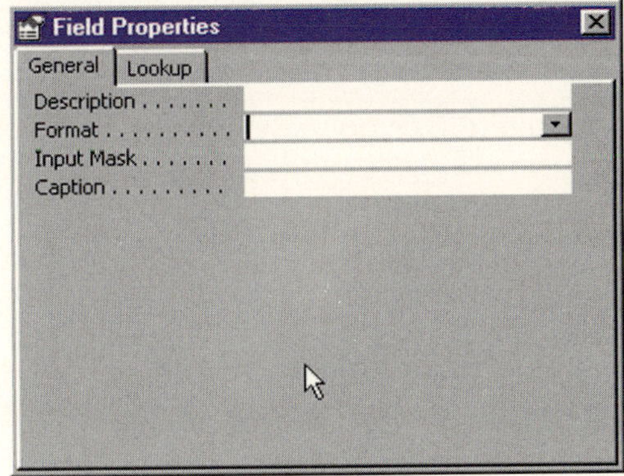

8 Click the drop-down list button. Drag the scroll bar until the Currency option is visible. Select Currency from the list.

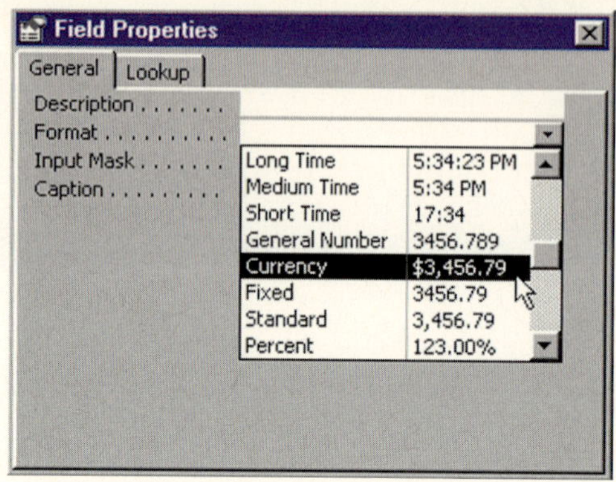

9 Close the Field Properties dialog box and run the query ! to view your changes. Adjust the view using the scroll bar if necessary.
Compare your results with the figure below. Note that the column title now reads "Member Fee" and that the data in that column is formatted for currency.

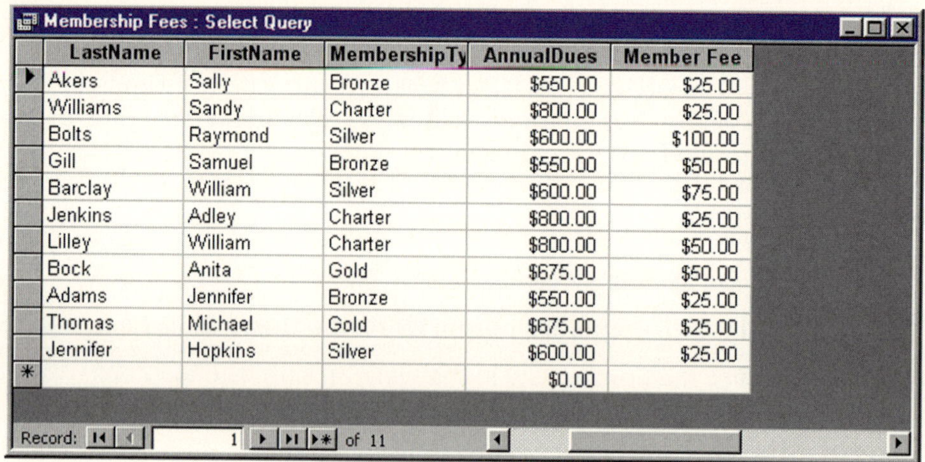
Membership Fees : Select Query

LastName	FirstName	MembershipTy	AnnualDues	Member Fee
Akers	Sally	Bronze	$550.00	$25.00
Williams	Sandy	Charter	$800.00	$25.00
Bolts	Raymond	Silver	$600.00	$100.00
Gill	Samuel	Bronze	$550.00	$50.00
Barclay	William	Silver	$600.00	$75.00
Jenkins	Adley	Charter	$800.00	$25.00
Lilley	William	Charter	$800.00	$50.00
Bock	Anita	Gold	$675.00	$50.00
Adams	Jennifer	Bronze	$550.00	$25.00
Thomas	Michael	Gold	$675.00	$25.00
Jennifer	Hopkins	Silver	$600.00	$25.00
			$0.00	

Record: 1 of 11

10 When you are finished, switch to Design view.

Building Additional Calculated Fields

You can create expressions in the Expression Builder in a variety of ways. One method is to type the expression directly in the upper pane of the Expression Builder dialog box.

> **Tip** You can also type expressions directly in the lower pane of the Query Design window when you know the proper syntax. Search for Expression in the Help system, and select the Creating topic. Then select the Create an expression topic.

TASK 6: TO BUILD AN EXPRESSION TO CALCULATE EACH MEMBER'S AGE:

1. Select the first row of the next available column in the query design grid.
2. Click the Build button on the Query Design toolbar.
3. Type **Current Age: DateDiff("d",[DateofBirth],Now())/365** as the expression in the upper portion of the Expression Builder.

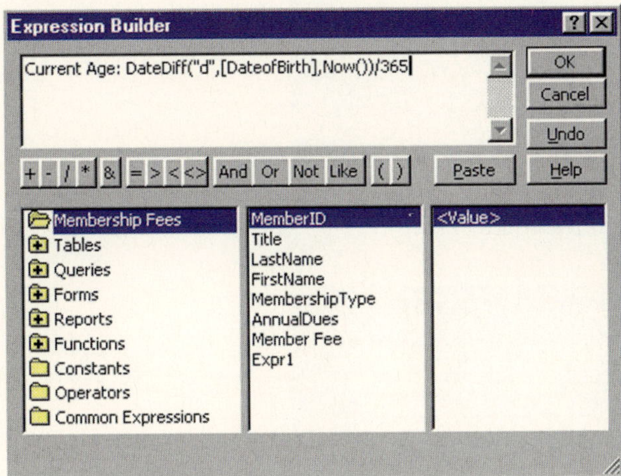

Hint This field calculates each member's current age, based upon his or her date of birth. For more information on the syntax for this expression, select Contents and Index from the Help menu, and search for DateDiff.

4. Click the OK button and run the query. Your results should be similar to those shown below. Note that the number of decimal places you see may differ.

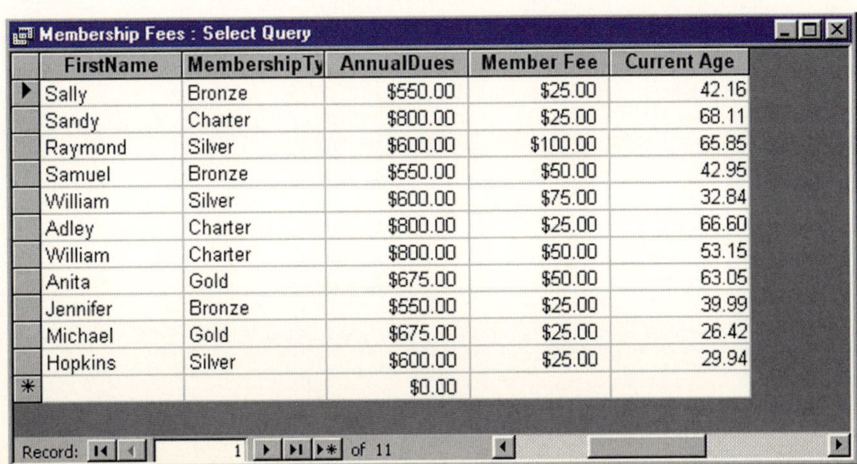

Membership Fees : Select Query

FirstName	MembershipTy	AnnualDues	Member Fee	Current Age
Sally	Bronze	$550.00	$25.00	42.16
Sandy	Charter	$800.00	$25.00	68.11
Raymond	Silver	$600.00	$100.00	65.85
Samuel	Bronze	$550.00	$50.00	42.95
William	Silver	$600.00	$75.00	32.84
Adley	Charter	$800.00	$25.00	66.60
William	Charter	$800.00	$50.00	53.15
Anita	Gold	$675.00	$50.00	63.05
Jennifer	Bronze	$550.00	$25.00	39.99
Michael	Gold	$675.00	$25.00	26.42
Hopkins	Silver	$600.00	$25.00	29.94
*		$0.00		

Record: 1 of 11

5. Click the View button to return to Design View. Click the Properties button on the Query Design toolbar.

6. Select Fixed as the format.

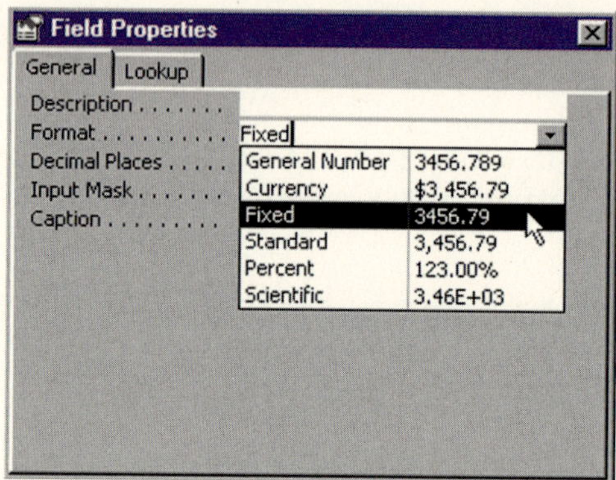

7. Set the decimal places to zero.

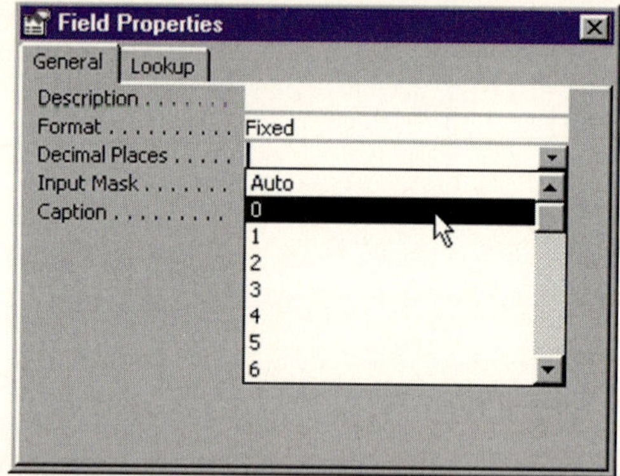

8. Close the Field Properties dialog box, and update the query design by saving the file.

9. Run the query. Use the scroll bar to display the results of the calculation.

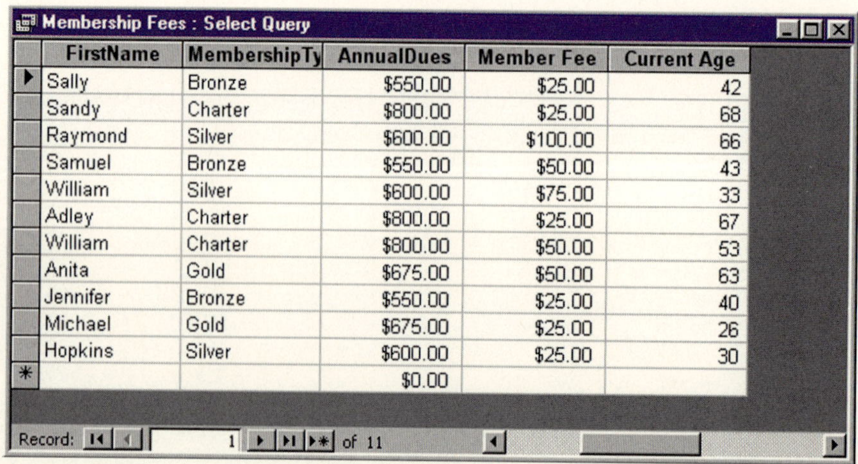

Membership Fees : Select Query

FirstName	MembershipTy	AnnualDues	Member Fee	Current Age
Sally	Bronze	$550.00	$25.00	42
Sandy	Charter	$800.00	$25.00	68
Raymond	Silver	$600.00	$100.00	66
Samuel	Bronze	$550.00	$50.00	43
William	Silver	$600.00	$75.00	33
Adley	Charter	$800.00	$25.00	67
William	Charter	$800.00	$50.00	53
Anita	Gold	$675.00	$50.00	63
Jennifer	Bronze	$550.00	$25.00	40
Michael	Gold	$675.00	$25.00	26
Hopkins	Silver	$600.00	$25.00	30
		$0.00		

Record: 1 of 11

Troubleshooting The expression you created uses the computer's system clock to calculate each member's current age. If your computer's clock is set differently, the values will change.

10. Switch to Design view.

TASK 7: TO BUILD AN EXPRESSION TO CALCULATE THE AGE DISCOUNT:

1. Select the first row of the next available column in the query design grid.
2. Click the Build button on the Query Design toolbar.
3. Type **Discount: IIf([Current Age]>=65,0.15*[AnnualDues],0)** as the expression in the Expression box of the Expression Builder.

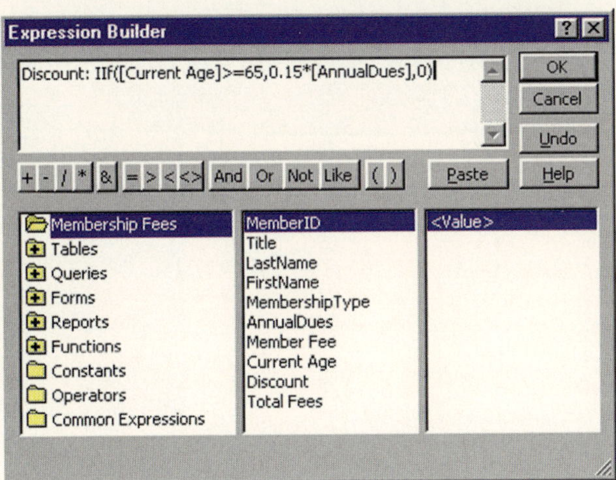

Tip This expression calculates a 15 percent discount for members who are 65 years of age or older, and no discount for members under 65 years of age.

4. Click OK to close the Expression Builder and run the query.
5. Switch to Design view and place the insertion point inside the Discount field. Click the Properties button. Select the Format row in the Field Properties dialog box.
6. Change the format to Currency.

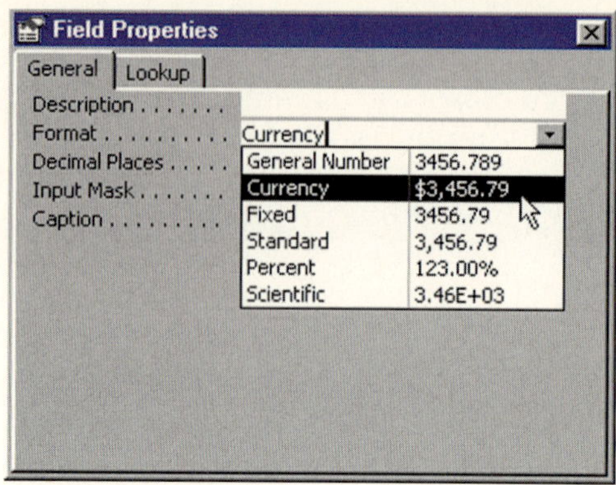

7 Close the Field Properties dialog box.

8 Run the query. The results should appear as shown below.

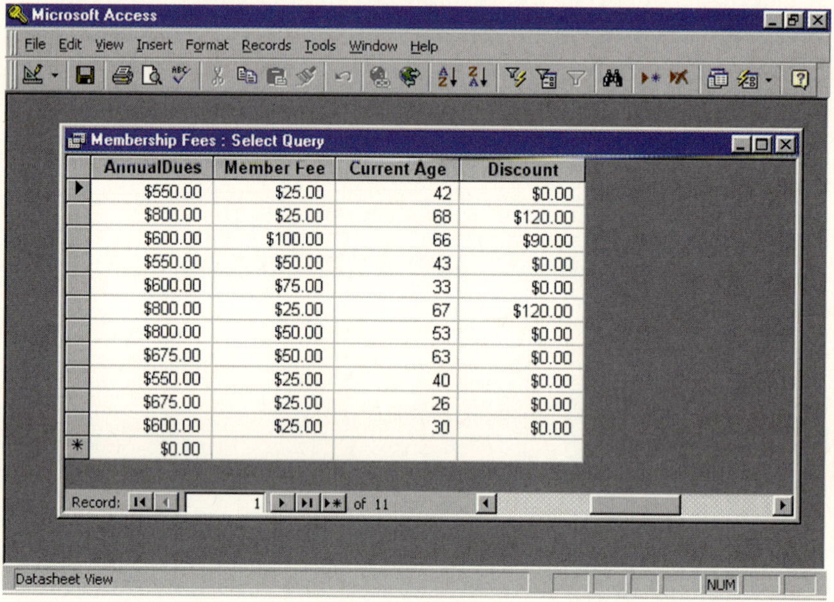

AnnualDues	Member Fee	Current Age	Discount
$550.00	$25.00	42	$0.00
$800.00	$25.00	68	$120.00
$600.00	$100.00	66	$90.00
$550.00	$50.00	43	$0.00
$600.00	$75.00	33	$0.00
$800.00	$25.00	67	$120.00
$800.00	$50.00	53	$0.00
$675.00	$50.00	63	$0.00
$550.00	$25.00	40	$0.00
$675.00	$25.00	26	$0.00
$600.00	$25.00	30	$0.00
$0.00			

9 Update your query by saving the file.

TASK 8: TO BUILD AN EXPRESSION TO CALCULATE THE TOTAL FEE FOR EACH MEMBER:

1 Select the first row of the next available column in the query design grid.

2 Click the Build button on the Query Design toolbar.

3 Type **Total Fees: [AnnualDues]+[Member Fee]-[Discount]** as the expression in the workspace of the Expression Builder.

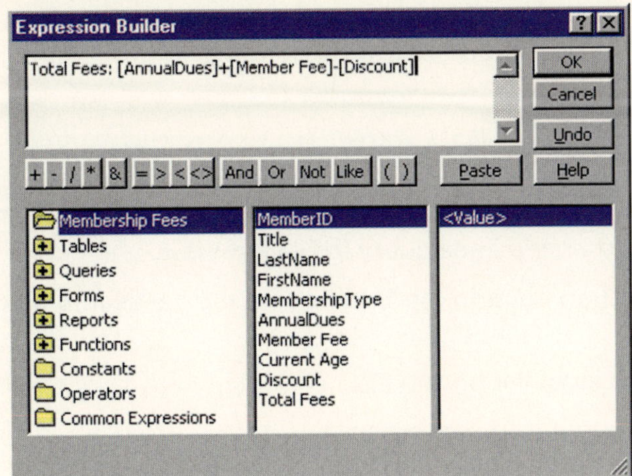

4. Click the OK button to close the Expression Builder.

5. Using the same procedure as in the previous task, change the format of this field to Currency.

6. Save your changes.

7. Run the query. Use the scroll bar in the datasheet window to display each of the calculated fields you created.

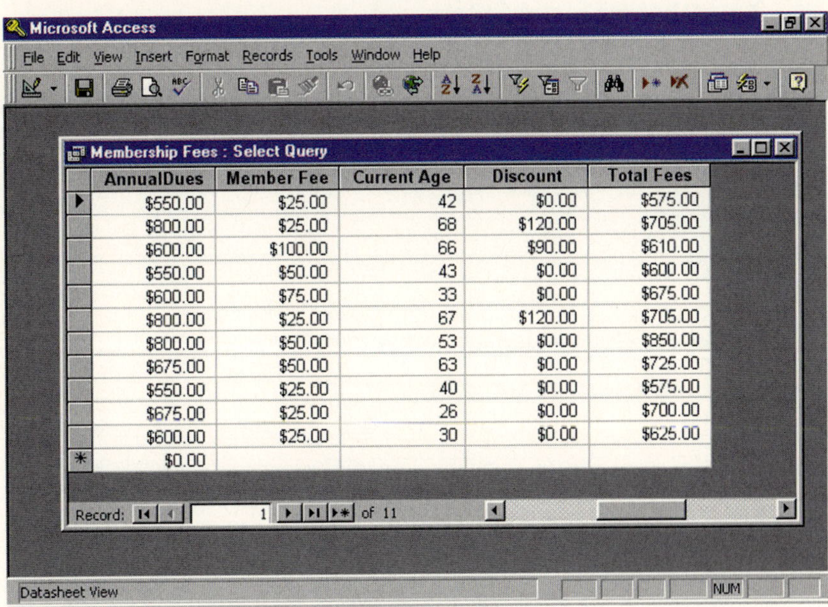

AnnualDues	Member Fee	Current Age	Discount	Total Fees
$550.00	$25.00	42	$0.00	$575.00
$800.00	$25.00	68	$120.00	$705.00
$600.00	$100.00	66	$90.00	$610.00
$550.00	$50.00	43	$0.00	$600.00
$600.00	$75.00	33	$0.00	$675.00
$800.00	$25.00	67	$120.00	$705.00
$800.00	$50.00	53	$0.00	$850.00
$675.00	$50.00	63	$0.00	$725.00
$550.00	$25.00	40	$0.00	$575.00
$675.00	$25.00	26	$0.00	$700.00
$600.00	$25.00	30	$0.00	$625.00
$0.00				

8. Close the query.

Defining the Sort Order and Criteria for a Query

You will frequently need to see records in a query that meet certain conditions and appear in a specific order. Remember that Mr. Gilmore requested a listing of the total fees for all charter members who also received a qualifying discount. He also wants this list alphabetized by last name. Query data can be sorted in either ascending or descending order.

TASK 9: TO ADD SORT ORDER AND FIELD CRITERIA TO THE QUERY DESIGN:

1. Open the Membership Fees query in Design View.
2. Place the insertion point in the Sort: row of the LastName field in the query design grid.
3. Click the drop-down list button ▾.
4. Select Ascending as the sort order.

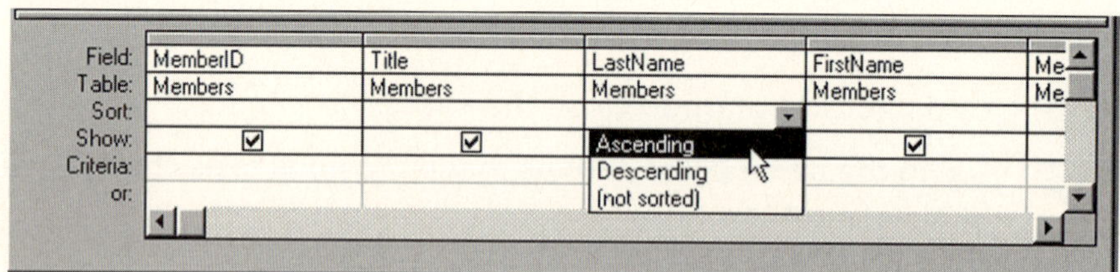

5. Use the scroll bar in the query design grid to display the MembershipType field.
6. Type **Charter** in the Criteria row.

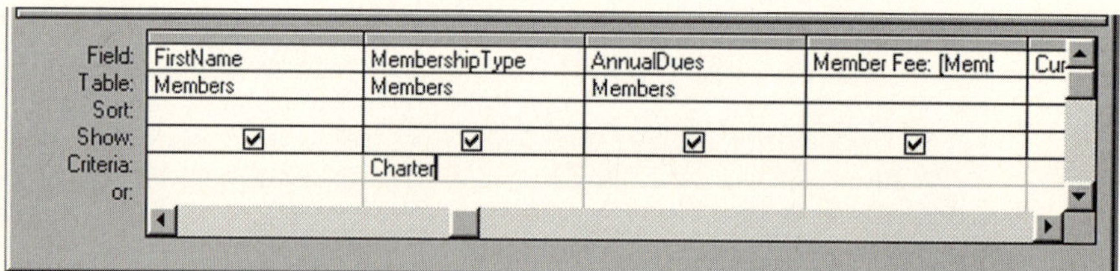

7. Use the scroll bar to display the Current Age calculated field.
8. Type **>=65** as the field criteria.

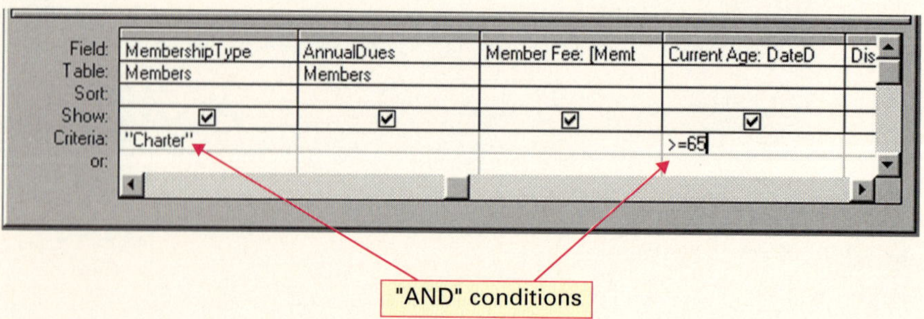

This is known as an ***AND condition***, since both conditions (records with Charter members who are not older than 65) must be met for any records to be returned. The criteria specifying an AND condition always occupy only one row in the Query Design window.

Tip You can also create OR conditions in Access, where records are returned that meet either one or the other condition. When constructing OR conditions, you will use more than one criteria row in the Query Design window. For more information, search for the topic *Ways to specify multiple criteria in a query* in the Access Help System.

9 Update the query design by pressing the save button on the toolbar and run the query. Two records meet the multiple conditions you specify.

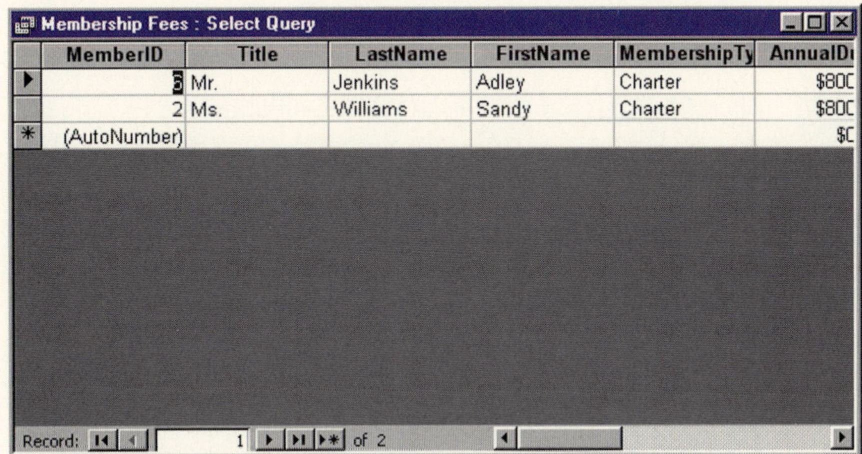

10 Use the scrollbar in the datasheet to verify that the conditions have been correctly met. When you are finished, close the query.

Creating an Autoform Based upon a Query

You can think of an Access query as being similar to a table because you can base other database objects upon it. Remember how easy it was to create a form based upon a table? It's just as easy to create an AutoForm from a query.

TASK 10: TO CREATE AN AUTOFORM BASED UPON THE *MEMBERSHIP FEES* QUERY:

1 Click the Forms tab in the Database window and then press New.

2 In the New Form dialog box, select AutoForm: Columnar as the form type, and select Membership Fees as the object upon which the query will be based.

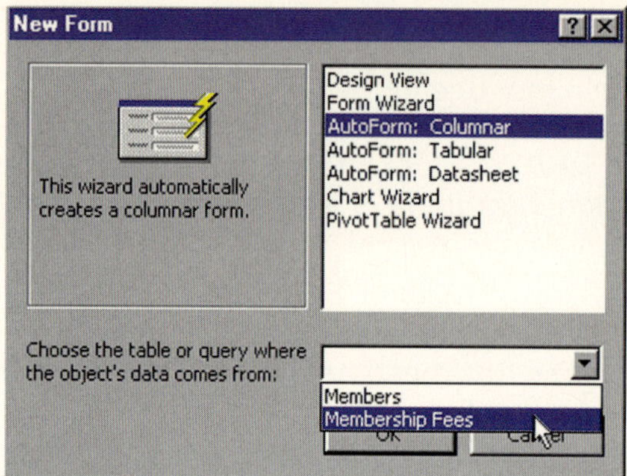

3 Click OK. After a moment, the form will appear.

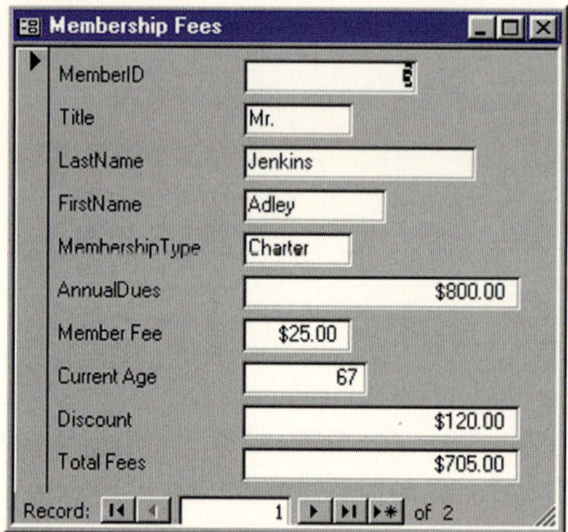

4 Close the form. Click Yes to save the changes, and accept the default name of Membership Fees

Tip By default, an AutoForm always uses the name of object upon which it was created as its own name.

5 Select Database Utilities from the Tools menu. Choose Compact Database from the cascading menu.

6 Close the Willows Membership database.

The Conclusion

As you can see, queries are much more powerful than filters for extracting information from a database. This is because in addition to supporting multiple criteria, queries can also include calculated fields that utilize the data stored in one or more tables to create additional fields. Calculated fields are not stored in the database, but are calculated whenever a query is displayed based on the commands that have been embedded in the query. Therefore, query results are always current even if users have changed information in the tables.

Summary and Exercises

Summary

- Queries are database objects that you use to view, change, and analyze data in different ways.
- Queries are often used as the source of records for forms and reports.
- A select query retrieves data from one or more tables and displays the results in a datasheet.
- You use the Query Design window to create queries in Access.
- The Query Design window consists of two panes — the upper pane contains a list of tables and fields; the lower pane contains the query design grid.
- Fields that appear in the query design grid return information in a query datasheet when the query is run.
- Queries can contain calculated fields that return data according to an expression.
- You can easily create expressions using the Expression Builder.
- You can add sort order and criteria specifications to return specific records in a specified order.
- A query object can be the source for an Access AutoForm.

Key Terms and Operations

Key Terms

AND condition
calculated field
expression
Expression Builder
query
query datasheet
query design grid
Query Design View
run
select query

Operations

add calculated fields to a query using the Expression Builder
add fields to a query using the query design grid
add tables to a query
create a new query
create an Autoform based upon a query
define the sort order and criteria for a query
run a query
specify sort order and criteria

Study Questions

Multiple Choice

1. The query design grid appears in the
   - **a.** Database window.
   - **b.** Query datasheet.
   - **c.** upper pane of the Query Design window.
   - **d.** lower pane of the Query Design window.

2. To sort the data returned by a query, you specify sort order in the
   a. Database window.
   b. query design grid.
   c. Query datasheet.
   d. upper pane of the Query Design window.

3. When you run a query based upon one table, the results are displayed in
   a. the Database window.
   b. a Query datasheet.
   c. a Table datasheet.
   d. the query design grid.

4. In Access, an AutoForm can be based upon
   a. tables only.
   b. queries only.
   c. tables and queries.
   d. neither tables nor queries.

5. Where do you add fields when designing a query?
   a. the Database window.
   b. the upper pane of the Query Design window.
   c. the query design grid.
   d. the query datasheet.

6. What do you use to create a calculated field in a query?
   a. an AND condition.
   b. an expression.
   c. a filter.
   d. an OR condition.

7. Which of the following statements is true?
   a. Select queries cannot be used to enter or edit field data in tables.
   b. Queries return records in a datasheet.
   c. Select queries do not reflect the most recent changes to an underlying table.
   d. Queries cannot be used as the source object for an Access form.

8. The expression =[Quantity]*[Cost] will most likely return the
   a. purchases made by an employee.
   b. total membership fee charged to a club member.
   c. total number of members belonging to a club.
   d. value of an inventory item.

9. Where is the data in a calculated field stored?
   a. The data comprising calculated fields are stored in the Database window.
   b. The data comprising calculated fields are stored in a query datasheet.
   c. The data comprising calculated fields are stored in a table.
   d. The data comprising calculated fields are not stored anywhere in a database.

10. Which of the following statements is false?
    a. Query results are returned in a datasheet.
    b. A query must be based upon one or more tables or another query.
    c. A query is similar to a filter in that it can be used to return specific records from a database.
    d. A query cannot be saved.

Short Answer

1. What is the query design grid?
2. What does the upper pane of the Query Design window display?
3. What do the columns in the query design grid represent?
4. How do you run a query?
5. What two options are available for sorting records returned by a query?
6. When you run a query, where is the data displayed?
7. How many criteria rows are required in the query design grid for an AND condition?
8. How do you specify conditions in a query?
9. What database objects can be used to create an AutoForm?
10. What kind of query returns data from one or more tables?

For Discussion

1. How does a query datasheet differ from a table datasheet?
2. What is a calculated field and where does it store data?
3. How do you specify the sort order for a query?
4. How does an AND condition differ from an OR condition?

Review Exercises

1. Enforcing referential integrity in table relationships

As you learned in this project, queries can be used to edit and modify data in the table or tables upon which a query is based. This can lead to potential problems in a database when data in two or more tables is related. By enforcing referential integrity, you can specify that tables related by a specific field MUST contain field data for the related field. In this exercise you will learn why referential integrity is important, and how to enforce referential integrity in table relationships. Complete the following steps:

1. Open the *Membership Payments.mdb* database from your floppy diskette.
2. Click the Relationships button on the Database toolbar.
3. Place the insertion point immediately over the line extending between the two tables.
4. Right-click to edit the relationship. Select Edit Relationship from the right-click menu.

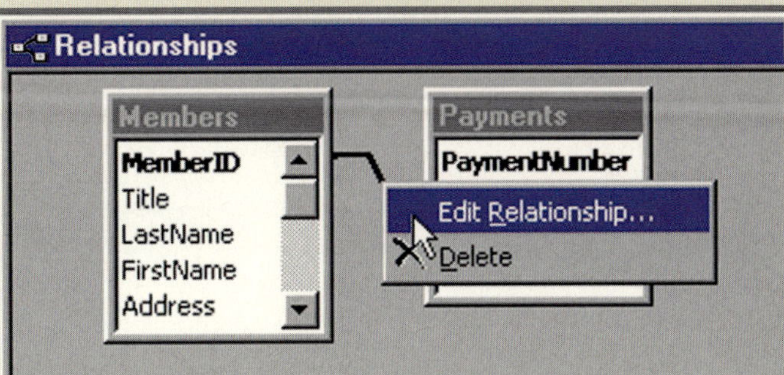

5. Click the Enforce Referential Integrity checkbox in the Relationships dialog box, which enforces referential integrity. Click OK.

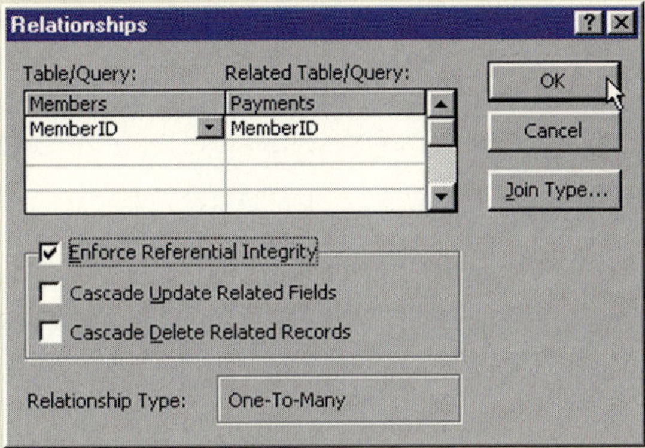

You will notice that the appearance of the line between the tables has changed. The graphical representation depicts a one-to-many relationship. In a one-to-many relationship, the related table (the "many" table) can contain one or more records that relate to the table on the "one" side of the relationship. In other words, there can be more than one payment record for each member.

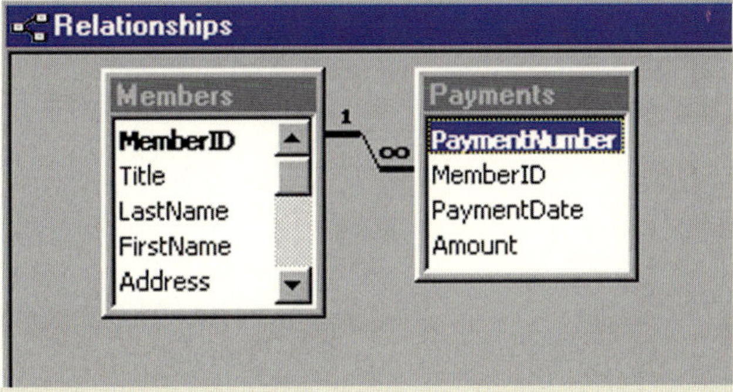

Enforcing referential integrity means that all records in the Payments table must have a MemberID entry that matches a primary key value in the *Members* table. Thus, you will never be able to enter a payment that is not related to a specific member.

6. Close the Relationships dialog box.
7. Close the database.

2. Creating a query based upon two tables

In this exercise you will see how a query can return data from more than one table. Complete the following:

1. Open the *Membership Payments.mdb* database.
2. Click the Queries tab in the Database window.
3. Click the New button and select Design View then press OK.
4. Select both tables, click the Add button, and click Close.

Tip You can select more than one table by dragging the pointer over all the tables you want to select, or pressing the SHIFT key as you click on the additional tables. Or you can click each table individually and then click the Add button after you have selected each one.

5. Add the MemberID field from the Payments table to the query design grid.
6. Add the LastName field to the query design grid from the Members table.
7. Add the PaymentDate and Amount fields to the query design grid from the Payments table.

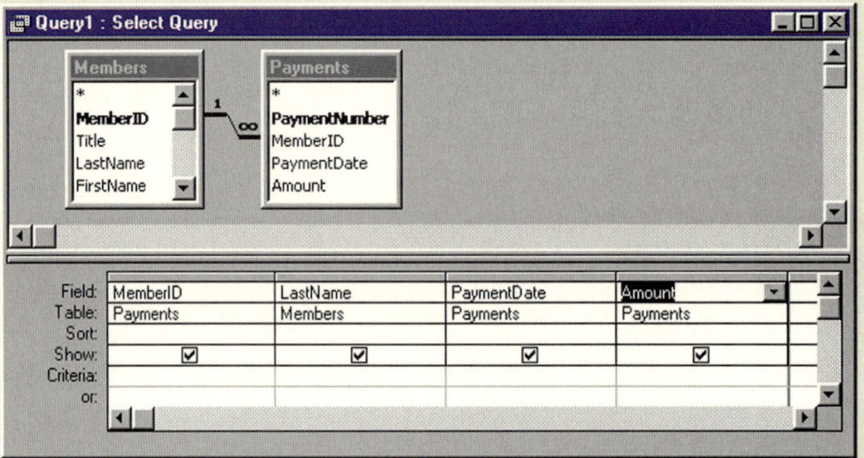

8. Click the Save button. Type **Payments (Query)** as the name for the query.

Tip A query cannot have the same name as an existing table object.

9. Run the query by pressing the Run button. Your screen should resemble the one shown in the next figure.

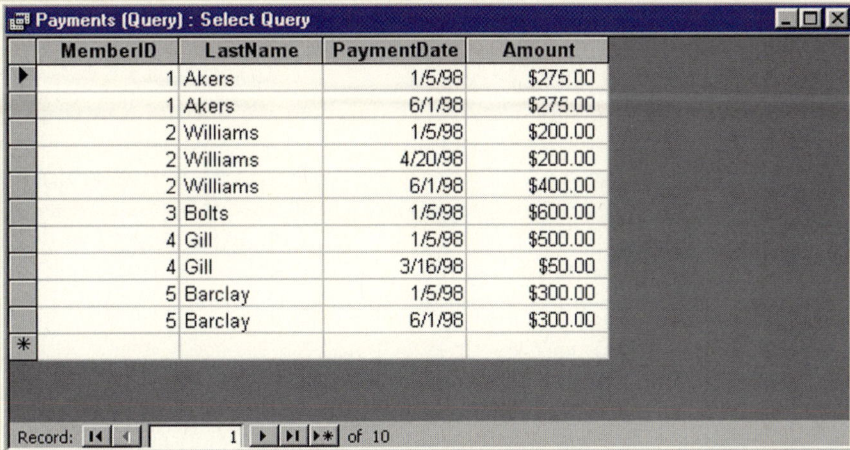
Payments (Query) : Select Query

MemberID	LastName	PaymentDate	Amount
1	Akers	1/5/98	$275.00
1	Akers	6/1/98	$275.00
2	Williams	1/5/98	$200.00
2	Williams	4/20/98	$200.00
2	Williams	6/1/98	$400.00
3	Bolts	1/5/98	$600.00
4	Gill	1/5/98	$500.00
4	Gill	3/16/98	$50.00
5	Barclay	1/5/98	$300.00
5	Barclay	6/1/98	$300.00

Record: 1 of 10

10. Close the query and the database.

3. Creating and running a query

1. Launch Access and open the *High Point Food Orders.mdb* database.

Tip If you do not have a database named *High Point Food Orders.mdb*, ask your instructor for a copy of the file you should use to complete this exercise.

2. Create a query that includes the *Food Categories* table and the *Food Products* table, that provides a list of each product by product category. Save the query using the query name **Food Products by Category**.
3. Run the query and print a copy of the query run.
4. Run the query again, sorting the product names alphabetically and print a copy of the query run.
5. Run the query again to obtain a list of beverages only; print a copy of the list.
6. Save the changes to the query design and close the database.
7. Exit Access.

Assignments

1. Creating a query containing an OR condition

Open the *Willow Employees.mdb* database file. Create a new query in design view based upon the Employees table. Add the SocialSecurityNumber, LastName, StateOrProvince, and Salary fields to the query design grid. Type **CO** in the first criteria row for the StateOrProvince field, and **CA** in the next criteria row (labeled "or") for this field. Save the query as **Current Salary for CO and CA**. Run the query. Only record for employees from either Colorado or California will be returned. After you view the results, close the query and the database.

2. Creating an AutoForm based upon a query

Open the *Web Sites.mdb* database file from your diskette. Create a new query named *Financial Services* that contain all fields but returns only those records in which the primary product is financial services. After you save this query, create an AutoForm based upon it. Save the AutoForm, close the database, and exit Access.

PROJECT 5

Creating and Modifying Forms

After you have designed tables and queries in a database, it is usually a good idea to create forms for users. Tables hold data, queries return data, and forms make it easy to work with records in a database. Most of the information in a form comes from an underlying record source—a table or query. Other information in the form is stored in the form's design.

Objectives

After completing this project, you will be able to:

- **Delete a form from a database and rearrange fields on a form**
- **Select and remove fields from a form**
- **Create a new form in Design View**
- **Add controls to a form in Design View**
- **Save a form**
- **Modify a form's controls**
- **Add unbound controls to a form**
- **Add a picture to a form**

The Challenge

Mr. Gilmore has reviewed the forms in your database. He wants you to create a new form listing information about members at the Willows that will be as easy as possible for the data entry team to use. He wants a simpler layout that has fewer descriptive labels. Finally, he wants the Willows logo to appear on the Members form.

The Solution

You can easily modify existing forms and create new ones using Form Design View. Rather than modifying the Members form, it is easier to delete the existing one and create a new one in Design View that will meet Mr. Gilmore's specifications. You can use Design View to add fields to a form, modify the appearance of the form and add the Willows logo. Figure 5.1 shows the form you will create in this project.

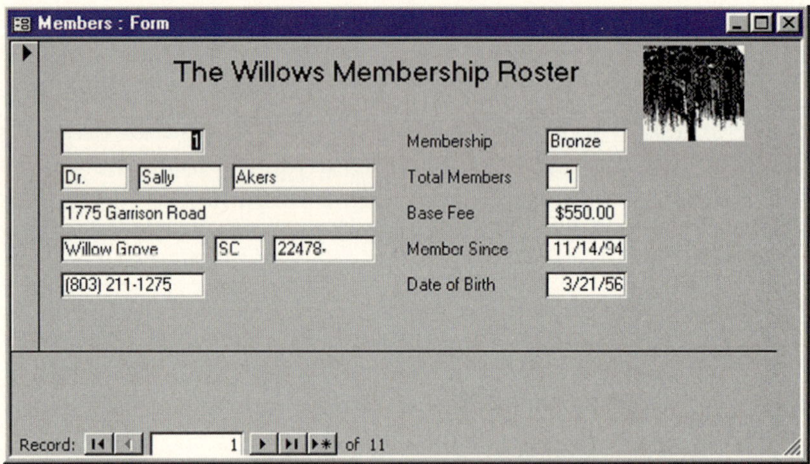

Figure 5.1

The Setup

After you launch Access and open your database, you should make sure the Database toolbar and the Status toolbar are displayed. These are the default settings in Access, but they may have been changed on your computer. (If you have forgotten how to do this, refer to Table 1.1 in Project 1.)

> **Troubleshooting** If you do not see the Database toolbar on the screen when you launch Access and open your database, choose Toolbars from the View menu. Select the Database toolbar to display it. If any additional toolbars are visible, close them. If you do not see the Status Bar at the bottom of the Application Window, choose Options from the Tools menu, click the View Page tab and change the Status Bar checkbox option.

Using the procedures you learned in Task 1 of Project 1, open the *Willows Membership.mdb* file from your floppy diskette.

Creating Forms

In Project 1 you used the Autoform Wizard to create the Members form that is currently in the database. Remember that a form is always based upon a ***record source***—a table or query that contains the records the form displays. You create the link between a form and its record source by using graphical objects called controls. A ***control*** is an object such as a text box that displays information in a form.

Although you have the option of modifying the current Members form in Design View, it is easier to delete the existing one and create a form in Form Design View.

TASK 1: TO DELETE AN EXISTING DATABASE FORM:

1. Click the Forms tab in the database window.
2. Select the *Members* form in the database window, if it is not currently highlighted.
3. Select Delete from the Edit menu or press the DELETE button on your keyboard.

Tip You can also delete a database object using the Cut button.

4. Click Yes when you are asked for confirmation.

Troubleshooting Make sure you have selected the Members form, as you cannot reverse this action with Undo!

The form is no longer visible in the database window.

Creating a New Form in Design View

You are now ready to create a form. As you will see, Access provides numerous tools for creating a form in Design View. As with tables and queries, you create a form by adding controls to the form's ***Detail section***, which is the area of the Form Design window that appears when you create a new form in ***Design View***.

TASK 2: TO CREATE A NEW FORM USING DESIGN VIEW:

1. Click the New button in the Form tab of the database window.
2. Select Design View to create a form without using a Wizard, and base the form upon the *Members* table.

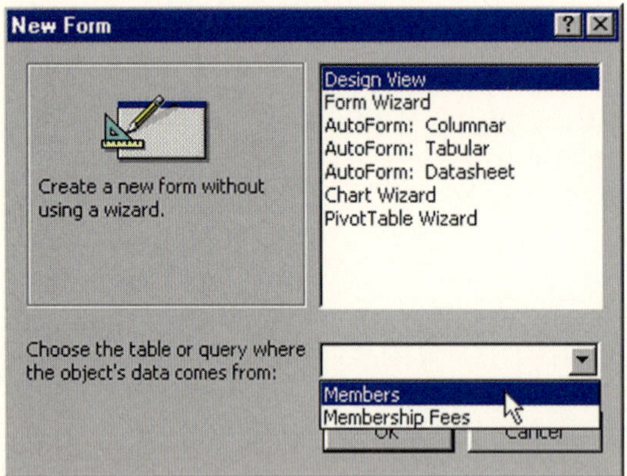

3. A blank form will appear in Form Design View.

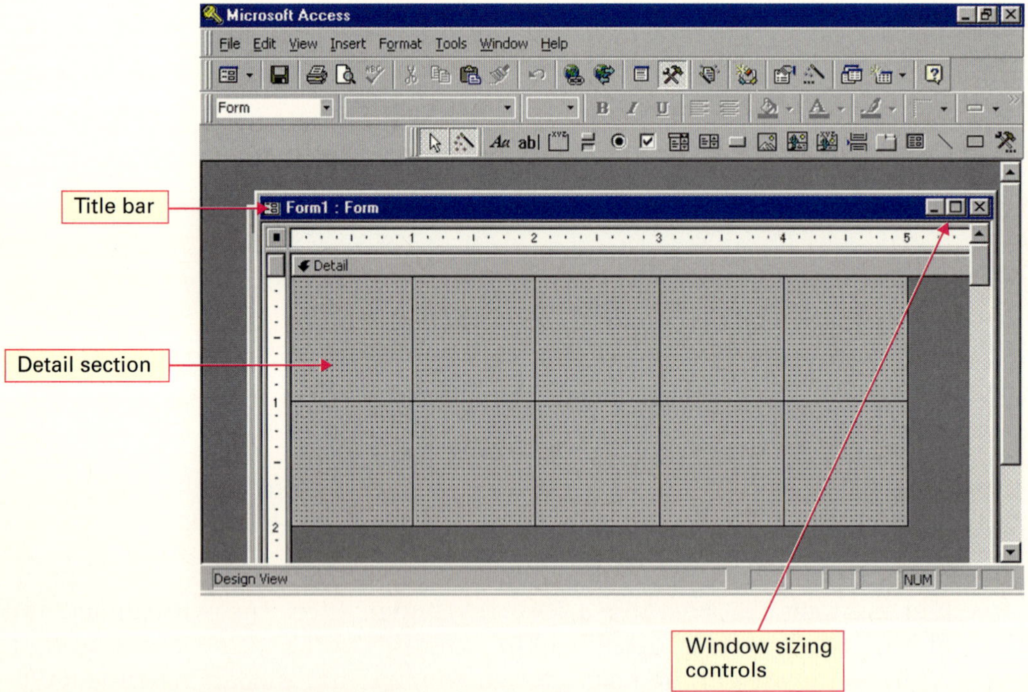

Note that a default name for the form appears in the form's title bar. The form design window contains the standard buttons in the upper right-hand corner for minimizing, maximizing, and closing the form. You will add form controls in the Detail section.

4. Click the Maximize button in the form's Title bar.

TASK 3: TO ADD CONTROLS TO THE FORM:

1. Click the Field List button on the Form Design toolbar.
2. Resize the Field List box so that all field names are visible.
3. Click the MemberID field name to select it. While holding the left mouse button, begin to drag the field name toward the form's Detail section. Notice that as you drag, the mouse pointer changes to a graphic representation of the field.

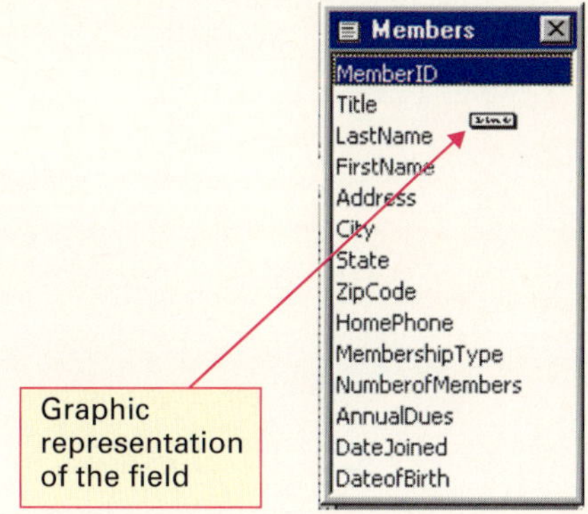

4. Drag the MemberID field into the upper left portion of the Detail section.
5. Release the mouse button. Two controls appear on the form.

Notice that both controls contain MemberID. The control on the right is a ***bound control***, which means that it is bound, or linked to a specific database object (in this case, a field). The leftmost control is a ***label control,*** which displays descriptive text. The bound control is a ***text box control***, which is used to display or enter field data from the underlying table or query.

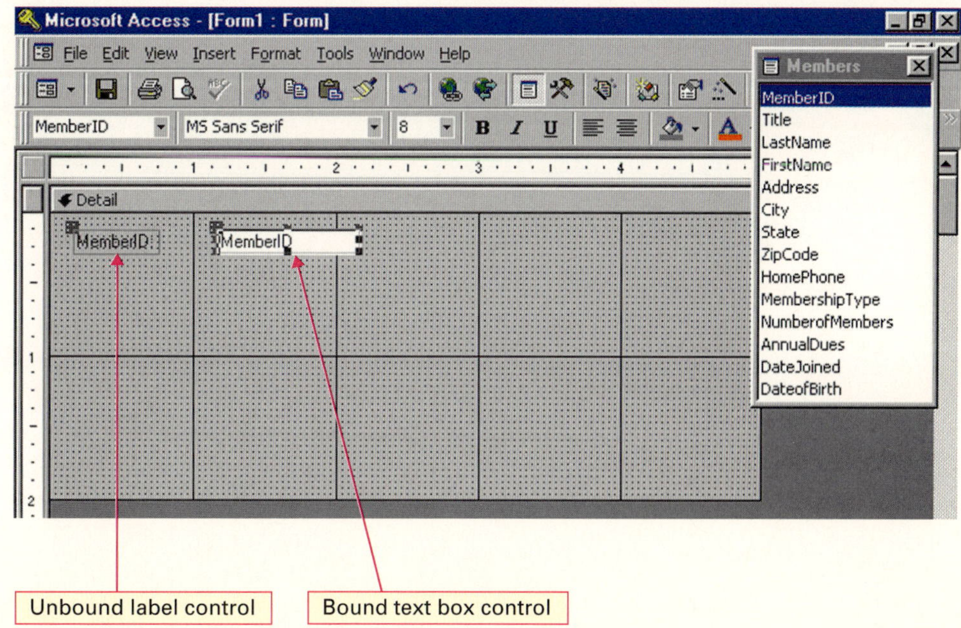

6 Using the same procedure as in the previous step, drag the remaining controls to the detail section of the form, approximately in the positions shown below.

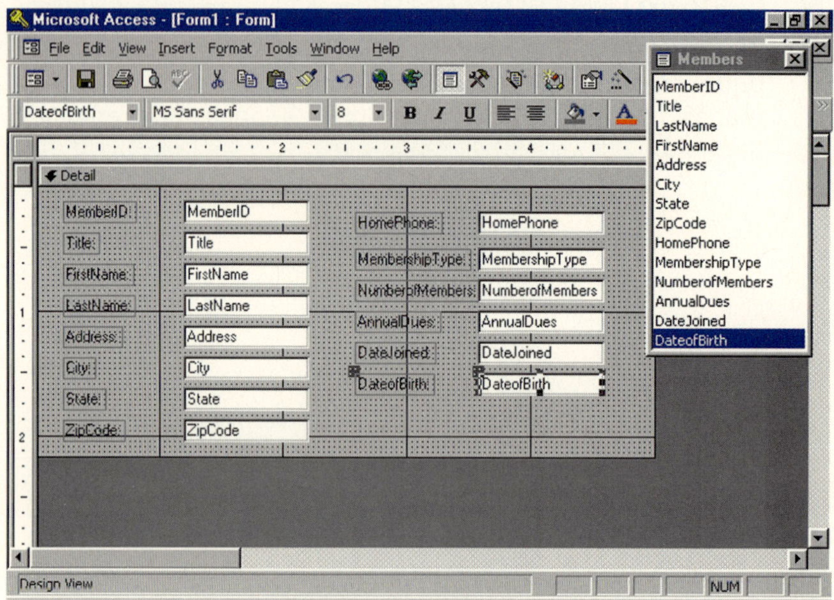

Troubleshooting Be careful not to place controls too close to the side of the form or the controls may overlap. Also, as you move the controls on the form you will notice that the label and the text box for each field move as a unit. If you inadvertently click the square selection handle in the upper-left portion of each control, it will move independently of the associated control.

TASK 4: TO SAVE THE FORM AND SWITCH TO FORM VIEW:

1 Save the form. Type **Members** in the Save As dialog box, and click OK.

2 Click the View button on the Form Design toolbar. The form displays the first record in the *Members* table in Form view.

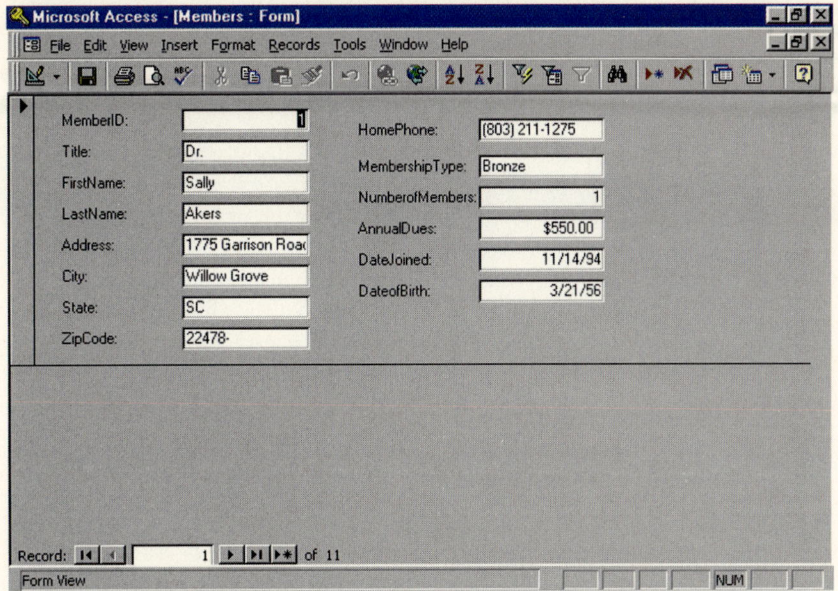

Tip The form is maximized, because you maximized the Form Design window.

3 Click the View button on the Form View toolbar to return to Design View.

Modifying a Form's Controls

Form Design View gives you complete control over the location and format of each control on a form. After you add controls to a form in Design View, the next step in designing a form is modifying the controls.

Some of the labels appearing on the Members form are not really necessary, and the size and location of each textbox should be changed as well. In the tasks that follow you will delete some of the labels on the form and change the text property of others. You will also reposition the text box controls to make the form easier to read. Finally, you will add a ControlTip to the text boxes that no longer have labels. A ***ControlTip*** is a descriptive message that appears when you move the mouse pointer over a control.

TASK 5: TO DELETE LABEL CONTROLS FROM THE MEMBERS FORM:

1 Move the mouse pointer over the MemberID label.

2 Click the left mouse button. The control is now selected. You can tell that it is selected because the sizing handles appear.

3 Click the Cut button on the Form Design toolbar.

4 Click the Title label. While holding the SHIFT key, click the FirstName, LastName, Address, City, State, ZipCode, and HomePhone labels.

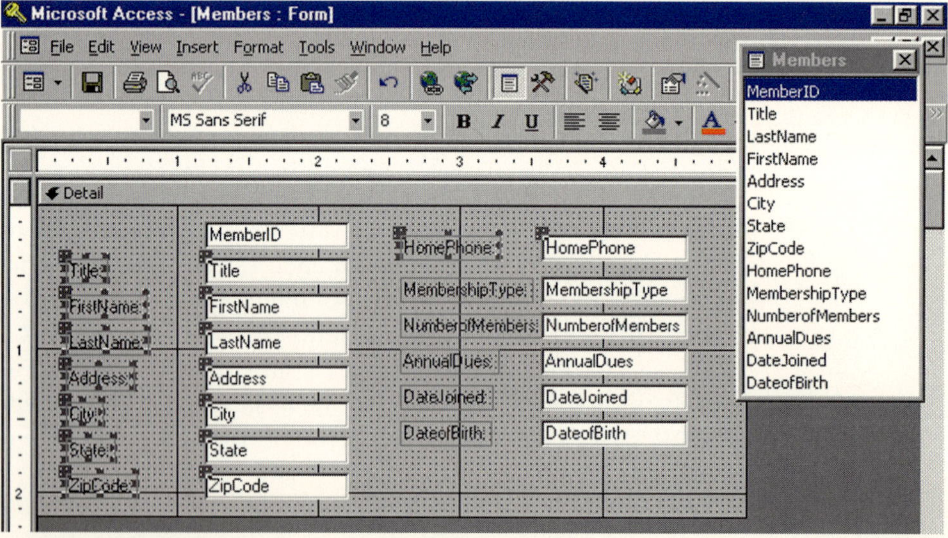

5 Select Cut.

6 Click the Close button on the field list to close it. The results of these actions are shown on the next page.

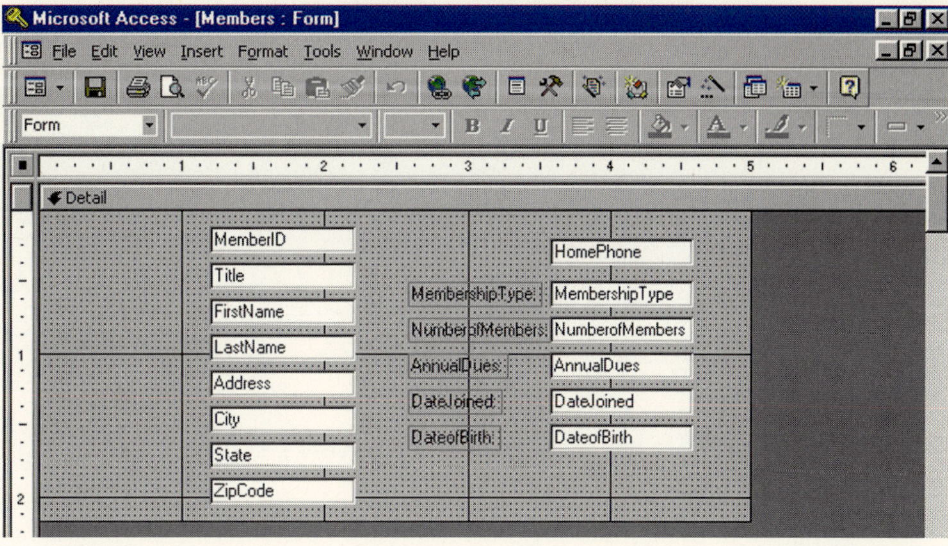

7 Save your changes [Save button].

TASK 6: TO REPOSITION TEXT BOX CONTROLS ON THE FORM:

1 Select the MemberID text box and move the insertion point to an edge until the pointer changes to a hand. You may now reposition the text box.

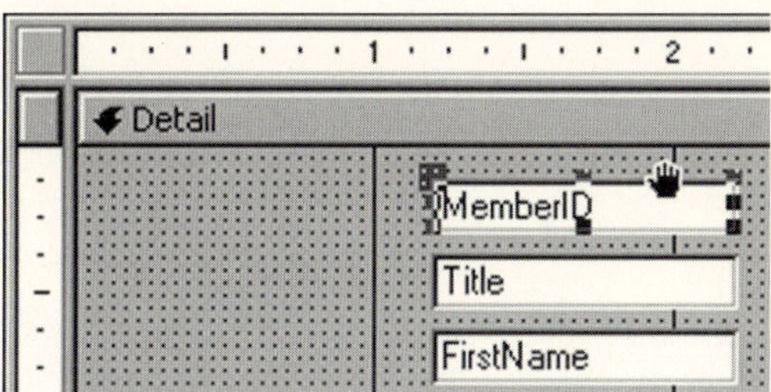

2 Move the MemberID text box to the left and below its present position.

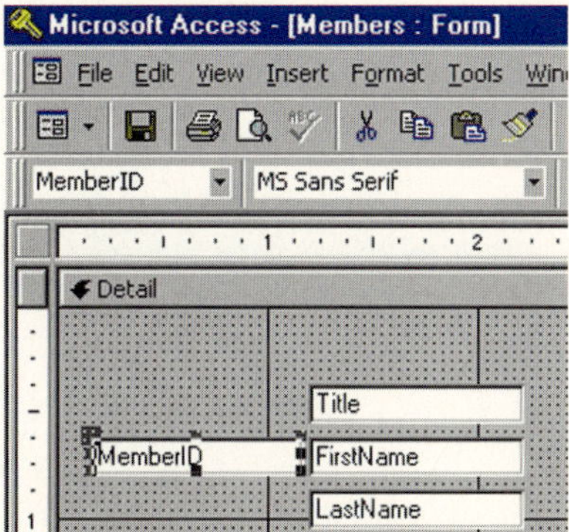

3 Move the Title text box immediately below the MemberID control.

4 With the text box still selected, move the insertion point over the selection handle on the right border of the text box until the resizing double arrow appears.

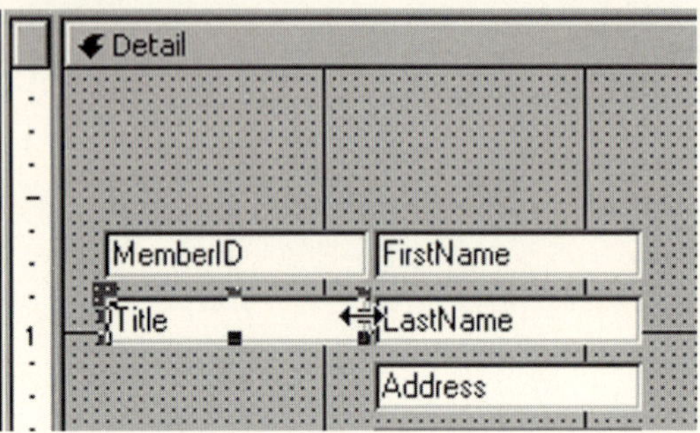

5 Use the left mouse button to resize the control.

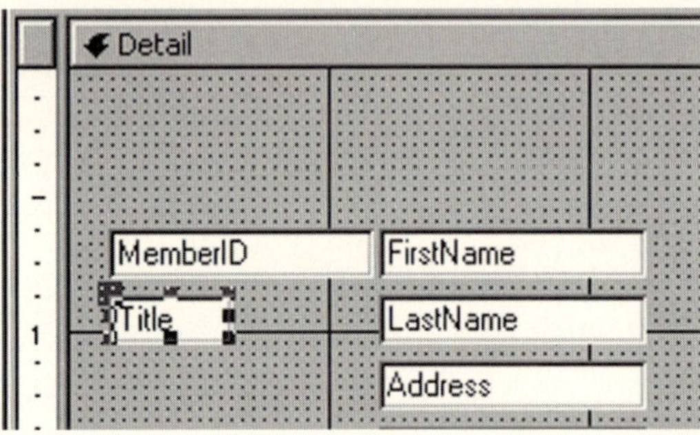

6 Using the figure below as a guide, reposition and resize the remaining controls as shown.

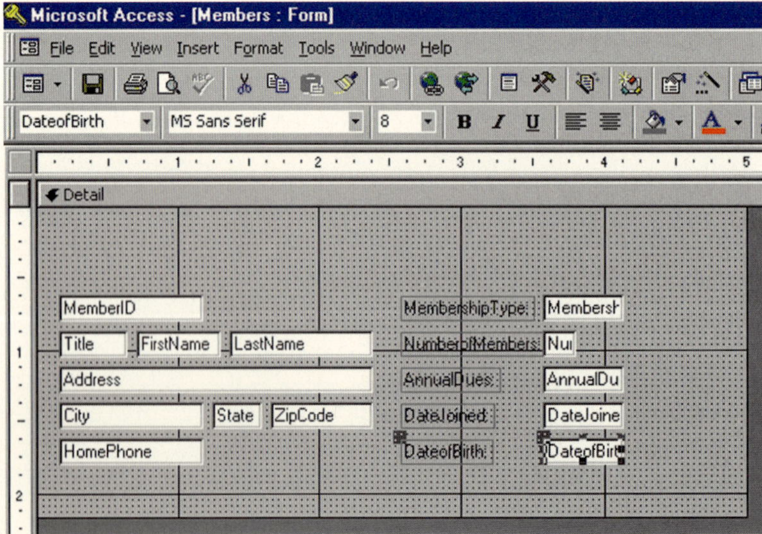

7 Click the Restore button in the Form's Title bar.

8 Resize the form as shown.

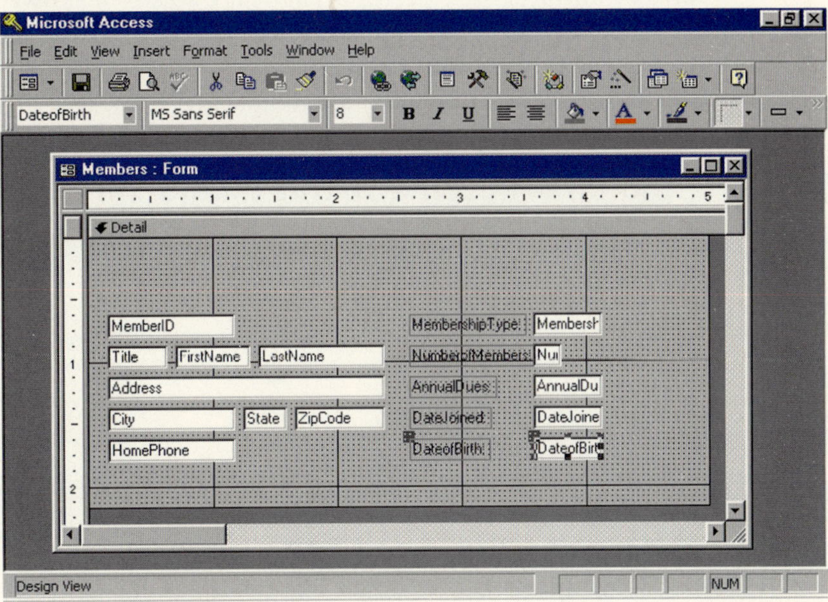

9 Click the View button to view your changes .

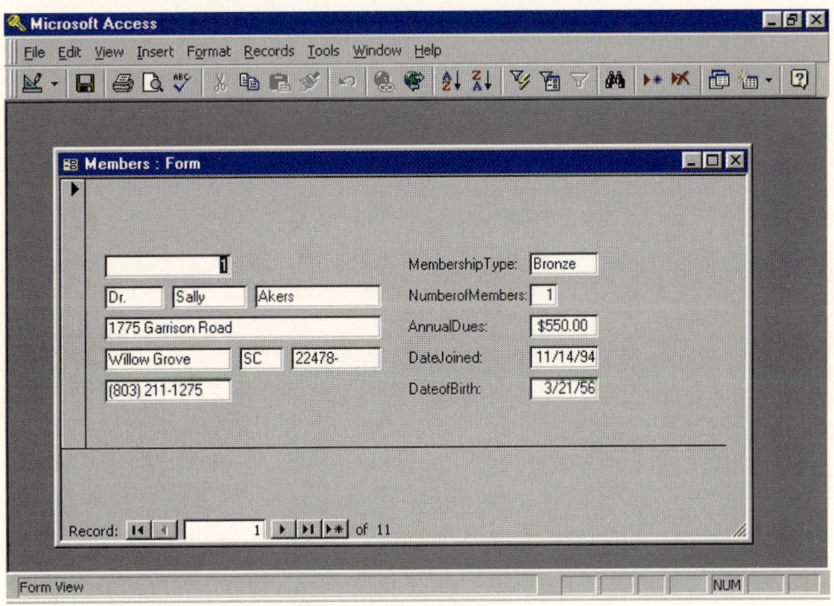

10 Save your form and switch to Form Design View.

Using ControlTips to Improve Data Accuracy

When the form displays a record, you can see from the field data which control is bound to which field. If you were to add a new record, you may not know exactly what to enter into some of the text boxes. A ControlTip tells users exactly what information to enter into a text box control when a form is used to add records to a database.

TASK 7: TO ADD CONTROLTIPS TO THE MEMBERS FORM:

1 Select the Title text box and click the Properties button on the Form Design toolbar.

2 Select the Other tab, and place the insertion point inside the ControlTip Text row.

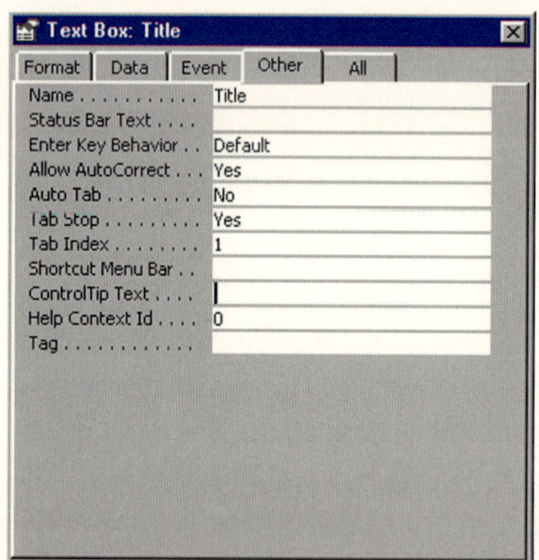

3 Type **Enter the Member's Title Here** in the row.

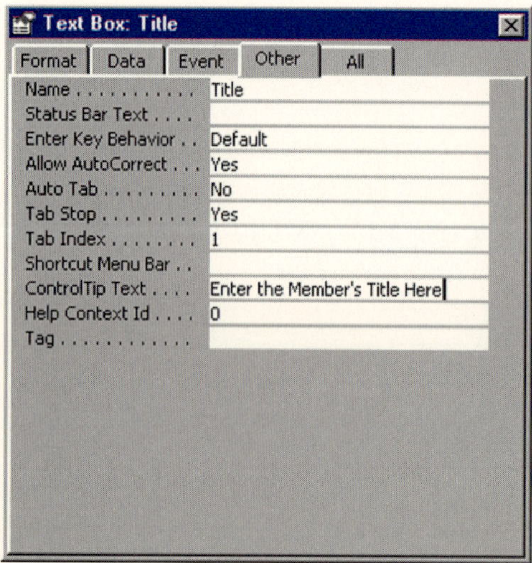

4 Close the Properties dialog box and switch to Form View.

5 Move the insertion point over the Title text box to see the ControlTip. Your screen should display the control tip shown in the next figure.

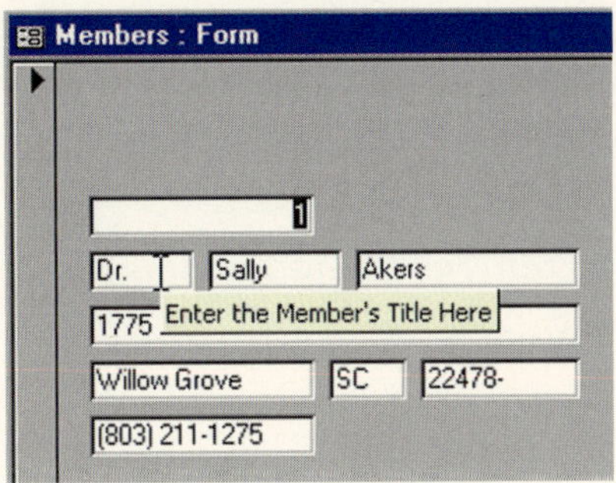

6 Switch to Design View.

7 Using the same procedure as in Steps 1–5, add a ControlTip to the FirstName, LastName, Address, City, State, ZipCode, and HomePhone text box controls. Type the appropriate field name in the text for the ControlTip.

8 Save your changes to the form.

Adding and Modifying Unbound Controls

Remember that a text box control is a bound control because it is bound, or linked to a specific record source. Labels, however, are ***unbound controls***, because they do not return data from a table or a query. Unbound controls are often used to add descriptive information to a form.

Working with Unbound Label Controls

When you added fields to the form using the field list, Access created a label to accompany each bound text box control. The text for each label corresponds to the name of the field the text box displays. You will now modify the text in the existing labels, and add a label control as a title for the form.

TASK 8: TO MODIFY EXISTING LABELS AND ADD A LABEL CONTROL:

1 Select the MembershipType label. Selection handles will appear on each of the label's borders.

2 Place the insertion point immediately after the letter *p* in the caption, and click the left mouse button.

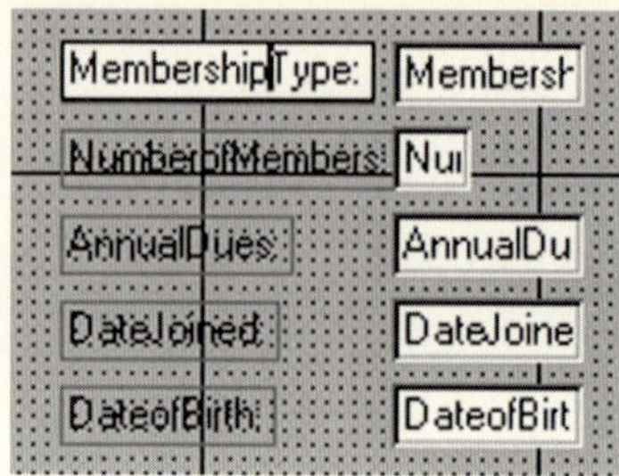

3 Press the (DEL) key five times to remove the remaining characters.

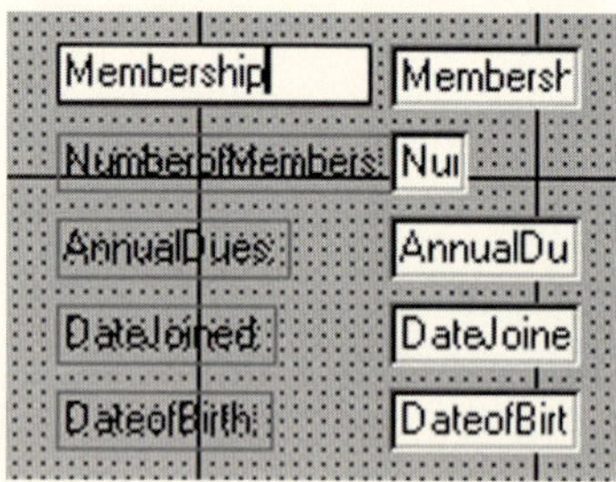

4 Using the same procedure, change NumberOfMembers: to Total Members, AnnualDues: to Base Fee, DateJoined to Member Since, and DateofBirth to Date of Birth. Note that the label width changes with your alterations.

5 Click the Toolbox button if it is not currently visible.

Troubleshooting The Toolbox may appear either as a docked toolbar, which is fixed at the top, bottom, or side of the Form Design window, or in an undocked state, and "float" anywhere within the Form Design window.

6 Click the Label button in the Toolbox.

7 Click inside the upper-left portion of detail section of the form, and drag the control down and to the right, approximately to the position shown in the figure below.

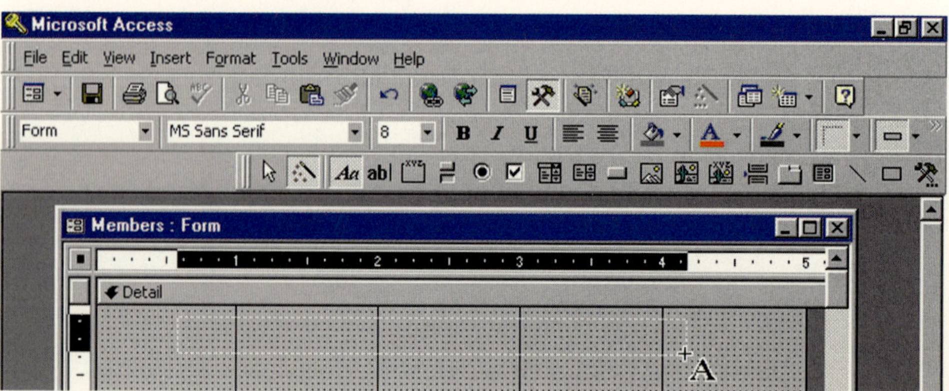

8 Release the mouse button. Type **The Willows Membership Roster** as the caption for the label and press (ENTER).

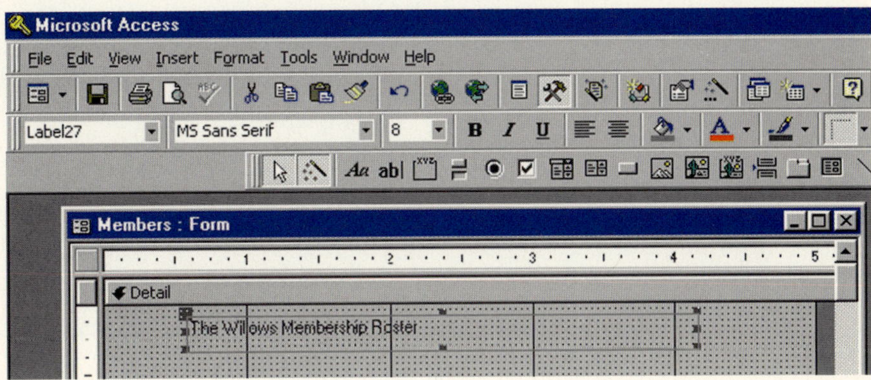

9 With the label control still selected, open the Properties dialog box. In the Format tab, change the Font Size property to 14 and the Text Align property to Center. You may have to scroll down in order to see these two properties.

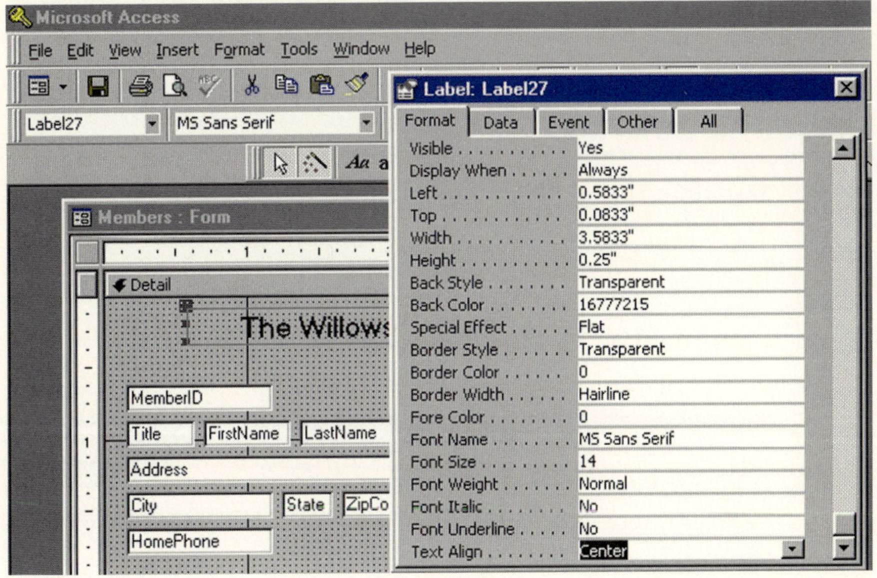

Tip Many of the properties can be set using a drop-down list. Click inside the property row to display the drop-down list button.

10 Save your changes. Now view the form. Your screen should look similar to the next figure.

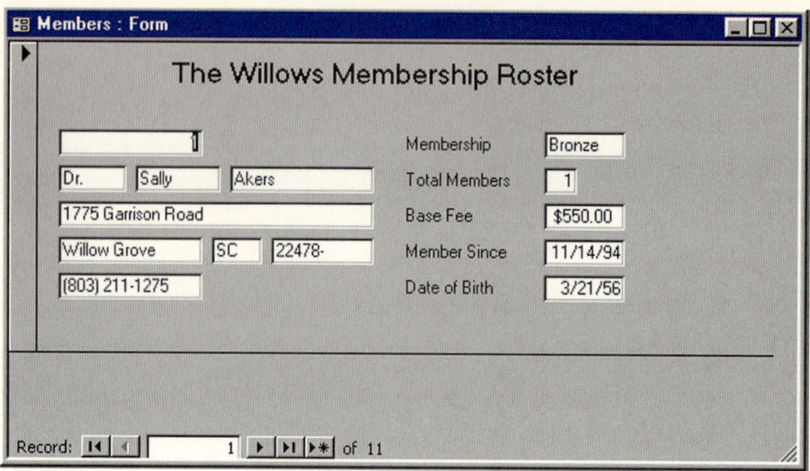

Adding an Image to the Form Using an Unbound Control

You can enhance the appearance of a form by adding an image to it. If the image will not need to be updated, you can insert or embed it into the form using an unbound image control, and the picture is stored with the database. An ***image control*** displays the embedded image file.

TASK 9: EMBEDDING AN IMAGE INTO THE FORM USING AN UNBOUND CONTROL:

1. Switch to Design View .
2. Close the Properties dialog box.
3. Select the image control from the Toolbox.
4. Drag an image control immediately to the right of the form's label.

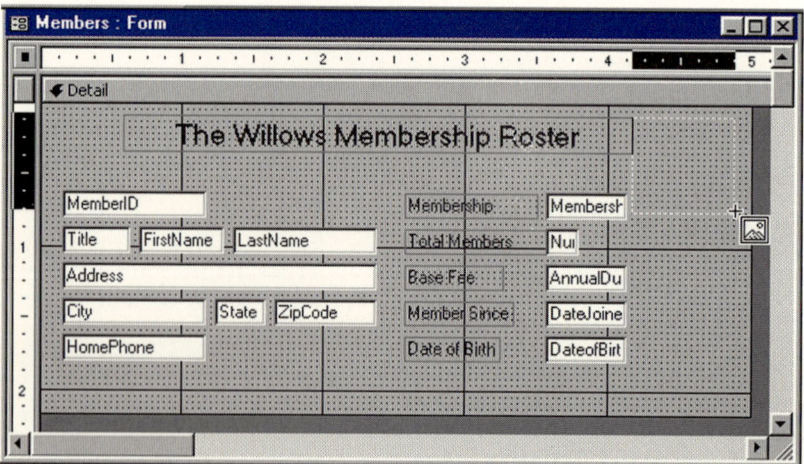

5. In the Insert Picture dialog box, select the *Willow.bmp* file from your diskette. Click OK.

Troubleshooting If you do not have a copy of the *Willow.bmp* file on your diskette, ask your instructor where it can be found.

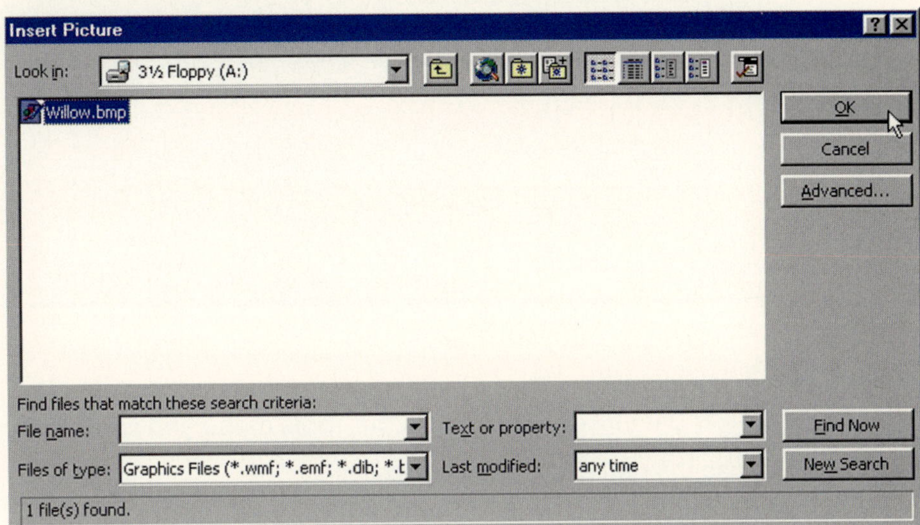

6 Position the image control as necessary using the method illustrated below.

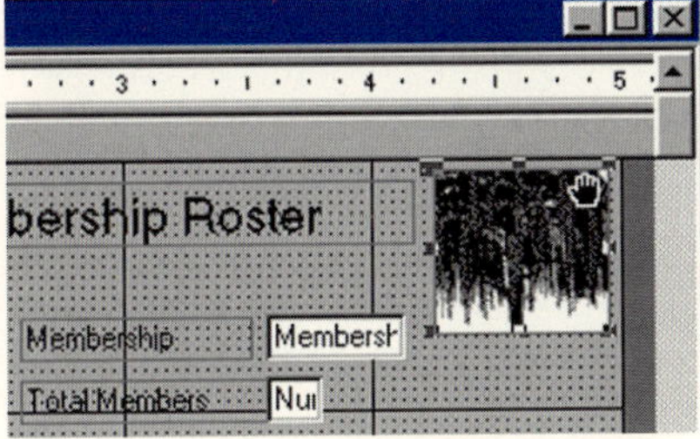

7 Update the form and switch to Form View . Your form should look similar to the one shown on the next page.

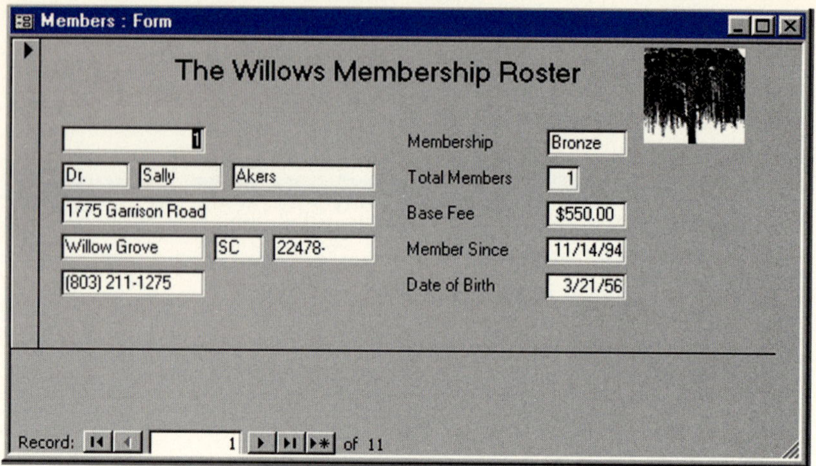

8. Close the form.
9. Select Database Utilities from the Tools menu and compact the database.
10. Close the database and exit Access.

The Conclusion

Mr. Gilmore should be pleased with how you have redesigned the Members form. Not only is the layout more visually appealing than the AutoForm you created in Project 1, but it is more user-friendly as well, because the ControlTips will assist users in entering the appropriate information in the form when it is used for data entry.

Summary and Exercises

Summary

- You have a great deal of flexibility in how you create a form using Design View.
- Forms often contain both bound and unbound controls.
- Bound controls are linked to an underlying record source such as a table or a query.
- Unbound controls are typically used to add descriptive information to a form.
- When a form will be used to enter data into a record source, ControlTips are useful for providing instructions for users.
- You can embed an image in a form using an unbound image control.

Key Terms and Operations

Key Terms

bound control
control
ControlTip
detail section
Form Design View
image control
label control
record source
text box control
unbound control

Operations

add fields to a form
add unbound controls to a form
create a new form using Design View
delete a form
embed an image in a form using an unbound control
modify bound controls
view a form

Study Questions

Multiple Choice

1. Which form element displays a message when a mouse drifts over a text box control?
   - **a.** label control
   - **b.** image control
   - **c.** bound control
   - **d.** ControlTip

2. To add controls to a form, you use
   - **a.** Form View.
   - **b.** the Toolbox.
   - **c.** Design View.
   - **d.** both B and C.

3. In Access, a form typically
   - **a.** is bound to a field.
   - **b.** is based upon a record source.
   - **c.** uses another form as its record source.
   - **d.** contains only unbound controls.

4. You can easily add fields to a form using
   a. the Toolbox.
   b. Form View.
   c. the field list.
   d. the View button.

5. Label controls are used to display
   a. descriptive text.
   b. data that is bound.
   c. field data.
   d. images or graphics.

6. A form displays records in
   a. Form Design View.
   b. Form Datasheet View.
   c. the database window.
   d. Form View.

7. To embed an image on a form, you generally use a
   a. label control.
   b. text box control.
   c. image control.
   d. bound control.

8. Which of the following statements is false?
   a. Label controls can be deleted from a form.
   b. A label can be resized on a form.
   c. A label can be moved on a form using the mouse.
   d. A label is a bound control.

9. You created a form using Form Design View and specified a table as the form's data source. How many record sources does the form have?
   a. one
   b. two
   c. four
   d. eight

10. A form can be based upon all except which of the following?
   a. a table
   b. a query
   c. a table and a query
   d. a form.

Short Answer

1. What do you use to add fields to a form in Design View?
2. What kind of control do you use to add descriptive text to a form?
3. What database objects can be used to create a form?
4. A text box is which kind of control?
5. What screen element assists in adding fields to a form?
6. Where do you find the tools you need to add controls to a form?
7. Do you use a bound or an unbound control to display field data?

8. A label is which kind of control?
9. The data in a form is displayed on the screen using which view?
10. What kind of control is used to display a bitmap graphic on a form?

For Discussion

1. How does Form Design View differ from Query Design View and Table Design View?
2. How do you remove controls from a form?
3. How do bound controls differ from unbound controls?
4. What is a ControlTip? Why is it sometimes helpful to include ControlTips on a form?

Review Exercises

1. Creating a form with data from two tables

At times you will want to create a form that contains controls bound to more than one table. For instance, the query you created in the Membership Payments database creates a record source based upon fields from two tables. In this exercise you will create a form with controls bound to that record source. You will then print the form. Complete the following:

1. Open the *Membership Payments.mdb* database file from your diskette.
2. Click the Forms tab, then click the New button.
3. Create a form in Design View using the Payments (Query) query as the record source as shown below. Click OK.

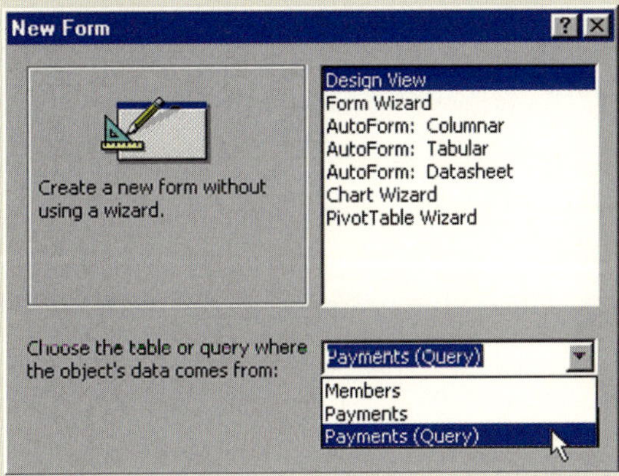

4. Add a label control at the top of the form. Type **Membership Payments** as the caption for the label. Change the Font Size property to 14 and the Text Align property to Center. Close the Properties dialog box.

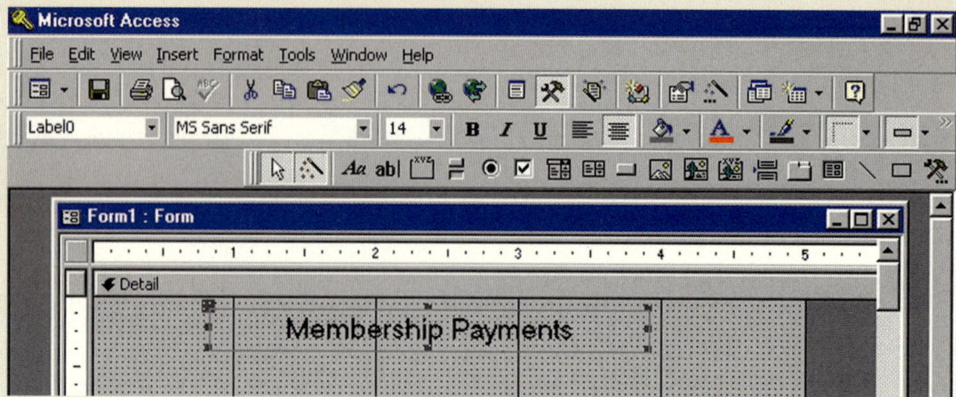

5. Display the Field List. Add the MemberID, LastName, PaymentDate, and Amount fields to the form. Modify the position of each control and resize the form as necessary.
6. Save the form design. Type **Membership Payments** as the name for the form.
7. Switch to Form View to view the form. It should look similar to the form shown in the figure below.

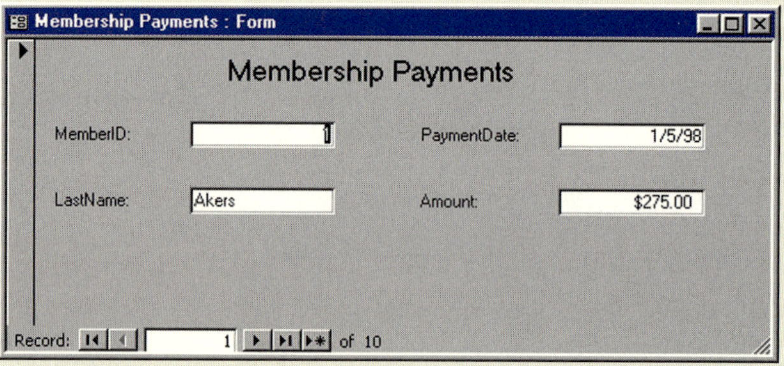

8. Click the Print button on the Form View toolbar to print the form.
9. Close the form.
10. Close the database.

2. Creating a main form with a subform using the Form Wizard

At times you will want to display multiple records in one table that relate to one record in another table. Recall from Review Exercises 1 in Project 4 that in a one-to-many relationship the related table (the "many" table) can contain one or more records that relate to the table on the "one" side of the relationship. You can display records from one table in a one-to-many relationship by creating one form that displays a single record and by creating a subform that contains one or more related records in another table. In this exercise you will create a form that lists each member in the Member Payments database. This form will include a subform that displays each member's payments.

1. Open the *Membership Payments.mdb* database file from your diskette.
2. Click the Forms tab, and create a new form using the Form Wizard. Base the form upon the *Members* table.
3. Click OK. In the Form Wizard dialog box, add the MemberID, Title, FirstName, and LastName fields to the Selected Fields list. Note that we are selecting the FirstName field before the LastName field.

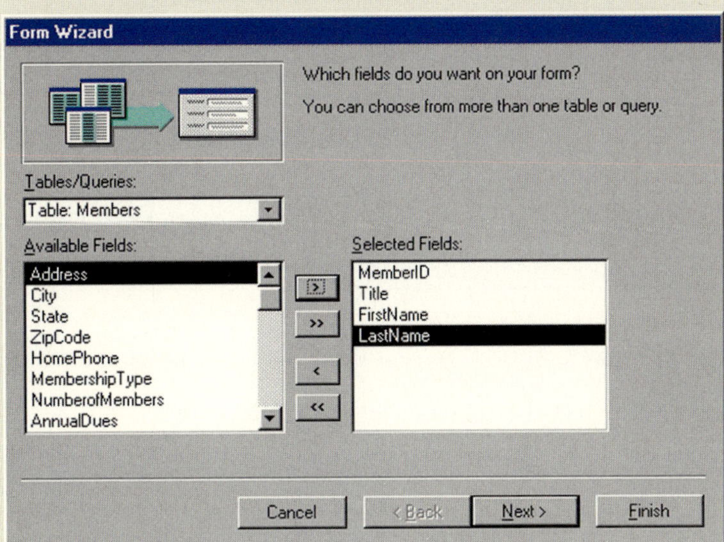

4. In the Tables/Queries list, select the Payments table.

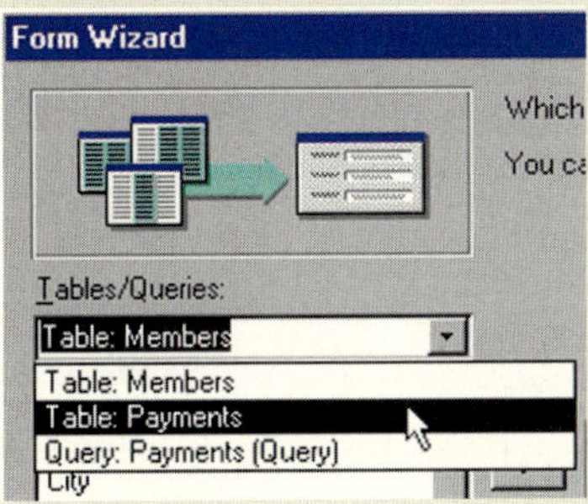

5. Add the PaymentNumber, PaymentDate, and Amount fields to the Selected Fields list.

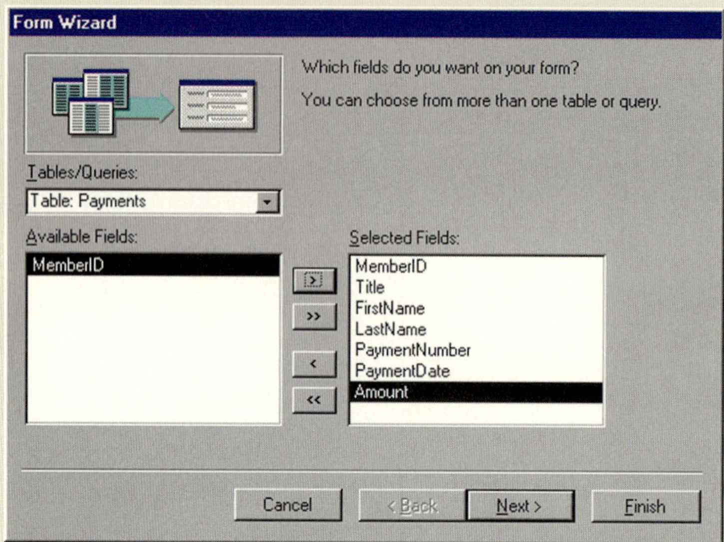

6. Click the Next button. Accept the defaults shown below and click the Next button.

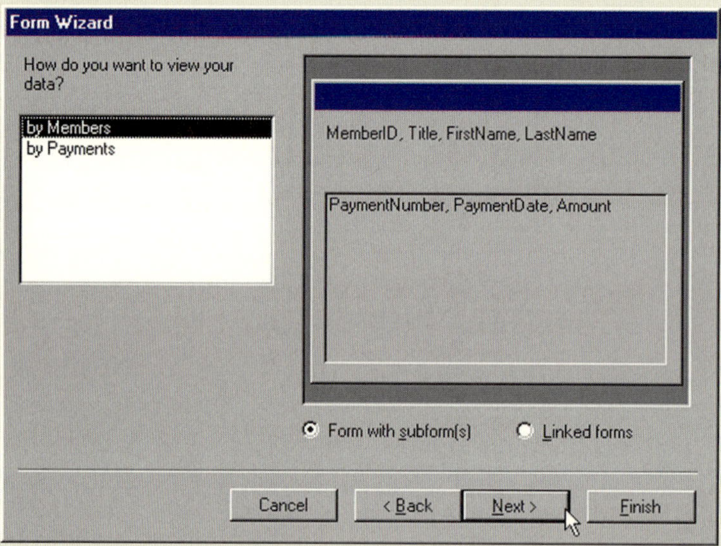

7. Select Datasheet as the layout for the subform. Click Next.
8. Select Standard as the style. Click Next.
9. Type **Payments by Member** as the name of the form, and accept the default name for the subform. Click Finish.
10. The form is displayed as shown on the next page. Close the form and the database when you are finished.

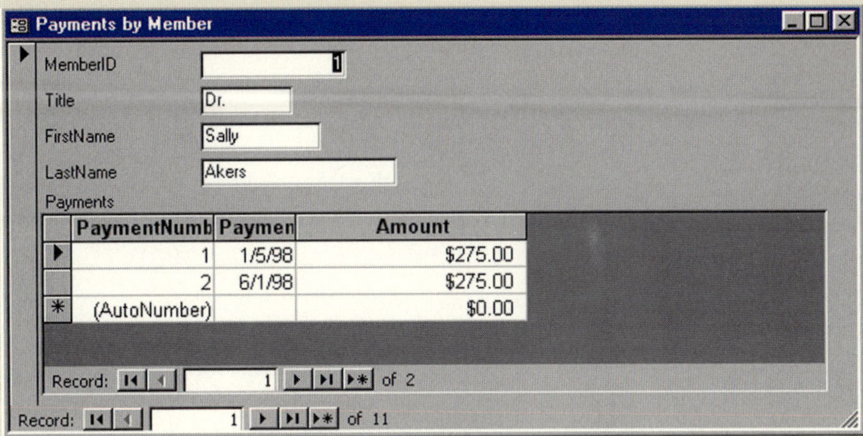

3. Creating and changing an AutoForm

1. Launch Access and open the database *High Point Food Orders.mdb*.

> **Notes** If you do not have a database named *High Point Food Orders.mdb*, ask your instructor for a copy of the file you should use to complete this exercise.

2. Create a new AutoForm named *Food Orders* based on the *Food Orders* table.
3. Use the Food Orders AutoForm to create the following form. Be sure to
   - Move fields to the positions shown.
   - Delete fields not shown on the figure.
   - Add a title to the form.
   - Adjust the length of fields so that they appear approximately as shown in the figure.
   - Change the field names so that they appear as shown on the figure.

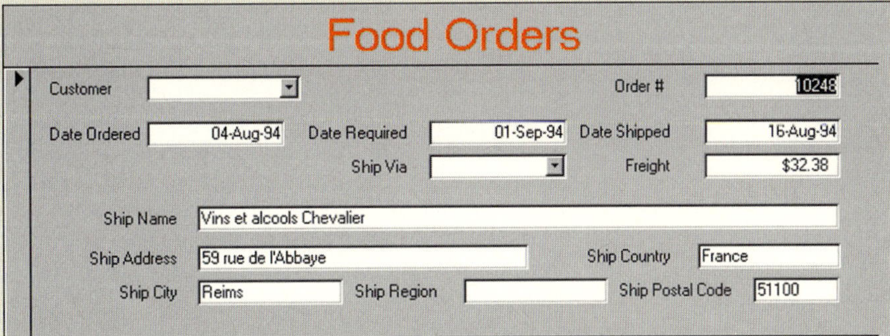

4. Print a copy of one record using the form design.
5. Close the database and exit Access.

Assignments

1. Creating a form using the Form Wizard

Open the *Willows Employees.mdb* file from your diskette. Using the Form Wizard, create a new form based upon the Current Salary for CO and CA query. Add all available fields to the form, use the tabular layout, and select a colorful style. Accept the default name when you finish the form. View the form and close the database when you are finished.

2. Modifying an AutoForm

Open the *Web Sites.mdb* database file from your diskette. Modify the controls to enhance the appearance of the Financial Services form. Add an image control to the form, and embed the *FSLogo.bmp* file on your disk in the control. Save your changes to the form and display it. Use the form to add one more record to the database for a financial service you located on the World Wide Web. Close the database when you are finished.

PROJECT 6

Creating and Modifying Reports

A report provides an effective way to present your data in a printed format. Because you have control over the size and appearance of everything included in a report, you can display the information exactly how you want to see it printed.

Objectives

After completing this project, you will be able to:

- **Create a report using the Report Wizard**
- **View a report in the Print Preview window**
- **Modify a report**
- **Print a report**
- **Create a report using Report Design View**
- **Sort data in a report**
- **Add a calculated control to a report**

The Challenge

Mr. Gilmore is very pleased with the work you have done on the membership database, and now he wants to begin distributing printed information from it. He has requested two reports: The first is a member address list that will be distributed to each of the club's committees. The second is a report listing the total fees each member owes the club, with the sum of all fees listed at the end of the report.

The Solution

You can easily create the first report using the Report Wizard. After you have designed the report, you can modify its appearance using Report Design View. You can create the second report using Report Design View in a manner similar to how you created forms. After adding the appropriate controls to the report's design, you can determine the total membership dues using a calculated expression in a text box control. Figure 6.1 shows the report listing each member's total membership fees that you will create in this project.

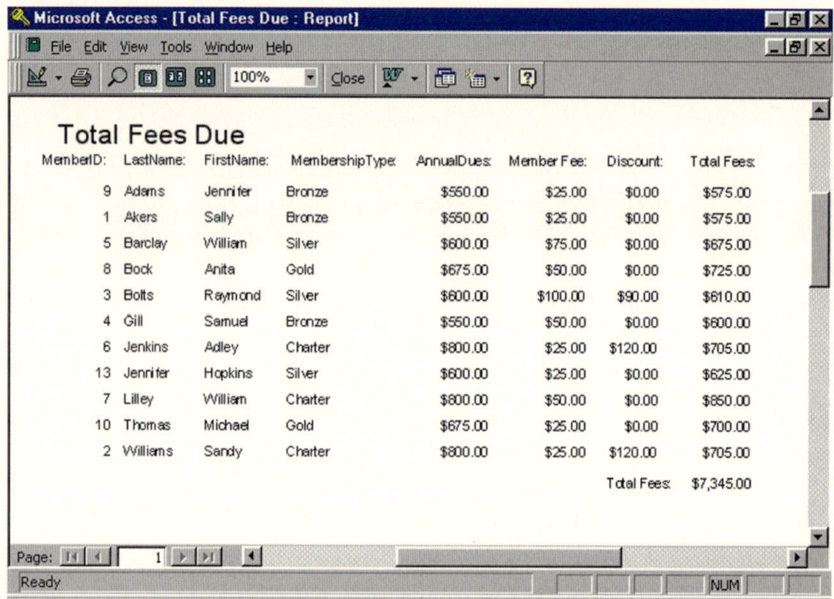

Total Fees Due

MemberID:	LastName:	FirstName:	MembershipType:	AnnualDues:	Member Fee:	Discount:	Total Fees:
9	Adams	Jennifer	Bronze	$550.00	$25.00	$0.00	$575.00
1	Akers	Sally	Bronze	$550.00	$25.00	$0.00	$575.00
5	Barclay	William	Silver	$600.00	$75.00	$0.00	$675.00
8	Bock	Anita	Gold	$675.00	$50.00	$0.00	$725.00
3	Bolts	Raymond	Silver	$600.00	$100.00	$90.00	$610.00
4	Gill	Samuel	Bronze	$550.00	$50.00	$0.00	$600.00
6	Jenkins	Adley	Charter	$800.00	$25.00	$120.00	$705.00
13	Jennifer	Hopkins	Silver	$600.00	$25.00	$0.00	$625.00
7	Lilley	William	Charter	$800.00	$50.00	$0.00	$850.00
10	Thomas	Michael	Gold	$675.00	$25.00	$0.00	$700.00
2	Williams	Sandy	Charter	$800.00	$25.00	$120.00	$705.00
						Total Fees:	$7,345.00

Figure 6.1

The Setup

After you launch Access and open your database, you should make sure the Database toolbar and the Status toolbar are displayed. These are the default settings in Access, but they may have been changed on your computer. (If you have forgotten how to do this, refer to Table 1.1 in Project 1.)

Troubleshooting If you do not see the Database toolbar on the screen when you launch Access and open your database, choose Toolbars from the View menu. Select the Database toolbar to display it. If any additional toolbars are visible, close them. If you do not see the Status Bar at the bottom of the Application window, choose Options from the Tools menu, click the View Page tab and change the Status Bar check box option.

Using the procedures you learned in Task 1 of Project 1, open the *Willows Membership.mdb* file from your disk.

Creating Reports

The process of creating reports is similar to that of creating forms. The ***Report Design window*** contains a graphical workspace displaying the report's bound and unbound controls. This window contains five sections where you can add controls. You add the controls to a specific section depending upon whether the information should appear at the beginning or end of the report; this requires a control in either the ***Report Header*** or ***Report Footer*** section, respectively. If your information should appear on every page of the report, add a control to the ***Page Header*** or ***Page Footer*** section. For information that is bound to a specific field in the record source, use a bound control such as a text box, and add this to the Report ***Detail section*** in the Report Design window. These sections are identified in Figure 6.2.

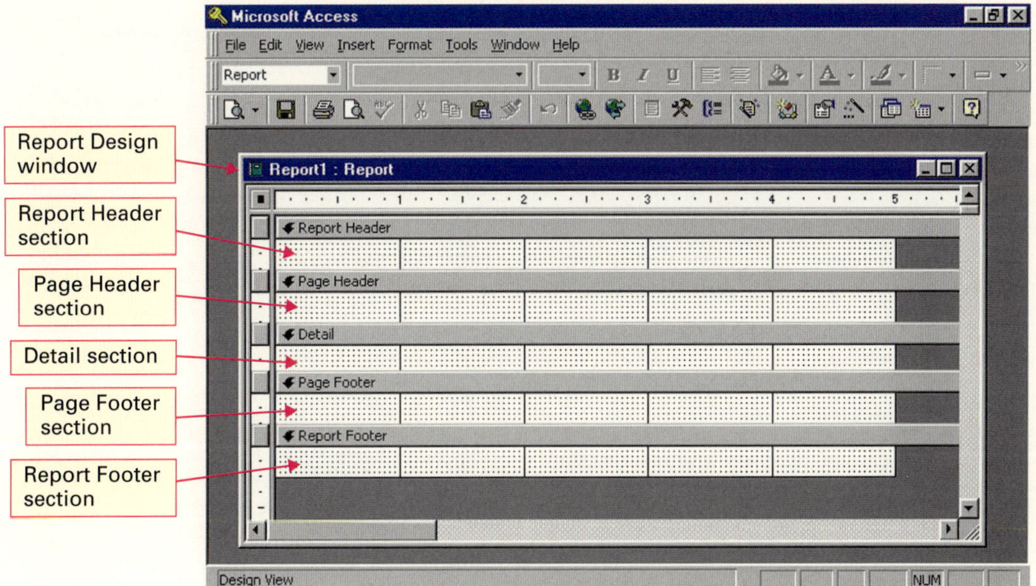

Figure 6.2

Creating a Report Using the Report Wizard

The easiest way to create a report is to use the Report Wizard, view the report, and then switch to the Report Design window to make any necessary modifications.

TASK 1: TO CREATE A REPORT USING THE REPORT WIZARD:

1. Click the Reports tab in the database window.
2. Click the New button.
3. Select the Report Wizard, and base the report upon the *Members* table.

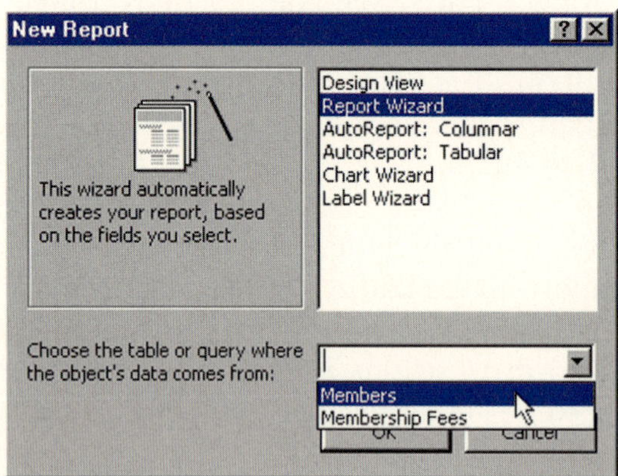

4. Move the MemberID, Title, LastName, FirstName, Address, City, State, ZipCode, and HomePhone fields from the Available Fields list to the Selected Fields list.

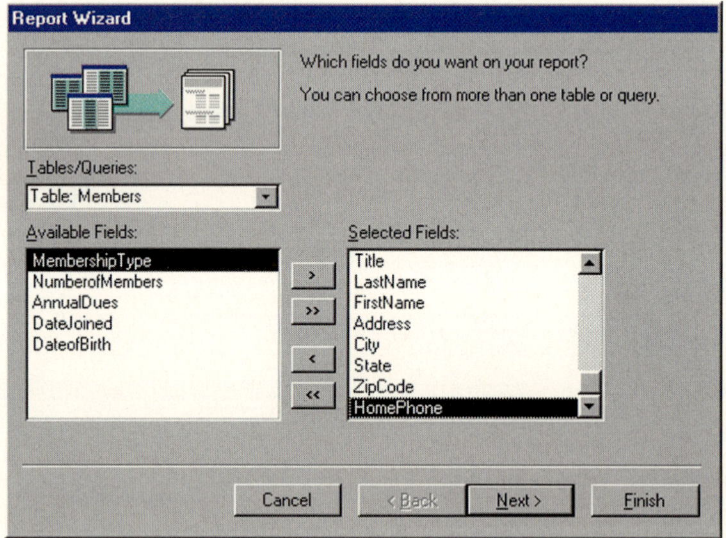

5 Click the Next button. The Report Wizard now asks if you want any grouping levels. Accept the default settings as shown below.

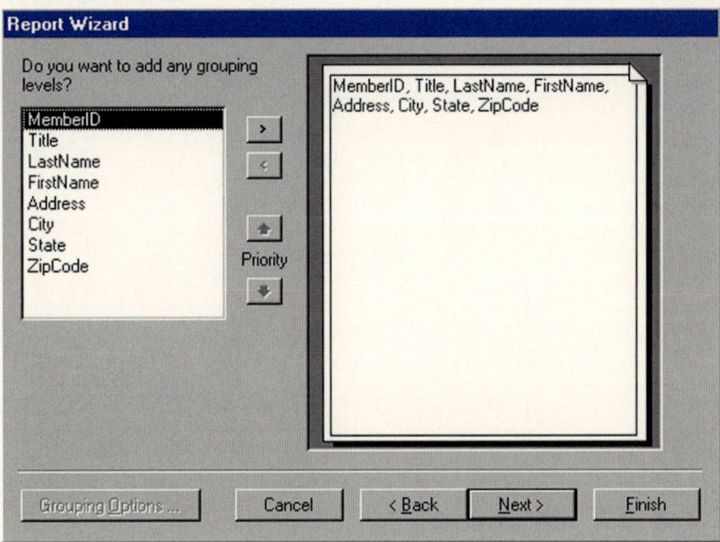

6 Click Next. Select LastName in the first sort drop-down list and select FirstName in the second list.

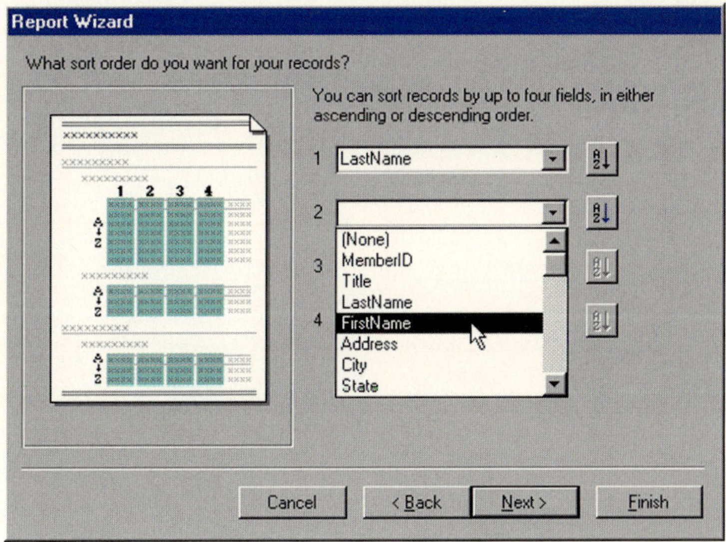

7 Click Next. Select a Tabular layout in Landscape orientation. Also select the check box to adjust all fields to fit on the page.

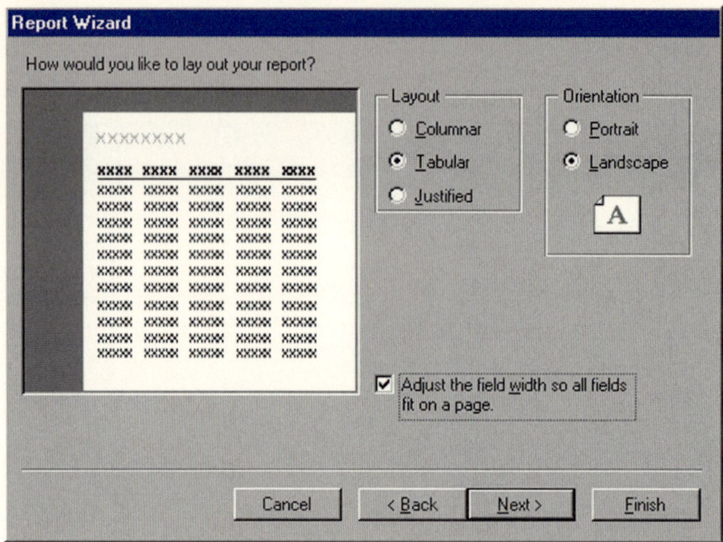

8 Click Next. Select Formal as the style.

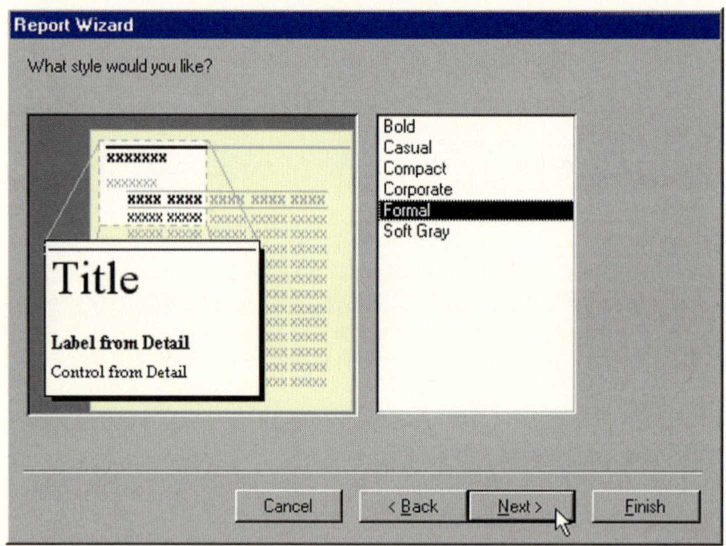

9 Click Finish to accept the default name for the report.

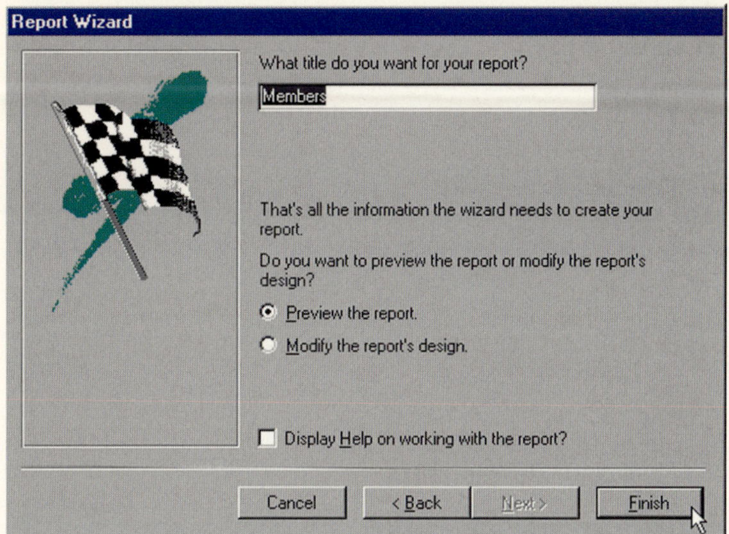

10 Access will display the report in Print Preview.

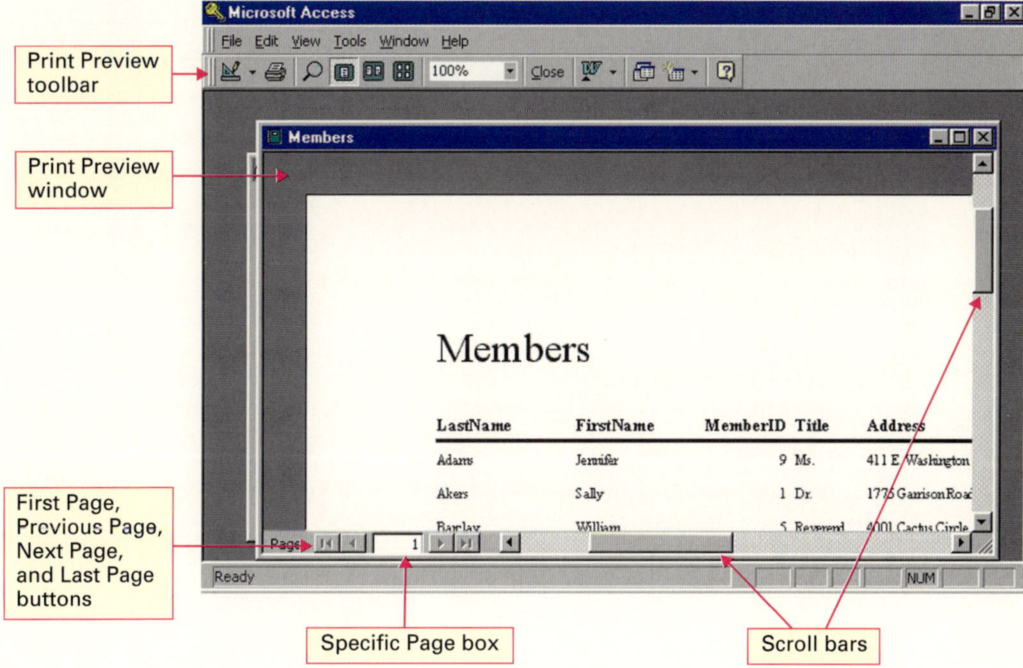

Viewing a Report in the Print Preview Window

When you create a new report using the Report Wizard, or when you preview an existing report, Access displays the report information in the Print Preview/Layout window. The information is displayed here exactly as it will appear when printed.

The preview typically displays at 100 percent of its size. You can use the scroll bars in the Print Preview window or the Zoom box on the Print Preview toolbar to change how the preview displays.

TASK 2: TO CHANGE THE PREVIEW DISPLAY:

1. Drag the horizontal scroll bar to reposition the preview. At 100 percent, it is difficult to see the entire layout of the report.
2. Click the Zoom box 100% on the Print Preview toolbar and change the view to 75 percent.
3. Reposition the preview using scrollbars. The entire report layout is now visible, as shown below.

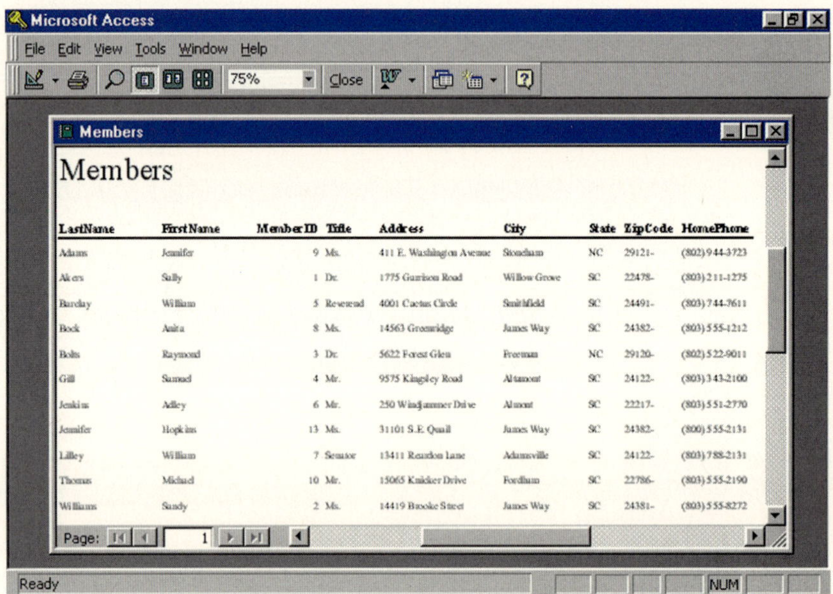

Tip You can also maximize the Report Preview window to view more of the report on the screen.

4. Close the report.

Modifying the Report Design for Printing

Rarely does a Wizard create a report that does not need modification. You can easily modify a report's layout by adjusting the size and position of its bound and unbound controls in the Report Design window. After you have modified the Members report, it will be ready for printing.

TASK 3: TO MODIFY THE DESIGN OF THE MEMBERS REPORT FOR PRINTING:

1. Click the Report tab in the database window if it is not currently active, click the Members report, and then click the Design button. Maximize the Report Design window.

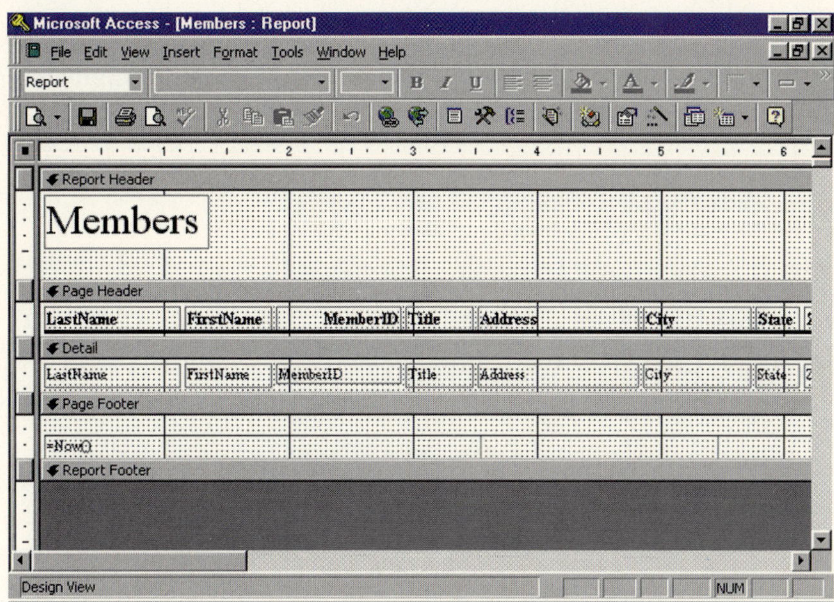

Notice that the current report used four report sections.

2. Double-click the caption of the label in the Report Header section to select the caption. This will bring up the label's property box. Type **The Willows Address List** as the new caption for the control, as shown in the next figure. Resize the label if necessary.

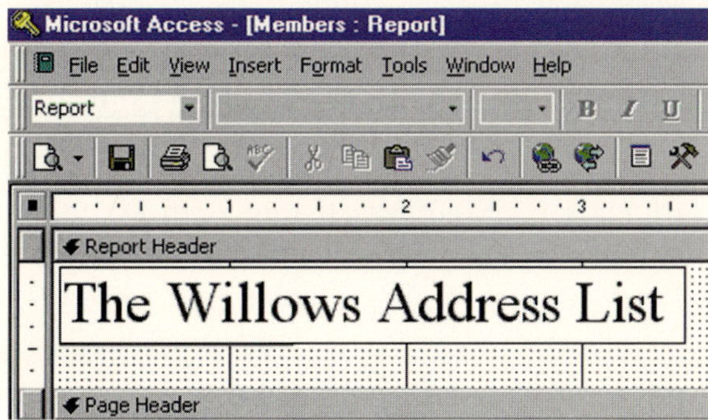

3. Select the MemberID text box control in the Detail section. Move the insertion point to the border of the control so it changes to the hand icon.

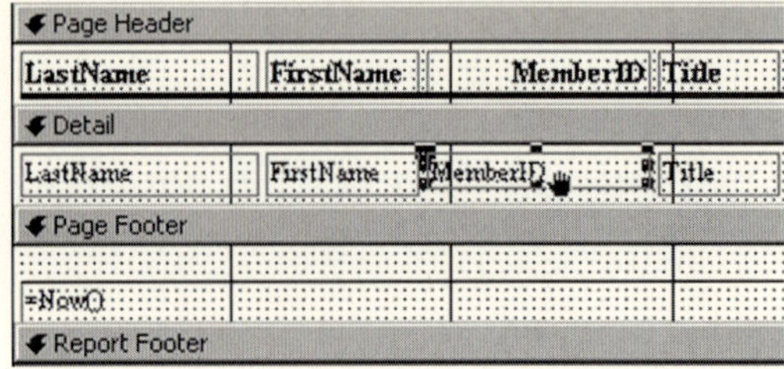

4 Hold the left mouse button and drag the control immediately under the LastName text box control.

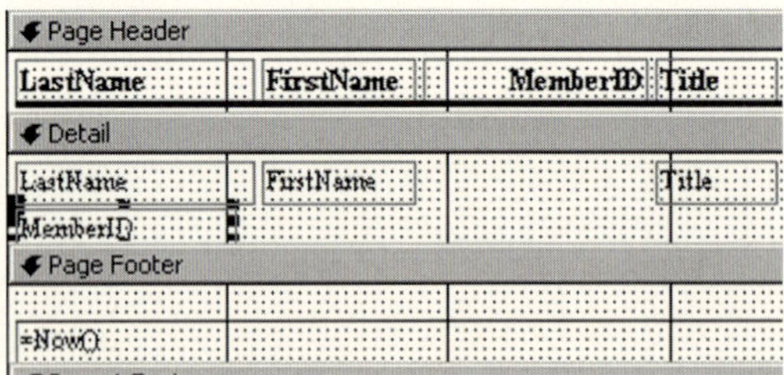

Troubleshooting Depending upon where you move controls in the report, the sections may resize automatically. You can also manually resize any of the report sections.

5 Reposition and resize the MemberID, Title, LastName, and FirstName text box controls so that they correspond with the controls shown below.

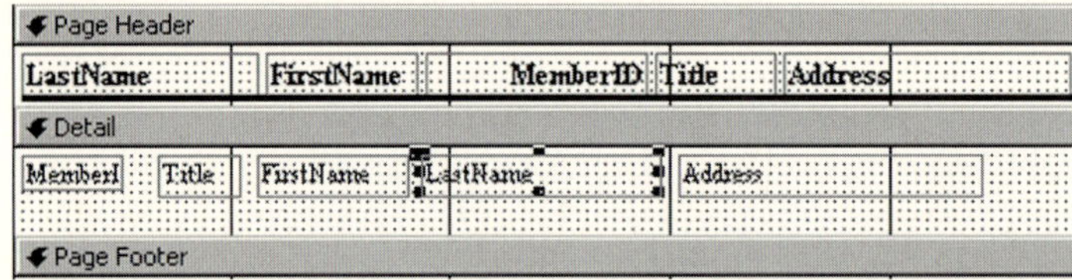

6 Select the FirstName label in the Page Header section, hold the SHIFT key, and select the Title label. Both labels should now be highlighted.

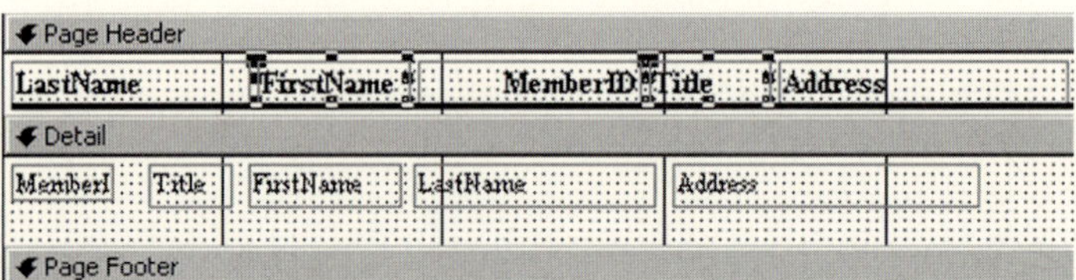

7 Select Cut. Reposition, rename, and change the captions for the MemberID, LastName, and Address label controls so that they correspond with the controls shown in the next figure.

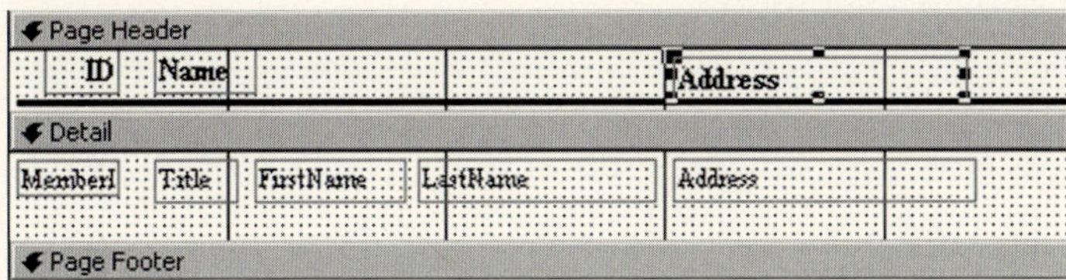

8 Move the insertion point to the lower edge of the Detail section, and hold the left mouse button to resize it. Your screen should now look similar to the one shown below. Save your changes.

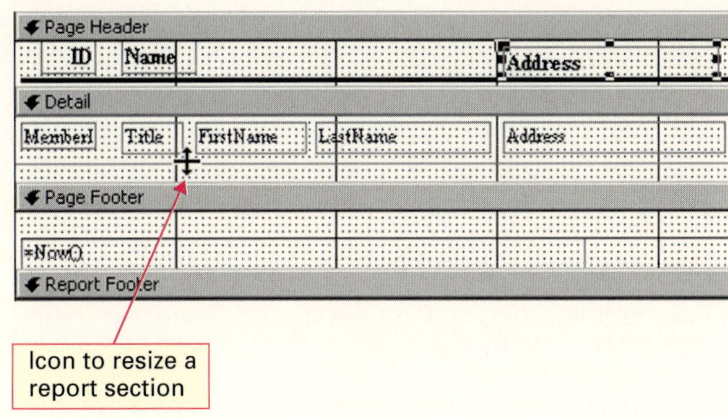

9 Click the View button on the Report Design toolbar to preview the report.

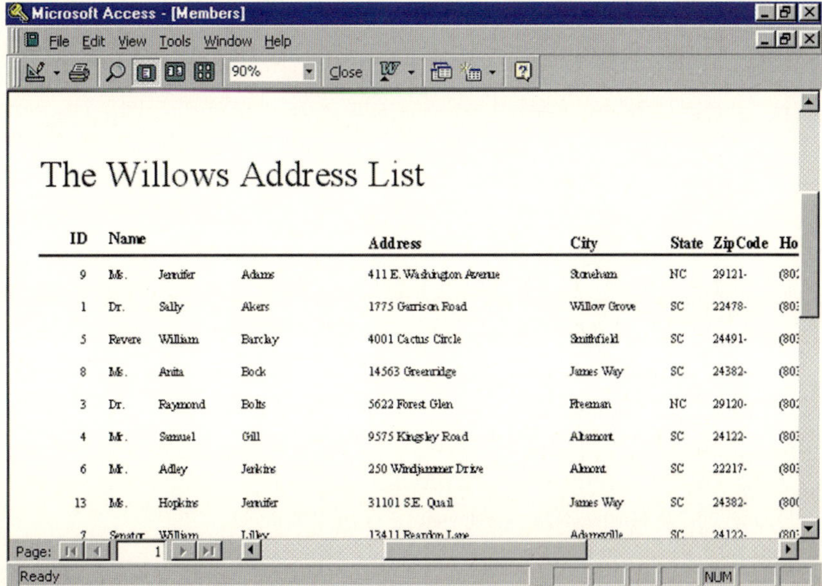

Tip Reports have three views: Design, Print Preview, and Layout Preview. You use Design View to create or change a report. Print Preview displays the report's data as it will appear on the printed page. Layout Preview displays the report's layout, which includes just a sample of the data in the report.

10 Click the Print button on the Print Preview toolbar to print the report. Close the report when it is finished printing.

Creating a Report Using Report Design View

Although the Report Wizard quickly generates reports, you have the greatest control over what a report contains when you create a new report using Design View. By placing bound and unbound controls in the various sections of the report, you specify exactly how you want the report to look.

TASK 4: TO CREATE A NEW REPORT USING DESIGN VIEW:

1 Click the New button in the database window.

2 Select Design View, and base the report on the Membership Fees query.

3 Click OK. Click the Field List button on the Report Design toolbar to display the field list if it's not already visible.

4 Drag the MemberID, LastName, FirstName, MembershipType, AnnualDues, Member Fee, Discount, and Total Fees fields into the Detail section.

Tip Don't be concerned with where these fields are currently placed, because you will modify the report design.

5 Select the MemberID label, and click the Cut button .

6 Place the insertion point inside the Page Header section and click the Paste button .

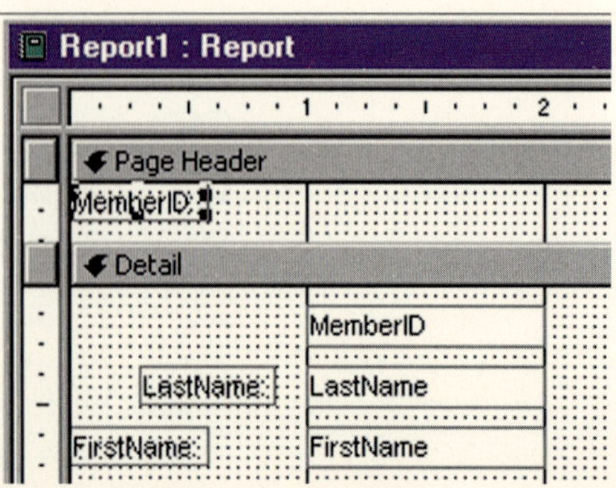

7 Cut the remaining labels from the Detail section, paste them into the Page Header section, and reposition each one. Resize the report as necessary, so it appears similar to the one shown below.

Troubleshooting You will have to reposition each control when you paste it into the Page Header section, because by default Access pastes the control in the upper-left corner of the section.

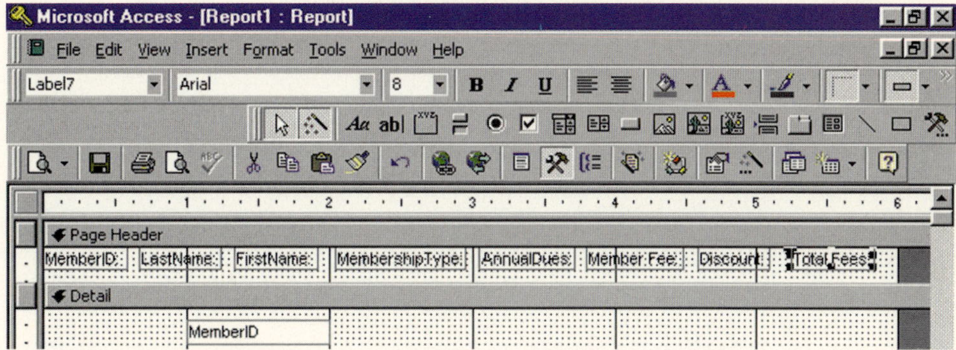

8 Position the text box controls as shown below. Make sure you resize the lower edge of the Detail section so that there isn't too much empty space at the end. If you leave a lot of space at the end of the detail section, you will find that your report has the same amount of space between each record.

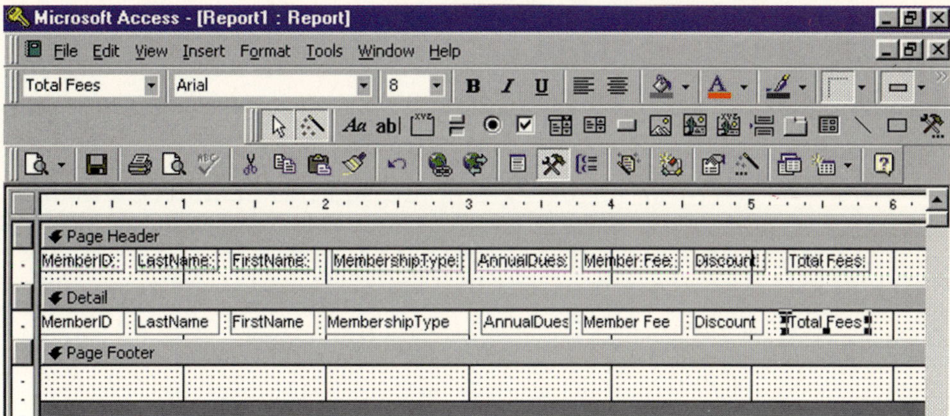

9 Save the report. Type **Total Fees Due** as the name of the report, and click OK.

10 Click the View button to preview the report. Depending upon how you sized the controls on your report, you may receive an error message stating that all of the information may not fit on the page.

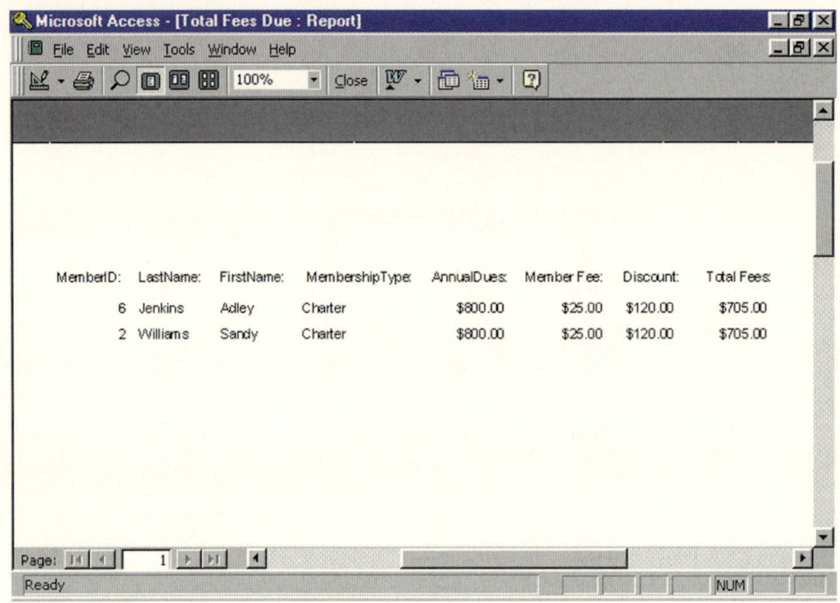

Tip You will notice that the report returns only two records. This is because in Project 4 you set multiple criteria for the Membership Fees query.

Adding a Calculated Control to the Report

Mr. Gilmore wants the report to display the total membership fees that are due by all members. You can add this figure at the end of the report in a ***calculated control***, which is a control containing an expression.

TASK 5: TO CREATE A CALCULATED CONTROL TO SUM THE TOTAL MEMBERSHIP FEES:

1 Click the view button on the Print Preview toolbar to return to Design view.

2 Select Report Header/Footer from the View menu.

3 Select the Text Box control tool from the toolbox.

4 Add a text box control to the right side of the Report Footer section, immediately below the Total Fees text box in the Detail section.

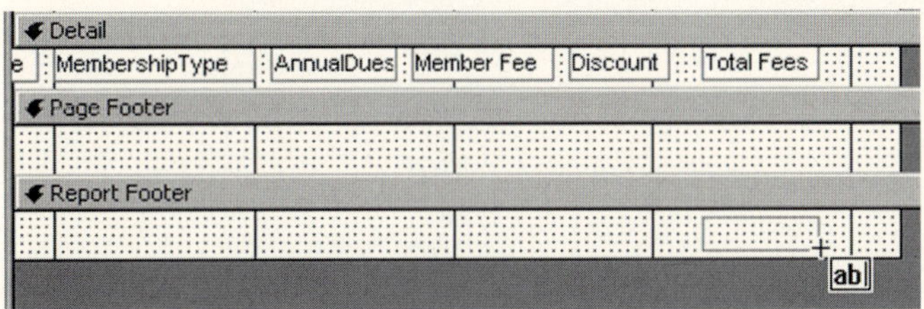

Tip Notice that the text box is currently not bound to a specific object.

5 Delete the label that is associated with the text box control.

6 Select the text box control, and click the Properties button on the Report Design toolbar.

7 Click the Data tab in the Text Box Properties dialog box to display the data properties. Click the ellipsis button ..., as shown on the next page.

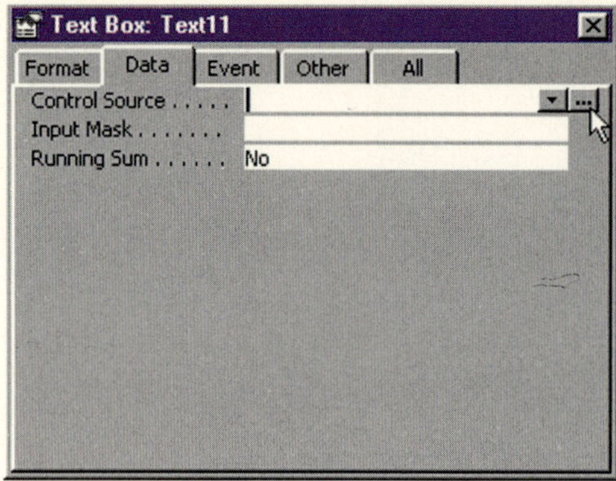

8 Type **=sum([Total Fees])** in the Expression box, then click OK.

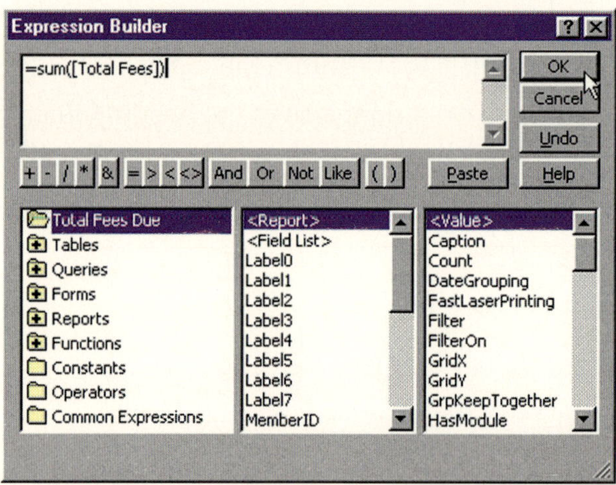

Tip For more information about the Expression builder and the syntax required for specific expressions click the Help button in the Expression Builder and select the Read more about expressions option.

9 Click the Format tab in the Properties dialog box, and set the Format property to Currency.

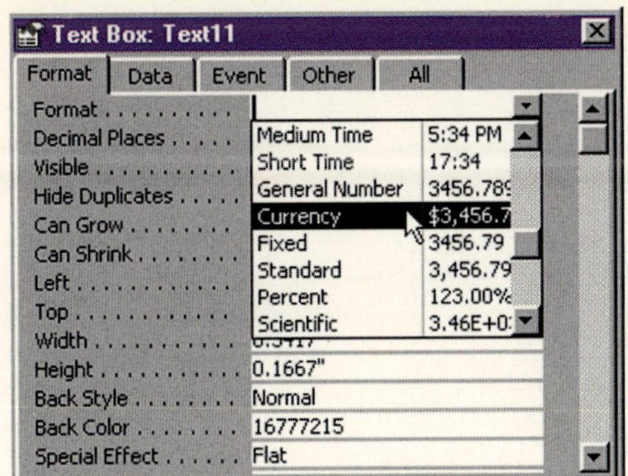

10 Save and preview your report. Your report should look similar to the one shown below.

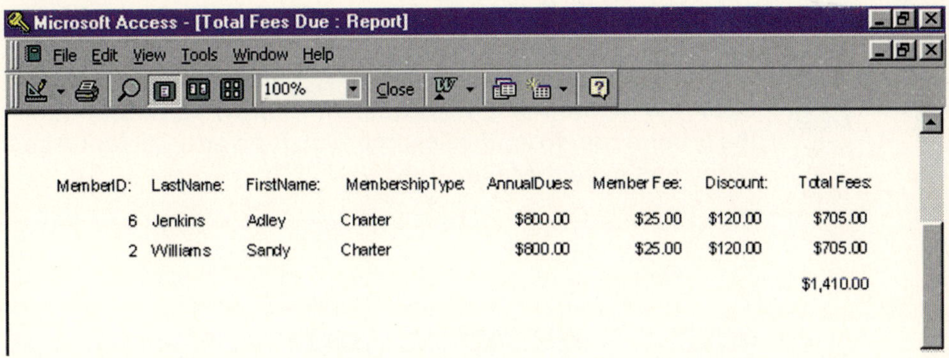

Modifying the Report

The report still needs slight modification: It will look better if you add a label in the Report Header section and add a descriptive label explaining exactly what information the calculated control displays. Finally, the query underlying the report needs to be modified so that the report lists records for all members.

TASK 6: TO MODIFY THE REPORT:

1 Click the View button to return to the Report Design window.

2 Add a label control to the Report Header section. Type **Total Fees Due** as the caption in the label.

3 Change the Font Size property to 16.

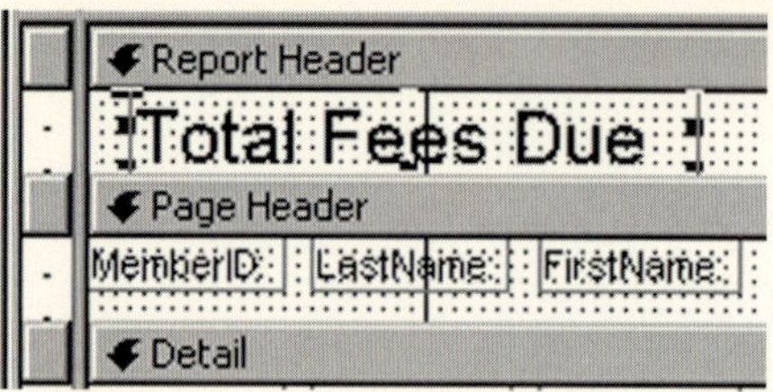

4. Add a label to the Report Footer section to the left of the calculated control.
5. Type **Total Fees:** as the caption.

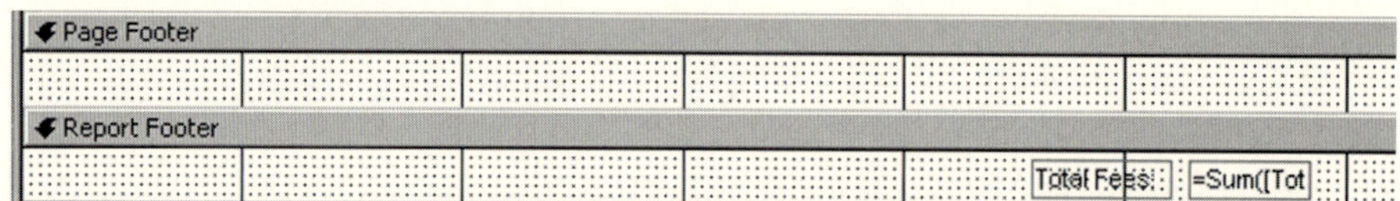

6. Save your changes to the report design, and close the report.
7. Open the Membership Fees query in Design View, and remove the entries in the criteria row from the MembershipType and Current Age fields. Close the query and save these changes.
8. Click the Reports tab in the database window, and preview the Total Fees Due report.

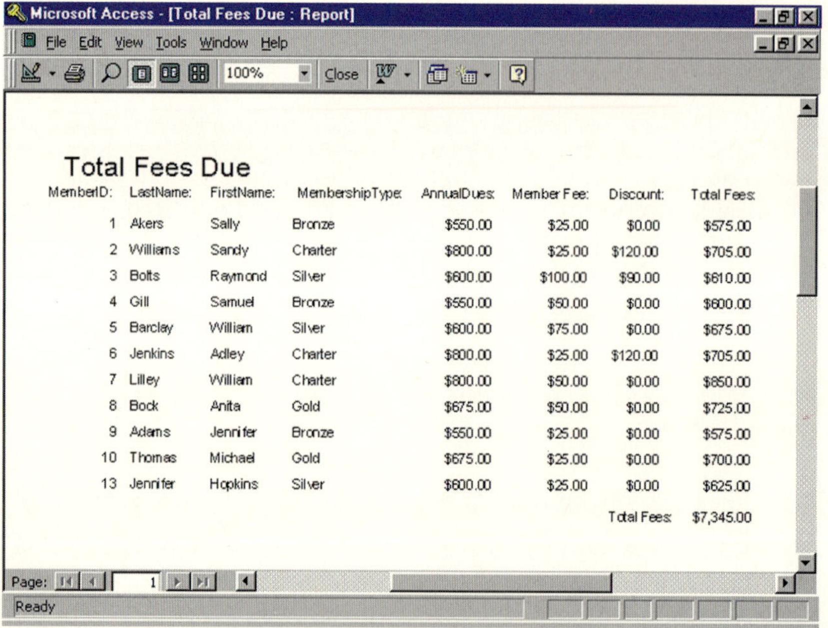

You will notice that the report is ordered according to MemberID. You can easily specify a different sort order for the report.

TASK 7: TO SPECIFY A DIFFERENT SORT ORDER FOR THE REPORT:

1. Click the View button to return to the Report Design window.
2. Click the Sorting and Grouping button on the Report Design toolbar.
3. Select LastName in the Field/Expression drop-down list.

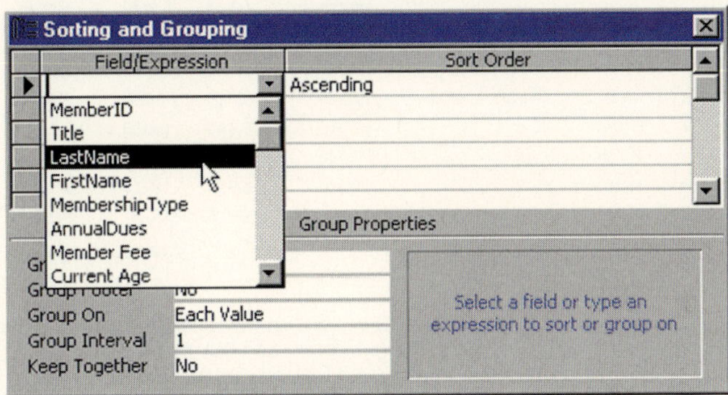

4. Make sure the settings in the Sorting and Grouping dialog box match those shown below.

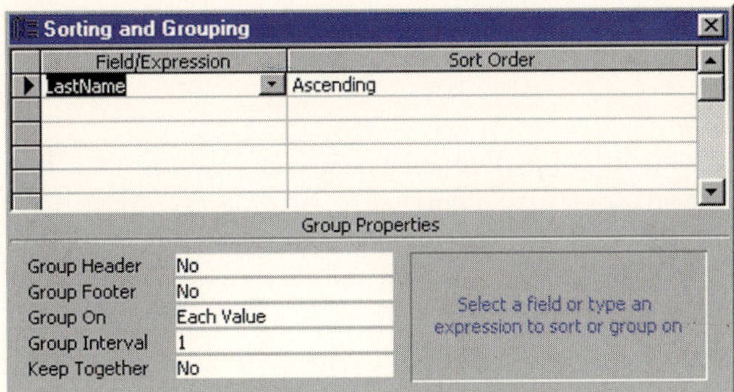

5. Close the Sorting and Grouping dialog box.
6. Save your changes to the report design and preview the report.

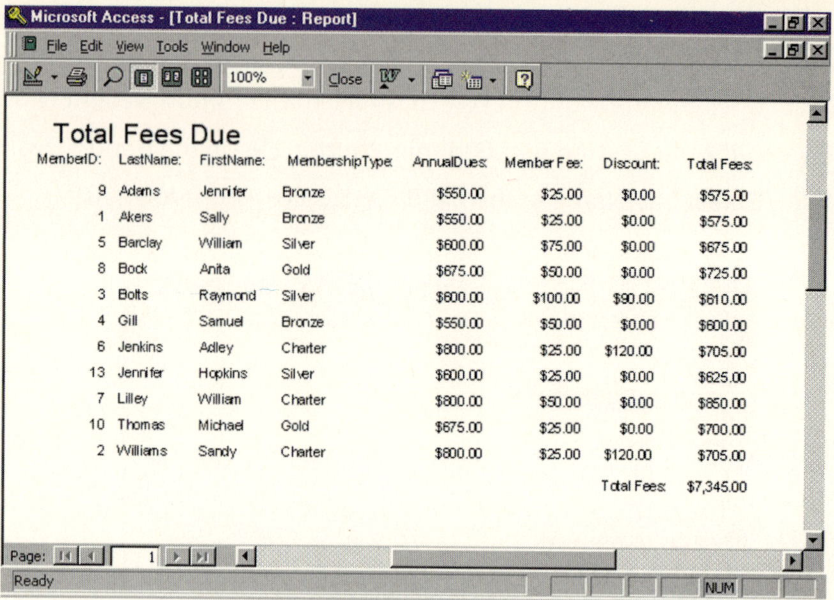

Total Fees Due

MemberID:	LastName:	FirstName:	MembershipType:	AnnualDues:	Member Fee:	Discount:	Total Fees:
9	Adams	Jennifer	Bronze	$550.00	$25.00	$0.00	$575.00
1	Akers	Sally	Bronze	$550.00	$25.00	$0.00	$575.00
5	Barclay	William	Silver	$600.00	$75.00	$0.00	$675.00
8	Bock	Anita	Gold	$675.00	$50.00	$0.00	$725.00
3	Bolts	Raymond	Silver	$600.00	$100.00	$90.00	$610.00
4	Gill	Samuel	Bronze	$550.00	$50.00	$0.00	$600.00
6	Jenkins	Adley	Charter	$800.00	$25.00	$120.00	$705.00
13	Jennifer	Hopkins	Silver	$600.00	$25.00	$0.00	$625.00
7	Lilley	William	Charter	$800.00	$50.00	$0.00	$850.00
10	Thomas	Michael	Gold	$675.00	$25.00	$0.00	$700.00
2	Williams	Sandy	Charter	$800.00	$25.00	$120.00	$705.00
						Total Fees:	$7,345.00

7. Close the report.
8. Close the database.

The Conclusion

Mr. Gilmore should be pleased with the reports you have designed. As you have seen, creating reports is similar to creating forms; you can quickly generate a report with the Report Wizard, which you used to create a printed address list, or you can create a report in Design View by adding controls to the various report sections. You can also add calculated controls to a report, such as the expression listing the total fees owed to the club.

Summary and Exercises

Summary

- Database reports are used to print information from a database.
- You can create a report by using one of the Report Wizards or by using Report Design View.
- A report contains bound and unbound controls that specify where information will appear on the report.
- After you create a report, you can view it in the Print Preview window.
- You can modify a report by changing the properties of each control in the report.
- Calculated controls perform calculations based upon an expression.
- A report can be sorted on up to four fields when you create a report using the Report Wizard.
- You can change the sort order of information in a report by using the Sorting and Grouping option.

Key Terms and Operations

Key Terms

calculated control
Detail section
Page Footer
Page Header
Report Design window
Report Footer
Report Header

Operations

change the datasource
change the Preview display
create a calculated control
create a new report using Report Design View
create a report using the Report Wizard
modify a report in Design view
modifying a report
specify sort order

Study Questions

Multiple Choice

1. Which view displays all the data in a report exactly as it will be printed?
   a. Design View
   b. Preview View
   c. Layout View
   d. Form View

2. When you create a report using the Report Wizard, how many fields can you specify for the sort order?
   a. one
   b. two
   c. three
   d. four

3. To arrange controls on a report you must use
   a. Design View
   b. Layout View
   c. Form View
   d. Preview View

4. In which section of a report do bound controls generally appear?
   a. Page Header
   b. Detail
   c. Page Footer
   d. Report Header

5. You can add fields to a report easily using the
   a. toolbox
   b. Properties dialog box
   c. database window
   d. field list

6. Unbound controls usually appear in all sections of a report except which section?
   a. Page Header
   b. Report Header
   c. Page Footer
   d. Detail

7. Data entered in the Page Header section of a report appears at the
   a. beginning of the report only.
   b. end of the report.
   c. top of every page
   d. bottom of every page.

8. Field data from a query appears in which section of a report?
   a. Page Header
   b. Detail
   c. Page Footer
   d. Report Header

9. A query displays an employee's last name, first name, address, Social Security number, and annual salary. To easily locate a given employee in a report based upon the query, the report should be sorted on which field?
   a. Last Name
   b. Social Security Number
   c. First Name
   d. Annual Salary

10. You want to add a descriptive title to a report that appears only on the first page of the report. To which section should you add the control?
    a. Page Header
    b. Detail
    c. Page Footer
    d. Report Header

Short Answer

1. What is the main purpose of a report?
2. What is a calculated control?
3. Where do bound controls generally appear in a report?
4. When should you use a query versus a table as the basis for a report?
5. How do you specify sort order in a report?
6. What is the fastest method for creating a report?
7. What control do you use to create a calculated control in a report?
8. How do you move labels from the Detail section of a report to the Page Header section?
9. How do you save a report?
10. What kind of unbound controls does a report usually contain?

For Discussion

1. What two database objects can you use to create a report? When might you use one rather than the other?
2. What are some ways you might use calculated controls in a report?
3. When do you use bound versus unbound controls on a report?
4. Describe the three views associated with reports.

Review Exercises

1. Modifying a query and creating a report

Because an Access report is always based upon a record source, it always displays the most recent changes to the table or query upon which it is based. In this exercise, you will copy the Current Salary for CO and CA query, modify it, and create a report that lists the salary paid to each employee. The figure below displays the report.

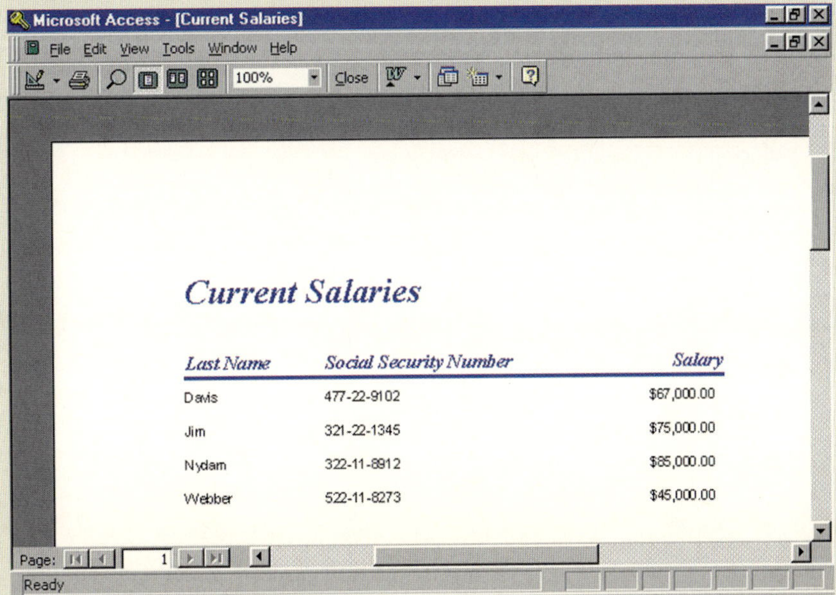

Troubleshooting Your data will be different than what is shown here.

1. Open the *Willows Employees.mdb* database from your disk.
2. Click the Queries tab in the database window.
3. Copy and Paste the Current Salary for CO and CA query. Type **Current Salaries** as the name for the copy of the query.
4. Open the query in Design View, and remove the criteria for the StateOrProvince field. Close the query, and save the changes to its design.
5. Click the Reports tab in the database window.
6. Using the Report Wizard, create a new report that is based upon the Current Salaries query.
7. Add the LastName, SocialSecurityNumber, and Salary fields to the Selected Fields: list. Press the Next button.
8. Do not add any grouping levels. Press the Next button.
9. Set the sort order by the LastName field. Press the Next button.
10. Choose a Tabular report in Portrait Orientation. Press the Next button.
11. Choose Corporate as the style for the report. Press the Next button.
12. Accept the default name for the report. Press the Finish button.
13. Close the report after you preview it.
14. Compact the database and close the file.

2. Grouping and Sorting Data in a Report

Mr. Gilmore wants a report listing the payments each member has made toward his or her annual dues. This report must be sorted by each member's last name, with each payment listed according to the date it was paid. The following figure shows a preview of the report.

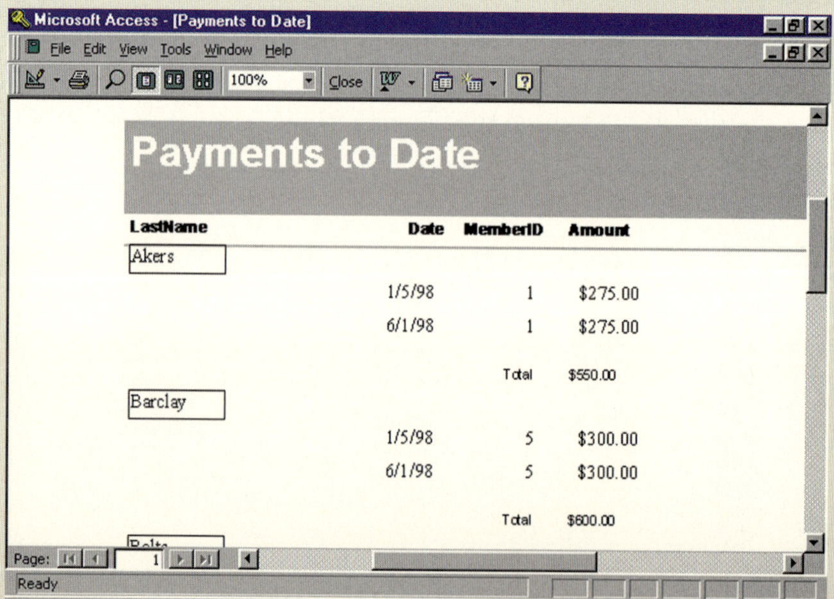

Complete the report as follows:

1. Open the *Membership Payments.mdb* database file from your disk.
2. Create a new report using the Report Wizard option. Base the report upon the Payments (Query) query. Click the Close button.
3. Add all the available fields to the Selected Fields: list. Click the Next button.
4. Group the report by Members, as shown below. Click the Next button.

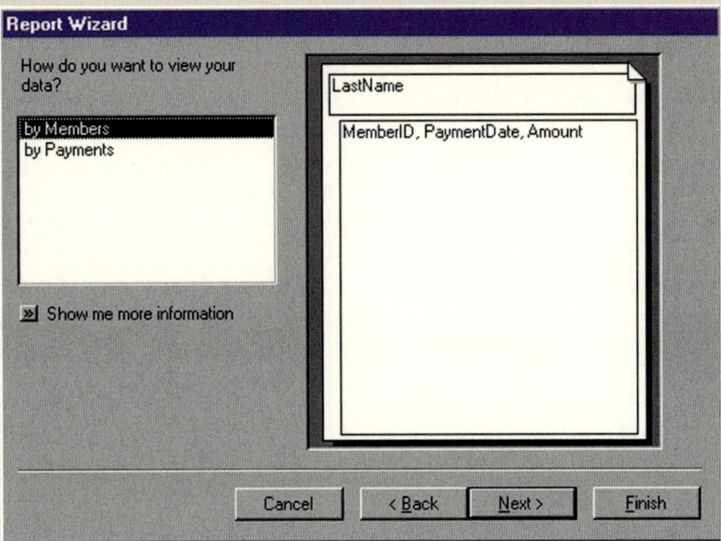

5. Do not add any grouping levels. Click the Next button.
6. Select PaymentDate as the sort order for the report.
7. Click the Summary Options button. Check the Sum box, and then select the option to show both the detail and the summary. Click OK. Then Click the Next button.

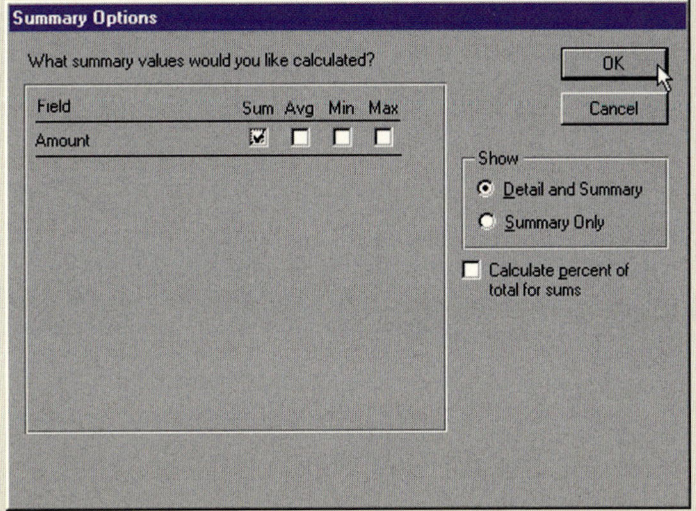

8. Choose the Stepped layout in Portrait Orientation. Click the Next button.
9. Select Soft Grey as the style. Click the Next button.
10. Type **Payments to Date** as the title for the report and click Finish.
11. Switch to Design View and modify the report design as necessary.
12. Close the report and save your changes.
13. Select Database Utilities from the Tools menu and compact the database.
14. Close the database.

3. Creating, saving, and printing a report

1. Launch Access and open the database *High Point Food Orders.mdb*.

Note If you do not have a database named *High Point Food Orders.mdb*, ask your instructor for a copy of the file you should use to complete this exercise.

2. Create the report layout as pictured based on the *Food Products by Category* query.

Food Products
by Category

Category Name	Product Name
Beverages	Chai
Beverages	Chang
Beverages	Chartreuse verte
Beverages	Côte de Blaye
Beverages	Guaraná Fantástica
Beverages	Ipoh Coffee
Beverages	Lakkalikööri
Beverages	Laughing Lumberjack Lager

3. Save the report using the report name *Food Products by Category.*
4. Print a copy of the report.

Assignments

1. Creating a grouped and sorted tabular report

Open the *Willows Employees.mdb* database file from your disk. Using the Report Wizard, create a report that is based upon the Current Salaries query. Include each employee's last name, Social Security number, state of residence, and current salary in the report. Add StateOrProvince as a grouping level, and sort the report by Last Name. Type **Current Salaries by State** as the name appearing on the report. Print a copy of the report and close the database when you are finished.

2. Creating a report of Web Sites

Open the *Web Sites.mdb* database file from your disk. Create a tabular report in landscape orientation that lists each company, the primary product, and the company's URL. Sort the data in the report by company name. Name the report *Sites*. Print a copy of the report, and close the database when you are finished.

More Access 97

We have made every effort in this book to cover the tasks and procedures you will need to know in preparation for becoming certified in Microsoft Access 97. You can download the *Microsoft Access 97 Exam Preparation Guide* from Microsoft's Web sit at www.microsoft.com/office/train_cert. This section covers a few additional topics that you should know before seeking your certification. These topics are:

- Data integrity
- Using Lookup fields to improve data integrity
- Using a switchboard to enhance a database presentation
- Analyzing data with queries
- Displaying related table information using subforms
- Designing custom reports
- Object Linking and Embedding (OLE)
- Importing data into Access
- Access and the World Wide Web

Database Design and Data Integrity

As you design a database, you will want to maintain ***data integrity*** whenever possible. Data integrity refers to the constraints you build into a database to ensure that the information it contains is accurate. Sound methods for maintaining data integrity include creating a database with multiple tables, establishing relationships among tables, adding validation rules, and using calculated expressions in queries. In addition, you can improve the accuracy of field information by setting the required property of a field to true. When you do this, users must enter data into the field and cannot delete the data or close the table, query, or form if the value is empty. In the *Willow Membership.mdb* database file, the Membership Fees query contains a calculated field. You can improve the data integrity of the database by making the fields used in the calculated expression required fields.

Using Lookup Fields to Improve Data Integrity

Another method for improving data integrity is utilizing Lookup fields wherever possible. A ***Lookup field*** is a field that displays a list of options either from an existing table or from a predefined list of values. In the Willows Membership database, the TypeOfMembership field will always contain one of a limited number of entries. Adding a Lookup field would serve as another good strategy for maintaining the data integrity of this table, because invalid data could never be entered.

The Integrity of Dates in Microsoft Access

And what about the integrity of dates in your Access database? Is Access safe from the Y2K (Year2000) problem? Yes it is, as long as your computer's BIOS chip will accept dates after 1999.

The Date/Time data type in Access uses an integer value to represent dates ranging from 1 January 100 to 31 December 9999, so your data is safe, even if the date is formatted in the short data format.

Improving the Presentation of a Database by Using a Switchboard

Finally, you may want to think about ways to keep users from opening tables or queries in which they might inadvertently change data or the object's design. By adding a ***Switchboard*** — a form with buttons that you can click to open forms and reports — you effectively limit the presentation of the database to those objects users need to use to enter, edit, and print information.

Analyzing Data with Queries

As you learned in Project 4, queries enable you to extract data from one or more tables based upon any criteria you specify. Queries also enable you to perform calculations using existing data and to summarize your data in different ways.

Summarizing Data with Queries

A ***summary query*** summarizes information in the underlying record source, such as counting the number of inventory items of a particular category currently in stock. A ***crosstab query*** is a specific summary query that displays summarized values (sums, counts, and averages) from one field in a table and then groups them by two sets of facts supplied from the data — one listed down the left side of the datasheet and another listed across the top of the datasheet. An example of a crosstab query is a datasheet listing the ages of the members at the Willows in rows, with separate columns displaying the membership categories. At the intersection of each row and column the average fees for members of an age and membership category appears. The format of a crosstab query is similar to a PivotTable, which is a method for designing cross tabulations in Microsoft Excel.

Modifying Queries

As you know, a query can be modified in the Query Design Window any time after you have created it. This means you can add or delete fields by either dragging them to the appropriate column or deleting the column completely from the Query Design grid.

Joining Tables in Queries

A query based upon multiple tables does not require a permanent relationship among the tables to display fields in a query datasheet. You can join two or more tables in the Query Design window by dragging a field from the field list in one table or query to the equivalent field in the field list for the other table or query. With this type of join, Access selects records from both tables only when the values in the joined fields are equal. You can remove a join in a query by deleting the line representing the relationship between tables.

Using Forms that Contain Subforms

If you completed Exercise 1 of Project 5, you know that a subform is a form within a form, and is useful when you want to show data from tables or queries with a one-to-many relationship. A subform is linked to a main form so that the subform displays only records that are related to the current record in the main form.

Entering Data into a Subform

When you use a form with a subform to enter new records, Microsoft Access saves the current record in the main form when you enter (display a record in) the subform. This ensures that the records in the "many" table have a related record in the "one" table. This method also automatically saves each record as you add it to the subform. Therefore, you can use a main form/subform combination to permit the user to enter data into multiple tables and still ensure that the data integrity constraints are met. See Exercise 3 of Project 5 for an example of how to create a form containing a subform.

Customizing Reports

As you may guess, reports are just as easy to modify as tables, queries, or forms. You can customize the pages in a report by selecting Page Setup from the File menu in Report Design view. You can also customize a report to display a chart. If Microsoft Graph 97 was installed with Access, you can use the Chart Wizard to create a chart from table or query data.

It is easiest to create a chart using the Chart Wizard. The Chart Wizard analyzes the existing data and determines whether it should display data from all fields in one global chart, or whether it is more appropriate to show a record-bound chart. If you use a record-bound chart, it represents only the data in the current record.

Sharing Information with Other Applications

One of the advantages of Microsoft Office Professional is that it enables you to easily share data among applications. You can add pictures to records, link your database to existing data, or import Excel or ASCII-delimited files into Access.

Using Object Linking and Embedding to Add Pictures to a Record

To add pictures to a record, you must use the OLE (Object Linking and Embedding) data type. The field will be bound to a specific bitmap image file that can be displayed on a form or in a report. You can also use the OLE data type to link an Excel or Word object to a bound or an unbound control. When information is linked, the source file is external to the database, and any changes to the source file are seen when the database displays this information. When you use embedding to share information with Access, the data becomes an Access object that does not change if the original information is subsequently changed.

Importing Data into Access

To import data from another source into Access, one or more import filters must be installed. Access can import text, existing workbooks, and data from a variety of database formats.

Access and the World Wide Web

One of the most exciting advances in the Office 97 suite is the degree of Web integration throughout. The End of Chapter Assignments in this book show you how to export the hyperlink data type, which you can use to link your Access form or report to the Web or other documents on your computer or network.

You can also develop static or dynamic HTML documents from your database, depending upon your application needs. Consider using static HTML format when your data does not change frequently and when your World Wide Web application does not require a form. If your data changes frequently and your Web application needs to store and retrieve live data from your Microsoft Access database using a form, you will need to use dynamic HTML. Dynamic HRML pages are more complex than static HTML pages. Search the Microsoft web site for more information about Dynamic HTML in Access.

Notes

Notes

Notes

Notes

Notes

Notes

Notes

Notes

Access 97 Function Reference Guide

Function	Mouse Action or Button	Menu	Keyboard Shortcut
Database, close	Click [X]	Choose File, Close	
Database, create new	Click [New]	Choose File, New Database	Press CTRL+N
display page of Database window	Click page tab	Choose View, Database Objects, and then choose desired database window page	Press CTRL+TAB until the database window page appears
Database, open existing	Click [Open]	Choose File, Open	Press CTRL+O
Exit Access	Click [X] in the application window	Choose File, Exit	
Field, delete	Display table in Design view, click field row, and click [Delete Rows]	Display table in Design view, click field row, and choose Edit, Delete Rows	Display table in Design view, click field row, and press DEL
Field, insert	Display table in Design view, click field row where new field is desired, and click [Insert Rows]	Display table in Design view, click field row where new field is desired, and choose Edit, Insert Row	
Field, sort	Select field and click [Sort Descending] or [Sort Ascending]	Select field and choose Records, Sort, Sort Order	
Form, create new	Open table or query and click [New Object]	Select table or query name in database window and choose Insert, Form	
Form, design	Select form name in database window and click Design OR open form and click [View]	Open form and choose View, Design View	
Form, open	Select form name in database window and click Open	Select form name in Forms page of database window and press ENTER	
Help	Click [Help]	Choose Help, Microsoft Word Help	Press F1
Object, create new	Click New on object page of database window		Press ALT+N on object page of database window
Preview	Click [Print Preview]	Choose File, Print Preview	

Function	Mouse Action or Button	Menu	Keyboard Shortcut
Primary key, assign	Display table in Design view, click field, and click	Display table in Design view, select field, and choose Edit, Primary Key	
Print	Click	Choose File, Print	Press CTRL+P
Query, add fields	Double-click field name		
Query, add table	Click	Choose Query, Show Table	
Query, design	Select query name in database window and click Design *OR* Open query and click	Open query and choose View, Design View	
Query, delete		Select the record and choose Edit, Delete Record	
Query, open	Select query name in database window and click Open		Select query name in Forms page of database window and press ENTER
Query, run	Click	Choose Query, Run	
Query, set criteria			Select Criteria row and type operator and symbol
Record, add data		Display Datasheet or Form view and type data into fields	
Record, delete	Click record selection bar or button, click	Select the record and choose Edit, Delete Record	Select record and press DEL
Record, insert	Display table to contain record and click	Open table to contain record and choose Insert, New Record	
Report, create	Display table or query and select AutoReport from drop-down list arrow	Select table or query name in database window and choose Insert, Report	
Report, design	Select report name in database window and click Design *OR* Open report and click	Open report and choose View, Design View	
Report, open	Select report name in database window and click Open		Select report name in Forms page of database window and press ENTER
Save	Click	Choose File, Save	Press CTRL+S

Function	Mouse Action or Button	Menu	Keyboard Shortcut
Send		Choose File, Send	Press ALT+F, E
Spelling check	Click	Choose Tools, Spelling and Grammar	Press F7
Table align		Click in the table and choose Table, Cell Height and Width	
Table, convert text to a table		Select the text and choose Table, Convert Text to Table	
Table, copy structure	Click table name in database window, click , click and type new table name	Click table name in database window, choose Edit, Copy, choose Edit, Paste and type new table name	Click table name in database window, press CTRL+C, press CTRL+V and type new table name
Table, create		Choose Table, Insert Table	
Table, design	Select table name in database window and click Design *OR* Open table and click	Open table and choose View, Design View	
Table, open	Select table name in database window and click Open		Select table name in Forms page of database window and press ENTER
Text, copy	Select the text and click	Select the text and choose Edit, Copy	Press CTRL+C
Text, cut	Select the text and click	Choose Edit, Cut	Press CTRL+X
Text, find	Click	Choose Edit, Find	Press CTRL+F
Text, paste	Select the text and click	Choose Edit, Paste	Press CTRL+V
Text, replace		Choose Edit, Replace	Press CTRL+H
Text, select	Drag through text		Press SHIFT+any cursor movement key, such as → or END
Toolbars, display or hide	Right click on toolbar	Choose View, Toolbars and select the toolbar	
Undo	Click	Choose Edit, Undo	Press CTRL+Z
View, change	Click or	Choose View, Type View	
Web	Click	Choose Help, Microsoft on the Web	

Glossary

AND condition A query expression using different criteria in the same criteria row of the Query Design grid. When Access uses the AND operator, only the records that meet the criteria in all the cells will be returned.

Ascending order A sort order in which you arrange records alphabetically from A to Z or numerically from smallest to largest.

AutoForm A feature that enables you to create forms using the fields and information stored as part of the table or query.

AutoNumber field A field that is set to automatically enter a sequential number as each record is added to the table.

AutoReport A feature that enables you to create simple report formats using the fields contained in a table or query.

Bound control A control that is tied to a field in an underlying table or query.

Calculated control A control that uses an expression as its source of data.

Calculated field A field in a query that contains an expression. When you display the results of a calculation in a field, the results aren't actually stored in the underlying table. Instead, Microsoft Access reruns the calculation each time you run the query so that the results are always based on the most current data in the database.

Class A category of objects used in an Access database. A specific table is an instance of an object from the table class.

Control A specific object, such as a text box, that is added to a form or report.

Controls Objects on a form or report that display data, perform actions, or decorate the form or report.

ControlTip A helpful tip that pops up over a control when you move the mouse pointer over the control.

Criteria Conditions you set in a grid to limit the information displayed in the datasheet.

Currency A data type that is useful for calculations involving money and for fixed-point calculations in which accuracy is particularly important.

Data type The characteristic of a field or a variable that determines what kind of data it holds.

Data validation Methods for controlling how data is entered into your database. Validation rules and input masks are two useful methods for data validation.

Database A collection of information related to a particular subject or purpose.

Database management system (DBMS) A computer application used to create and maintain databases.

Database object The tables, queries, forms, reports, macros, or modules that comprise an Access database.

Datasheet view The view in which you can see multiple records on-screen at the same time; this view makes data entry more efficient.

Date/time A data type that contains date and time values for the years 100 through 9999.

Descending order A sort order in which you arrange records alphabetically from Z to A or numerically from largest to smallest.

Design modifications Any enhancements you make to your database objects.

Design view The view of a table, query, form, or report object in which you can modify the object's properties.

Detail section The part of a form or report that holds the field data controls and pulls information from database tables.

Edit To change the field information contained in a record.

Expression A combination of symbols—identifiers, operators, and values —that produces a result.

Expression Builder A graphical workspace for designing expressions for a specific control object or control.

Field A field object represents a column of data with a common data type and a common set of properties.

Field properties A property is an attribute of a field that defines one of its characteristics; an example is the size property of a text field.

Filter To select only those records in a table that contain the same value in the selected field.

Find A feature available using the Find dialog box to locate one or more records displayed in a table or form.

Form An Access database object used to display data from tables or queries in an aesthetically-pleasing format.

Hyperlink Underlined text or a graphic that you use to jump to a location on the Internet or on an intranet, to an object in your database or in another database, or to a document on your computer or on another computer connected by a network.

Image control A control that is used to display pictures in an object such as a form or report.

Input mask A property of a control that you use to make data entry easier and to control the values users can enter into the database.

Label control An unbound control used to display descriptive text such as titles, captions, or brief instructions on a form or report.

Macro A set of one or more actions that each perform a particular operation, such as opening a form or printing a report. Macros can help you automate common tasks.

Memo A data type used to store random entries exceeding 255 characters.

Module A collection of Visual Basic programming procedures stored together to customize the Access environment.

Navigate To move from one record to another in a table or form.

Numeric (number) Data type used to hold numeric data used in mathematical calculations.

OLE Object Linking and Embedding, a way of automating how information is shared among applications.

Object A table, query, form, report, macro, or module in a database.

Office Assistant The new, on-the-spot Help feature that pops up frequently to offer help on the task you're performing. The Office Assistant enables you to ask questions about the task you want to perform.

Online help The help provided by the software and which is accessible from the computer.

Page Footer The section of a form that contains any information you want to appear at the bottom of every printed page of a form.

Page Header The section of a form that contains any information you want to appear at the top of every printed page of a form.

Property An attribute of an object that defines one of the object's characteristics, such as size, color, or screen location, or an aspect of its behavior, such as whether it is enabled or visible. To change the characteristics of an object, you change the values of its properties.

Query Used to view, change, and analyze data in different ways. You can also use them as the source of records for forms and reports. Query objects contain information that determines how underlying table data is displayed on the screen.

Query datasheet A window that displays the results of a query in a row and column format.

Query design grid The lower pane displayed in the query design window containing columns where you define the fields of data the query will display.

Query Design View A view for queries where you create or modify a query.

Record A collection of related field data stored in a table, such as a person's name and address.

Record source A table or query that contains the records the form displays.

Relational database management system (RDBMS) A database management system (DBMS) specifically designed to utilize the relational database model.

Replace An option available in the Find dialog box to replace field values.

Report An organized format for summarizing and grouping database data to provide meaningful information in a printed format.

Report Design window A graphical workspace displaying the report's bound and unbound controls.

Report Footer A report section for specifying the information that you want to appear at the end of an Access report.

Report Header A report section for specifying the information that you want to appear at the beginning of an Access report.

Run The action of applying query specifications to a table to display field information and records.

Select query A query that returns record information in a query datasheet without changing the underlying data.

Sort The action of displaying records in ascending or descending order.

Sort criteria Criteria added to a query or report specifying how the records shall be ordered.

Table The primary object of a database that stores field names, field descriptions, and field data. Tables display multiple records in a row/ column format similar to a spreadsheet layout.

Table Design view The view used to create or modify a table's structure.

Table Design window A window displaying the table design grid.

Table structure The field names, data types, and properties defining the physical arrangement of a table.

Text Text or combinations of text and numbers, as well as numbers that don't require calculations, such as phone numbers. Text fields may contain up to 255 characters of information.

Textbox control A bound control that is used primarily on a form to modify or add field data to an underlying field.

Unbound control A control on a form or report that is not bound to a specific field.

Update To change the field data contained in a record.

Validation rule A property used to specify requirements for data entered into a record, field, or control.

Validation text A property used to specify the message to be displayed to the user when a validation rule is violated.

Yes/no Yes and No values and fields that contain only one of two values (Yes/No, True/False, or On/Off).

Index

Windows 95 (WIN)

Active Desktop (WIN98)

Access 97 (ACC)

Notes

Notes

Notes

Notes

Notes

Contents

Six of the best

Left What a way to start! 1970 H-D Sportster street racer style. This detailing took Ed Kerr eight months to finish – he values all that for $10,000 US. Induction side of this Harley shows chrome and gold plating by South Shore and engraving and paint by Cycle Fabrication. That intake ram hides an S & S carb

Above Pure street racer style, a comparatively new 'lowrider' offshoot. Note solid rear end, long frame but short Honda forks. Zipton oil tank obvious now just beneath seat. Bike took first in class at '83 Rat's Hole

Kerr's street racer from the primary case side. That's the depth of detail needed to create a winner. Everything but everything is painted or plated

Cycle Fab is well known as the purveyor of much good custom work. Dave Perewitz did this superb paint on Kerr's H-D seat, plus the engraving

Below Detailing and more detailing. Honda forks and brakes certainly add variety to this Harley. Spokes are chromed and rims gold

Right Fuel tanks are recognized as the topping to any custom bike. Here's where you show off your best art. Just superb. Ed Kerr's Sportster is remarkable. Hails from Carlisle, Penn.

CYCLE FAB

Above Another street racer, this time from Rockland, Massachusetts. Mike Estabrook's '62 Sportster came second at the '83 Rat's Hole. Daytona Beach background. This one has a sprung rear end and big near-oval air cleaner for hidden Dell'Orto carburettor from a car

Right Originally built by Mark Shadley, Mike Estabrooks developed and finished this 80 cube Sportster courtesy Harley-Davidson. Incredible shine

Left New style of street racer – third in class at the '83 Rat's Hole. Built by Mark Shadley, who built the bike before last, this incredible engraving was accomplished by Dave Perewitz of Cycle Fab – no mean craftsman

Below Based on a 1977 Harley Sportster, Mark Shadley of Hanson, Mass. went for the 'slimstyle' lowrider look for this stunning street racer. Black and silver show off well on the Daytona sand

Harleys are always heavy, some more than others. Even this sylphlike street racer still needs a beer can under its side stand to prevent it sinking into the Daytona Beach sand. A fall would definately spoil this work of art

Here's the Cycle Fab man himself, Dave Perewitz, behind the Harley he built for himself. Not a radical design at all this one, just a vehicle to show off his paint and engraving skills. He worked on the first three in the street racer class at the '83 Rat's Hole show

Left Perewitz engraving. Axle shaft needs chrome but the design flair and engraving skill is just stupendous in his Harley's rear hub and exhaust

Above Tasty, understated look of black and chrome set off with a deep, subtle shade of purple maroon. Not a street racer, a lowrider or a chopper – just a regular custom street bike

Deep chrome from Cycle Fab

Careful, careful work in this '59 XLH Sporty of Walter Rasile. Lacquered paint is ice blue with dark blue flames over-painted with pearl white. Took six months

Below In fact nothing too drastic in the way of cutting and shutting but a perfect and tasteful paint and chrome job. Typical shorty pipes for this Sporty

Right Close up on the Rasile bike. Perfection slightly spoilt by the fuel tap and pipe although the shine's so bright you hardly notice

BMW
I JUST CAME FROM
the RAT'S HOLE
DAYTONA BEACH FLORIDA

Rat's Hole - Florida fun

Left Daytona Beach in Florida every early March means road racing to some but the Rat's Hole show for others. Billed as the largest chopper show in the world, it now means less choppers but a greater variety of custom bikes. Judge wears the official T-shirt

Above When Skinners Union first produced the SU carburettor it had no idea some would gold plate it and engrave it, even fit it to an American motorcycle

Above All hand work. Ingenious instrument mount, fuel tank and seat unit. Wing flat four engine hard to work with because of width and low exhaust exits

Right Futurethink. Most striking Honda Gold Wing, actually based on a GL 1100, built by Jim Greasey. Lowrider style with inevitable hard tail but with clever utilisation of the shaft drive. Big crowds around this one

'Old style' hard tail side valve Harley.
Headers are wild, leather tool pouch wacky

Nice touch just for the show David Brown's
Honda 750 four

Left Simple, tasty H-D Sportster, typical of the bikes which make up the vast numbers on show. Not a show winner but adding to the carnival atmosphere

Above Black Magic. Wally Hostetter's Honda 750 shows off careful balance of chrome, black paint, matt black alloy and nicely cleaned castings

Left Turbo Honda 750 (early single cam version) shows that custom power is what everyone wants. Harley style peanut tank won't take that engine far, and will it get hot!

Below Had to win a prize. Same bike belongs to Tom Summers who took first in class in '83. Bike's a '76 just warmed over. Stainless steel, heat resistent plug leads though

Below Custom Triumph twin with worked-over Amal carburettor. Kink in fuel line won't help either

Right Gold valve covers for this XLCH Sportster is just typical of what can be done. Gold on the head nuts too. Mural works well

SILICONE

SILVER
STREAKER

Left *Silver Streaker* shows nearly as much gold as silver. Actually a Honda 750 chopper, but look how clean underneath

Below That Turbo Honda again. Drag rear end, lowrider front. Best pipework in the show

Z1R Kawasaki lookalike. Two engines coupled for 2084 cc, weight 680 lb – but all for 240 mph. Not only does it have drag strip speed of no mean level but it's also street legal and a custom show winning potential. Only requirement is long arms

Historical accuracy? Is that an American Civil War naval engagement? Carburettor is actually an English SU and the bike's a Harley with yet another style of pipework

Left Rose bud Harley. Stark contrast to all the other bikes but still worthy for all that. Pink usually sticks to Dressers

Below Some of the show bikes do get ridden. Honda chopper with canard aerodynamic device and bizarre style

Left Strange choice. Honda 450 twin is uncommon with custom bikers. Martingly and Gosnell own this one. Nothing special, just neat

Above Not neat. Home made, not store bought, this one from owner Dunnelly Hall. Olds 215 cu. in. is what it says – that should mean their all-alloy V8. Some power but what about the handling? Rat's Hole show takes anything interesting

OPEN
RIDING FOR THE SON

Seven more of the best

Far left Greg Heinritz from Brookfield, Wisconsin has ridden 100,000 miles on this Guzzi for the Christian Motorcycle Association. He's the United States Road rep riding for the 'Son'

Left Greg did all the work himself on this 850 T3 (?). All the murals run a biblical theme

MOTO GUZZI
MOTO GUZZI

Left Noah's Ark

Right Into the depths . . .

Below Neat work here but a heavy front end for this Italian sports touring motorcycle

Spare parts big-inch Harley, actually
93 cu. in. Frame is courtesy SBF, all built
by Mallard Teal of White Bear Lake, MN.
He runs Motorworks which rebuilds H-D
engines and transmissions

Hidden behind that primary cover, nicely vented. Neat, but wide belt drive.

Candy brandywine with flames with
appropriate upholstery

Right A multitude of different Harley parts make no odds to this magnificent beast. Just beautiful. Note Police Special speedo in tank top

Below Belt drive to the rear wheel too, à la Sturgis

Harley 'Duo Glide' called *The Barbarian*. Custom everything. Prominent here are Drag Specialties saddle bags, Janner seat; invisible is Andrews cam

S & S Two-Throat carburettor hidden beneath that cleaner. Two-throat is twin-choke to the British. John McCarthy did the paint on Bernie Tatro's '62 Panhead

HARLEY-DAVIDSON
M
I
5486
GA 83
MADE IN U.S.A

Left Licence plate frame says it all. Custom motorcycles and Harley-Davidson are more American than apple pie

Right Here's where the time is invested. Bike took one and half years to complete. Now you can see why. Mural figure is hard to do

Below Clever mural from John McCarthy; he did all the paint and the striping on Tatro's H-D. Gas cap plating came from Browns

Heavyweight front end features special disc wheel, Dunlop rear tyre and Duo Glide mudguard. Note green 'mother of pearl' tinge

Left is John McCarthy, the bike's builder. Right is owner Bernie Tatro. Location is Wendy's (hamburger joint) parking lot, Daytona Beach

Left Neat trick.Mother of Pearl and warm red. Bike's a '74 XL H-D Sporty. Took owner Dan O'Connell of Stamford, Conn. nine months to build although he's had it from new

Below Sweet simplicity. Frame is a C & J custom but rest is mostly stock Harley handsomely turned out

Owner Dan O'Connell on his pride and joy. Shows in his face. Just custom street motorcycle

Above Chrome and neat blue paint

Right The other *Barbarian*. Ken Goldsbury astride his '72 Hog. Hailing from Hialeah, Florida he didn't have far to go to get to Daytona Beach. Fierce but gentle

BARBARIAN
BARBARIAN

Below Paint by Kent Imperial on Goldsbury's peanut tank

Right Plating by London Plates, engraving by Del Mar, money by Ken Goldsbury, bike by Milwaukee's finest, sand by Daytona

THE BARBARIAN

GOODRIDGE
Lockheed Brakes
Lucas
Batteries
CIBIE
DELLORTO
Aeroquip
DUNLOP
HESKETH
130/90 V 17

Above Made in England, and proud of it. Malcolm Cox can match the American scene throughout the game. Vee-twin aristocratic Hesketh unusual scooter

Left You can read who's done what on Malcolm Cox's Hesketh. Working in the centre of the Black Country in Britain's industrial backbone, he can find the finest craftsmen but it's he who has the ideas and assembles the bike. He's coming on

ROADRUNNER
AVON

One of the very best from Uncle Bunt. Innovator, craftsman and promotor of the British custom motorcycle. Bike might make 'street legal' at a pinch. It's a Triumph called *Roadrunner*

A M A
HONDA

Full Dresser

Moody Honda Gold Wing on the beach. Paint's special, most of the bits come from Drag Specialities, but it's one loaded dresser

Below Fourteen hundred little lamps! Well-known bike but no 'dresser book' would be without this one. Weight is not quoted

Right Same bike from the front. Where's the battery and generator?

1200
TAG NUMBER 421
YEAR
MAKE

Left Less heavy but still in full dress uniform. This one's a '72 1200 Glide waiting to win. Bring your own grass

Below *Purple Passion*. '79 Glide this time, getting dressier all the time. Don't fall over!

Holiday Inn

Big

H G
Daddy O
AX 8242
MASS 83
Harley-Davidson
Electra Glide
BACK OFF

Left Somewhere under there is a little ol' Electra Glide

Below Weight

Oh so careful work on this dresser

Nearly a dresser. Actually an Electra Glide but farily stock except for paint and chrome

'Possum Gair

Salted or dry roasted?

Left American passion for inflatables

Above Quite one of the best tanks ever to grace a Hog. Old British traditional tank line

80
100
120
140
160
40
20
MPH

Left She's back with cats. Love the 160 mile speedo

Below Back again, this time with teeth and Mr SciFi

DOE
BILL
DIANE
ED
RICH

Left Lovely work of the very finest. Names are unknown to the photographer but look like fond memories

Below Trad. But so superbly executed. Trick Harley below

THE
Black Dahlia
II

Thank you for your order, Main Address!

Thank you for shopping with Half Price Books! Please contact Support@hpb.com. if you have any questions, comments or concerns about your order (113-4388110-2808230)

Visit our stores to sell your books, music, movies games for cash.

SKU	ISBN/UPC	Title & Author/Artist	Shelf ID	Qty	OrderSKU
S468703994	9780850455083	Custom Motor Cycles (Osprey colour series) Morland, Andrew	TRN3.5	1	

SHIPPED STANDARD TO:
Main Address
800 Avondale Ave
1033647-1-0802
Grandview Heights OH 43212
3ks0spkqsbh0r38@marketplace.amazon.com

ORDER# **113-4388110-2808230**
AmazonMarketplaceUS

Left Sad memory on well-known tank style

Below Coffin style tank, *The Gray Remnant*

Below 'If pigs had wings'

Right Seen before in these pages but this is a better view of that paradise mural

Standard passion but difficult paint

Left Fantasy world

Below Cycle Fab at their most inventive. She's returned again

1982
FLA.
1107

Above *Free Bird* is finished. John McCarthy is ready to clean off the chalk guide marks and take your $30 (or thereabouts)

Left How to do it. John McCarthy from Hinsdale, NH, has been professional for ten years. At Daytona he worked a full seven days in Wendy's parking lot applying gold leaf, custom lettering or anything in paint you might have fancied. Not pricey either

Three, four, five, oddball

Left Nice thing if you don't fall over in the water. Folks have done lots of things to VeeDubs, but this is one of the nicest trikes ever seen

Above Sawn in half? Not quite, but watch stark contrast with Daytona Beach buildings in the background

Star Trike sports rear mounted V8 power, just like a drag boat. Driver and Mom sit either side

STAR TRIKE
GILLETTE SPRINT GT 60

Harley trike in the style of a horsedrawn van-delivery

1977
WINNERS
ATH HOUSE-SAF
The
BEAR
CATCHER
THOMPSON 60
INDY PROFILE

Trike hot rod in conventional dress. Cobra decal on valve cover suggests hot performer. Spectating Honda's something else

Ice cream simple; VW engine in the back
there

Airplane style. Novel arrangement with
driver outrigged as though riding shotgun

Chopper trike with beer barrel fuel tank. Rear-end VW engine and drive train make ideal base

Ground Control comes courtesy of Honda although an American has done all the work to make this turbo powered 750 four trike fun to run

Chuck wagon, boat, trike, or is it a plane?

Left First in the unusual class at the '83 Rat's Hole show went to Trooper Trudeau's sidecar car. That's a '41 Harley vee twin sitting aside a '36 sidecar body. Read on

Above right Registered as a motorcycle it's Trooper's best project yet. His Ormand Beach, FL based company Southern Custom did all the fabrication work to turn this 45 cu. in. Flathead into a 100 mph scoot

Below right Underneath most of the motive parts come from the H-D dealership. Outside it's all Trooper

1729
BFGoodrich
Radial T/A
BFGoodrich

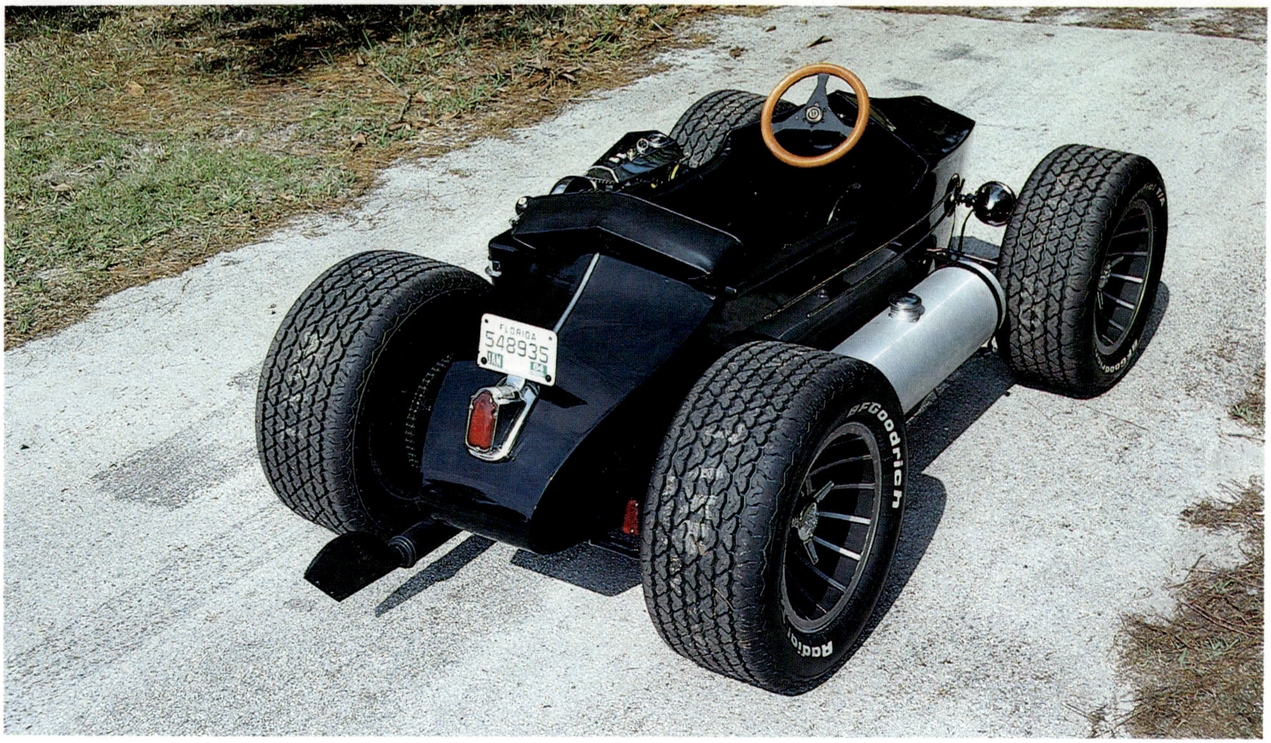

Wrecker trike, with five wheels.
What will we see next?

GRAND PRIX
SUPER WIDE G/T

UFO?

It'll be a big rig if it tows a trailer

Vee-three Harley. This extraordinary bike ran well. So hard to do. The vee-twin Harley with a cylinder missing is now running too with but one

John Tatro's special '73 FLH sidecar was designed and built by him and his family and friends. He's a paraplegic. John can get on and off the bike into his wheelchair without help. His wheelchair sits on the back, as does sister Marie. Some people can never leave Harleys alone – this one's dedicated to Jim Sullivan

AMERICAN
MOTORCYCLES
ARE
CHEVROLET
Holley

Left There's no stopping some. Chevy power will make a mess of your left jeans' leg if the exhaust heat doesn't melt it first. Some car-a-bike kits exist

Above There's a car engine hiding under this one too. British built Quasar promotes feet-forward stance – Mike Scott supports the package

Second generation feet-forwards also from the pen of Malcolm Newell. These are the Phasars. Power comes from shaft driven Honda, Guzzi and Kawasaki for these four

Guzzi 1000 cc Convert (read automatic) Phasar shows Newell's high feet-forward riding position. Defazio style centre-hub steering points up front. All from England's West Country design studios!

Newell's Kwaker Phasar with the chief pretending to be the pilot. His work is as radical and 'custom' as anything from Stateside